Second Edition

Identity DEVELOPMENT

Adolescence Through Adulthood

Jane Kroger

University of Tromsø

SAGE Publications
Thousand Oaks ▪ London ▪ New Delhi

Copyright Acknowledgments

Credit: Photographs of eight sculptures by Gustav Vigeland taken by Jane Kroger. ©2005 The Vigeland Museum/Artists Rights Society (ARS), New York/BONO, Oslo.

Grateful acknowledgment is made for permission to quote from the following sources:

Excerpt "Towards new shores—?" from MARKINGS by Dag Hammarskjöld, trans., Auden/ Sjoberg. Translation Copyright ©1964 by Alfred A. Knopf, Inc. and Faber & Faber, Ltd. Reprinted by permission of Alfred A. Knopf, Inc.

Excerpt from Alzheimer's sufferer in *On the Loss of Self: A Family Resource for the Care of Alzheimer's Disease and Related Disorders* by D. Cohen and C. Eisdorfer. ©1986 by W. W. Norton & Company, Inc. Reprinted by permission of W. W. Norton, Inc.

Statement from Pär Lagerkvist. Reprinted by permission of Elin Lagerkvist.

Excerpt from *Saint Augustine's Confessions*, trans., Henry Chadwick. Translation Copyright ©1991 by Oxford University Press. Reprinted by permission of Oxford University Press.

For information:

Sage Publications, Inc.
2455 Teller Road
Thousand Oaks, California 91320
E-mail: order@sagepub.com

Sage Publications Ltd.
1 Oliver's Yard
55 City Road
London EC1Y 1SP
United Kingdom

Sage Publications India Pvt. Ltd.
B-42, Panchsheel Enclave
Post Box 4109
New Delhi 110 017 India

Printed in the United States of America.

Library of Congress Cataloging-in-Publication Data

Kroger, Jane, 1947-
Identity development: adolescence through adulthood / Jane Kroger.— 2nd ed.
    p. cm.
Includes bibliographical references and index.
ISBN 978-0-7619-2959-8 (cloth) — ISBN 978-0-7619-2960-4 (pbk.)
    1. Identity (Psychology) 2. Developmental psychology. I. Title.
BF697.K76 2007
155.2′5—dc22

                                                                        2005037837

This book is printed on acid-free paper.

08   09   10   10   9   8   7   6   5   4   3   2

Acquisitions Editor:	Cheri Dellelo
Editorial Assistant:	Karen Ehrmann
Project Editor:	Tracy Alpern
Copy Editor:	Amy Freitag, Four Lakes Colorgraphics
Typesetter:	C&M Digitals (P) Ltd.
Proofreader:	Joyce Li
Indexer:	D. Teddy Diggs
Cover Designer:	Candice Harman

Second Edition

Identity
DEVELOPMENT

For Sandy
Der Erlkönig kommt zu früh

Contents

Preface

Erikson's concept of identity has been as important a contribution to the social sciences in the second half of the 20th century as Freud's concept of the unconscious was to the first half of the 20th century. With Erikson's understandings of identity came a focus on the roles not only of one's biological and psychological foundations, but also of cultural contributions to the ways in which one both shapes and is shaped by the surrounding milieu. The field of identity research has expanded so much over the past three and a half decades that virtually every major textbook on adolescent development contains a significant section on identity development and a discussion of Erikson's writings. In addition, there are now at least four English-language social science journals that include the word *Identity* in their titles and focus upon the interplay between the individual and context in shaping the course of the human life cycle.

What is identity and how does it change as well as remain the same over the course of one's life span? This volume provides a synthesis of theory, research, and practical consequences of the identity-formation process during the years of adolescence and adult life and attempts to answer these questions. I begin Part I by defining identity, tracing its origins from Erikson's original concept through five general theoretical frames by which identity is currently being studied among social scientists. These frameworks include: a historical focus, addressing conditions that have precipitated a contemporary concern with identity; a structural stage approach, which addresses changing internal structures of ego development through which one interprets and gives meaning to one's life experiences; a sociocultural approach, which emphasizes the role society plays in shaping the course of individual identity over time; a narrative approach, which stresses how people tell stories about their lives in order to bring many diverse elements together into an integrated whole and to provide some sense of sameness and continuity to these life experiences; and finally through a psychosocial approach, which seeks to integrate the roles played both by society as well as an individual's psychology and biology in developing and maintaining personal identity. All frameworks have their strengths and limitations, and a brief critique of each is also included. Erikson's psychosocial approach to identity has been selected to provide the organizing framework for remaining chapters of this volume because of the theory's integration of historical, biological, psychological, and sociocultural forces.

Parts II and III center on identity development through the years of adolescence and adulthood, respectively. The chapters in Part II focus on issues of identity in early, middle, and late adolescence. An additional chapter in Part II addresses selected issues posing special identity challenges for a substantial number of adolescents in the general population; all of these special challenges involve coming to terms with differences resulting from a nonchosen identity element. Part III also contains chapters addressing identity development during the early, middle, and later years of adulthood, respectively. This section similarly concludes with a final chapter on selected topics that pose particular identity-related challenges to Erikson's psychosocial tasks of intimacy, generativity, and integrity at various stages of adult life. Part IV, an epilogue, provides a contemporary analysis of identity research that has been conducted within an Eriksonian perspective.

During each of the chapters focusing on specific adolescent and adult phases of the life span, I have attempted, in line with Erikson's notions, to outline key biological characteristics, psychological features, and social influences that interact to shape the course of individual identity over time. All chapters in Parts II and III additionally focus on both process and content questions of identity—on how identity development normatively proceeds during the phase of the life span under discussion and on what issues serve as key, identity-defining markers for most individuals, at least in industrialized nations. A final section of each chapter addresses selected key contexts that are likely to interact with psychological and biological factors to shape the evolution of identity through this selected phase of the life span. The focus of this volume is on the normative course of identity development throughout adolescent and adult life. As such, many important questions and issues surrounding nonnormative patterns of identity development simply could not be addressed in this volume. In addition, there are still numerous identity-related issues that may be paramount for large percentages of individuals that similarly could not be addressed in this volume due to length constraints. It is hoped that this volume might stimulate research attention to various adolescent and adult identity issues in the future through some of the design strategies noted in the epilogue.

A number of new features appear in this second edition to *Identity Development: Adolescence Through Adulthood*. In keeping with Erikson's emphasis on the importance of the social milieu to individual development, I have made special efforts to include researches, personal statements, and examples of identity-related literature from a variety of contexts around the world. As national boundaries have changed and new economic alliances have formed in many regions of the world over the past two decades, identity themes have often emerged among individuals attempting to maintain some sense of personal continuity and integrity under such altered social conditions. Many researches on both adolescent and adult development over the past decades reflect such identity issues. The contents of this second edition have also been thoroughly updated. Of the more than 650 references contained in this volume, about one-quarter are to theoretical commentaries and research published within the past two to three years. Additionally, Chapter 1 now contains examples of measurement instruments commonly used to assess identity from the variety of theoretical orientations overviewed in the chapter. And the epilogue also reflects new, critical comments on the course and contents of identity from adolescence through adulthood, as well as suggesting new research directions for this burgeoning field of study.

The inspiration for this second edition of the volume has come from many sources. The growing body of literature now beginning to address interactions among biological, psychological, and contextual issues of adolescent and adult development begged for integration within an identity framework. Through such integration, it becomes clear where gaps in our understanding of identity process and content issues still lie. Certainly identity processes involved in balancing Integrity Versus Despair during the later years of adult life pose a rich area for ongoing study. Additionally, comments from research participants through my many years of undertaking identity research have also sparked my interest in and curiosity about the twists and turns of identity over time. I have again included some of their statements, anonymously, in the text of this edition, alongside examples from literature to highlight relevant research findings. Though a U.S. citizen, I have also lived for extended periods of time in three additional and different cultural settings. These varied cultural experiences have brought into clearer focus for me the fascinating and often subtle ways in which varied cultural norms and expectations cast broad boundaries around individual identity alternatives. I hope the material presented in this volume may again lead you to understand and further question the course, contents, and consequences of identity development over the exciting and challenging years of adolescent and adult life.

Acknowledgments

I am grateful for the support of many individuals during the preparation of this volume. Jim Brace-Thompson, Psychology Editor at Sage, and his assistant Karen Ehrmann have helped me to keep on target throughout the writing process. My student helpers, Hilde Jensen, Kjersti Lillevoll, and Gro Åsli provided invaluable assistance with searches and reference checks. Hilde Jensen's additional aid in the final stages of manuscript preparation, with endless checks and balances, have helped ensure the accuracy and continuity of material presented in this new edition. I again wish to express my special appreciation to Drs. Emmy Werner and Stanley Jacobsen for providing me with current demographic and statistical information from the United States Government Printing Office in San Francisco. Drs. Jim Marcia, Gerald Adams, Ruthellen Josselson, Hal Grotevant, Carol Markstrom, Jim Côté, Luc Goossens, and many other identity researchers have also provided me with the most current work available in their own research programs. Their contributions have certainly strengthened the timeliness of this volume.

A number of anonymous reviewers have also given valuable suggestions for shaping this work. Many of their ideas have been included in this new edition, along with those of my professional studies students in developmental psychology. I must also give special thanks to Hege Raklev, head psychology librarian at the University of Tromsø, who remained unphased with yet more of my endless interlibrary loan requests—tusen takk til deg (many thanks to you). And finally, to participants in research projects I have cited in this book, I am especially grateful for the time and insights you have shared with me about the process of identity development through various stages of your own lives. Your input has provided a human face to the many identity research projects in which you have been involved.

—*Jane Kroger*
Havnes, Håkøya
Eidkjosen, Norway

PART I

Introduction

At every moment you choose yourself. But do you choose your self? Body and soul contain a thousand possibilities out of which you can build many Is. But in only one of them is there a congruence of the elector and the elected. Only one— . . . which is your I.

—Dag Hammarskjöld, *Markings*

1

Perspectives on Identity

- What is identity?
- Are there aspects of identity that change over time?
- Are there aspects of identity that remain the same over time?

Well, again there is this feeling that I am the same person that I was as a child though my body has changed, and people's expectations of me have changed. Now, though, I find myself searching . . . searching once again for the meaning of life, searching for myself. It seems like I should have finished with all of this ages ago.

—Elaine, 55-year-old housewife, returning to university study

What is identity? When does identity form? What aspects of identity change over time? What features of identity remain the same over time? Can identity ever be lost? If so, can it be regained? How do early life experiences affect one's later sense of identity? What roles do one's family, friends, schools, places of work, houses of worship, and cultural values play in the development of identity? Questions such as these have caught the attention of social scientists interested in identity, and numerous perspectives have been taken in an effort to define its dimensions.

Identity is a complex entity. Over the past 60 years, an understanding both of what identity means and how it evolves over the course of the life span have been the inspiration for many theoretical writings as well as numerous research investigations. A search for personal meaning has also been the quest of many individuals, often featured in literary works ranging from Erikson's (1958) *Young Man Luther* to Salinger's (1951) *Catcher in the Rye* to McCarthy's (1994) *The Crossing*. Common to all pursuits has been the need to define individual identity and to show how identity leads one to find (or not find) meaningful connections and pursuits within a larger cultural milieu.

This volume has been written to introduce some of the many and varied understandings of identity and to chart key issues related to identity's evolutionary course from early adolescence through the later adult years of life. Although identity has often been presented as a key developmental task of adolescence (e.g., Erikson, 1968), its reverberations throughout the years of adulthood have also been attracting increasing research attention over the past two decades. I hope to convey some of the current issues and controversies in this expanding and exciting field through the presentation of various theoretical approaches, research investigations, and exemplary statements from some well-known and other lesser-known individuals going about their daily lives. Whereas numerous writings have addressed various identity-related pathologies experienced by some adolescents and adults seeking clinical assistance, the focus of this volume will be primarily on normative identity issues experienced by most individuals through various phases of their adolescent and adult lives. Before outlining the ideas of some major theorists on the meaning of identity, however, I would like to approach the issue from a somewhat different perspective.

In teaching, I have often found it instructive to ask my students at the beginning of a new academic term for their definitions and understandings of a particular psychological construct that we will be studying in some detail during the semester. One early September afternoon, I asked my second-year undergraduate human development class to note down, anonymously, if they wished, how they knew or how they would know when they had achieved their own sense of adult identity. The class encompassed a broad spectrum of ages, ethnicities, and socioeconomic groups. Students' responses, some poignant, some humorous, captured the array of emphases given to the meaning of identity by many of the theorists in the pages to follow:

- **Laura, 22** I knew I had my own identity when I stopped changing "how I was," depending upon the people surrounding me [*sic*]. Only when I became clear on what I wanted to be and could be, regardless of the people around me, did I know I had my own identity. It has only happened very recently and I'm still working on it!

- **Margaret, 25** I don't think anyone can ever say they have reached a stable sense of adult identity. I believe the sense of identity will change, depending on the different situations you face throughout life. Therefore, without ever reaching a stable identity, you can't say you have an adult identity. I'm always reassessing values and beliefs.

- **Jason, 40** I think identity is present when other people's opinions become something to reflect upon, rather than to live by.

- **Fiona, 30** For me, self-identity is on a continuum. I'm still exploring some aspects of my identity, while other parts feel more secure, like my cultural heritage. Today, I'm 30, divorced, a full-time student, while just three years ago I was 27, married, and employed full time. The only thing I'm sure about in life is that nothing is for sure.

- **Samuel, 19** I think that one's sense of identity changes all the time. I don't believe I have a firm identity yet—I have values and stuff, but I can't really say this is who I am, this is what I believe. Period. I don't know if I will ever feel that, or rather I don't know what it is that will make me feel as though I do have a definite identity. I cannot qualify what an identity will involve for me.

- **Gillian, 20** I am always me, the same person, unchangeable, though I will age, get new insights, and circumstances in my life will, of course, change over time.

In these passages, themes of stability and change, of psychological autonomy and connection, and of intrapsychic and contextual components have all been aspects of identity addressed and given differential emphasis by various identity theorists over the past 50 years.

For 19-year-old Samuel, identity is rather elusive, difficult to define or even to anticipate any possible outcomes of who and what he in the future might be. Erik Erikson, one of the first writers to address the issue of identity, found it easiest to understand identity's meaning by probing the psychological worlds of those for whom a sense of identity had become elusive. It might be that Samuel could offer many further insights regarding identity processes through identity's elusive nature in his own life.

Laura, at 22, still working toward her own sense of identity as well as a definition of the term, describes a shift from an earlier identity seemingly dependent upon group approval or support to one more driven by internal factors. Jason, at 40, offers a more succinct and perhaps personally comfortable expression of this definition. Some identity theorists such as Jane Loevinger and Robert Kegan have focused on such internal structural changes that enable people to filter through more complex and differentiated developmental perspectives such as those expressed by Laura and Jason.

However, Gillian, 20, views identity as a more static entity, existing in unaltered form across time and space. Such developmental writers might view Gillian as one who may yet undergo such a process of structural transition, thus expanding her understanding of identity as well as her own identity-formation experience. However, trait theorists such as Costa and McCrae (1994), would argue that particular personality features, to which Gillian may have been referring, are relatively stable across the late adolescent and adult life span.

Margaret, 25, and Fiona, 30, have a definition of identity more contingent upon social circumstance, continually subject to change. Mead (1934) defines the self as basically a social structure, emerging through social experience and activity; the unity of one's total self is merely a reflection of the unity in one's social experience. More recently, Shotter and Gergen (1989) and Gergen (1991) have furthered arguments that identity is formed, delimited, and constrained within ongoing relationships and the cultural context; identity, in their view, is ascribed by the demands of the culture.

Thus, identity can be understood from many perspectives, and these perspectives are elucidated through the work of selected writers and researchers in the following pages. I begin this chapter by providing a somewhat detailed overview of the concept of identity elucidated by Erik Erikson, for his framework will serve to organize the presentation of theoretical and research investigations in the remaining chapters of this volume. I then describe five general contemporary approaches to identity, discussing the work of one or two representative writers working within each framework and giving an overview of their understanding of what identity is. A brief critique of each approach is offered, and the focus returns to how each model would view two of the questions asked at the beginning of this chapter: Are there aspects of identity that change over time? And are there aspects of identity that remain the same over time?

A final comment must be made on terminology. Differing approaches to identity are described in the following sections of this chapter. *Self, ego, identity, I,* and *me* are all terms that have been used by psychologists interested in identity. In this volume, I will retain the terminology each theorist or researcher uses to describe various identity-related phenomena. Thus, though a particular theorist or researcher may not use the term *identity*, the phenomenon he or she is addressing relates closely to the identity construct described by Erik Erikson. The study of identity, of who I am and of how my biology, psychology, and society interact to produce that subjective sense of the person who is "genuinely me" is the focus of this volume. Additionally, questions of how I can meaningfully express who I am within the various circumstances afforded to me by my society are also key considerations in the chapters ahead.

Origins of Identity: Erik Erikson

Erik Erikson (1956) has generally been credited with first focusing both popular and scientific attention on the meaning of identity. Erikson originally trained under Freud in Vienna, after accepting a teaching position at the school Freud had established to teach the children of colleagues and patients undergoing analysis. Erikson noted that, to his knowledge, Freud had used the term *identity* only once. This usage held a deliberate psychosocial connotation, as Freud spoke of his link to the Jewish people and of having an "inner identity" based on a shared system of values and the unique history of a people. Erikson first used the term *ego identity* to describe a central disturbance in the psychological lives of some veterans returning from World War II, whom he saw in a clinical treatment center:

> What impressed me the most was the loss in these men of a sense of identity. They knew who they were; they had a personal identity. But it was as if, subjectively, their lives no longer hung together—and never would again . . . this sense of identity provides the ability to experience one's self as something that has continuity and sameness and to act accordingly. (Erikson, 1963, p. 42)

It is often easier to understand a psychological phenomenon such as ego identity, which most can take for granted, when its presence has been disrupted, Erikson argued.

Encouraged to illuminate his concept of identity further, Erikson (1968) described identity as involving a subjective feeling of self-sameness and continuity over time. In different places and in different social situations, one still has a sense of being the same person. In addition, others recognize this continuity of character, and respond accordingly to the person "they know." Thus, identity for the holder as well as the beholder ensures a reasonably predictable sense of continuity and social order across multiple contexts.

Erikson (1969b) also spoke of identity as both a conscious and unconscious process—as a conscious sense of individual identity as well as an unconscious striving for continuity of personal character. He also used the term *identity* to refer to that which results from the "silent doings of ego synthesis" as well as that sense of inner solidarity with the ideals and values of a significant social group. He furthermore described identity as "a configuration gradually integrating constitutional givens, idiosyncratic libidinal needs, favored capacities, significant identifications, effective defenses, successful sublimations and consistent roles" (Erikson, 1969b, p. 116). Given these many and varied meanings attached to identity by just the one writer, the complexity of the concept becomes readily apparent. However, Erikson defended the multiple meanings he gave to the term by arguing that the construct of identity can only be made more explicit from a variety of angles; the term, he indicates, must "speak" for itself through this variety of connotations.

Tripartite Nature of Ego Identity

Erikson (1968) further noted how one's sense of ego identity is shaped by three interacting elements: one's biological characteristics; one's own unique psychological needs, interests, and defenses; and the cultural milieu in which one resides. Physiological characteristics such as an individual's gender, physical appearance, physical capacities, and limitations provide one with a sense of "bodily self." As one ages, physical features and capacities will change and healthy identity adaptation requires altering one's sense of identity in accordance with differing physical changes. Psychological elements of identity include one's unique feelings, interests, needs, and defenses, which give one a sense of *I* that remains the same across time and circumstance. One's social and cultural milieus provide opportunities for expression as well as recognition of biological and psychological needs and interests. For Erikson, optimal identity development involves finding social roles and niches within the larger community that provide a good "fit" for one's biological and psychological capacities and interests. Initial resolutions to this task normally are undertaken during mid- to late adolescence as one sets up vocational and interpersonal structures for adult life. However, identity reformulations will continue throughout the life span as one's biological, psychological, and societal circumstances change.

Identity in Life Span Perspective

Erikson (1963) has developed an eight-stage life cycle scheme of development, which identifies key psychosocial tasks requiring resolution at different stages of the life span. Identity Versus Role Confusion, that central task of adolescence, both builds upon resolutions to preceding stages and serves as a building block for that which will be encountered throughout the years of adult life. Identity work is, thus, not confined to the adolescent years, but rather brings resolutions to earlier psychosocial stages of Trust Versus Mistrust, Autonomy Versus Doubt and Shame, Initiative Versus Guilt, and Industry Versus Inferiority into focus as youth encounter the work of learning how best to recognize and actualize their own individuality within a larger social order. Identity Versus Role Confusion, like preceding and succeeding stages, requires finding some optimal balance between two polarities, ideally tilted more toward the positive end of the spectrum.

For adolescent identity, resolution to Trust Versus Mistrust provides a legacy of how best to approach the world; the subtle yet vital learning conveyed through the trustworthiness of the first relationships of infancy set the groundwork for one's general life outlook as well as approach to later relationships. From Autonomy Versus Doubt and Shame comes the will to be oneself with whatever manner of confidence the social response to this developmental task of toddlerhood has allowed. Through negotiation of Initiative Versus Guilt, the preschooler's experience of anticipating future roles is reflected in the degree of guilt carried forward to their later implementation. The task of Industry Versus Inferiority for the primary school-aged child establishes the basis for one's attitudes toward finding and completing later identity-defining tasks.

Identity Versus Role Confusion is normatively encountered during adolescence, according to Erikson. Not only does society impose its demands on youth to find appropriate ways to enter adult roles, but newfound sexual drives as well as the use of more sophisticated cognitive operations from within also press toward different forms of expression. Some role confusion under such circumstances is to be expected.

Role confusion is the counterpoint of identity. Role confusion refers to the inability to make moves toward identity-defining commitments. There may be problems with a sense of industry, a disturbance in the experience of time, and difficulties with relationships. Sometimes, there is the desire to "merge" with a leader as some kind of identity resolution or, alternatively, a distancing to avoid enmeshment. There may be the experience of an inner void and the inability to gain satisfaction in accomplishing any activity. Life is being lived passively, not by the individual's own initiative, according to Erikson. At the same time, it is necessary for adolescents to experience some kind of role confusion in undergoing the identity formation process. Letting go of early childhood identifications to forge one's own commitments in life is a sobering task, often resulting in feelings of loss and confusion.

Resolution to this task of Identity Versus Role Confusion lays the groundwork for entry into adult life, with its own further psychosocial tasks. The balance found between Identity Versus Role Confusion during adolescence indeed sets the quality of resolution that is possible for subsequent psychosocial stages of Intimacy Versus Isolation, Generativity Versus Stagnation, and Integrity Versus Despair to be found through the years of young, middle, and later adulthood, respectively. The sense of identity established during late adolescence is that which allows (or does not allow) engagement in an intimate relationship, a counterpointing of identities. Constriction, in identity terms, is associated with constriction in the style of intimacy experienced during adult life. Similarly, one's style of resolution to Identity Versus Role Confusion appears also to be associated with one's style of being able to give during adulthood—giving to one's children and/or making a personally meaningful contribution to one's community or larger social context. And last, identity issues resurface in life's final psychosocial task of Integrity Versus Despair—an existential task of finding ultimate meaning in and acceptance of one's life before it ends. Erikson's scheme of personality development emphasizes the interdependence of all stages and provides a helpful model for understanding the relationship of identity to other psychosocial tasks pressing for resolution at different stages of the life cycle.

The Identity Formation Process

Erikson (1968) also devoted considerable attention to the identity formation process. He described its evolution, beginning in childhood and continuing its developmental course throughout the life cycle, but coming to the fore as a central task of adolescence. "If we consider introjection, identification, and identity formation to be the steps by which the ego grows in ever more mature interplay with the available models, the following psychosocial schedule suggests itself" (p. 159). Initially, the infant begins to establish a sense of self through *introjection*—literally the incorporation of another's image based on the (hopefully satisfactory) experience of mutuality in early relationships. An ideal experience of early relationship thus gives the infant a haven of safety from which to begin exploring further relational potentials beyond that with the primary caregiver. Through later *identifications,* the child *becomes like* those significant others with characteristics or features that are admired. *Identity formation,* however, can begin only when the process of seeking identifications as the basis of one's identity ends.

Identity formation, finally, begins where the usefulness of identification ends.
It arises from the selective repudiation and mutual assimilation of childhood
identifications and their absorption in a new configuration, which, in turn,

is dependent on the process by which a society (often through subsocieties) identifies the young individual, recognizing him as somebody who had to become the way he is and who, being the way he is, is taken for granted. (Erikson, 1968, p. 159)

Identity formation, then, involves the emergence of a new, intrapsychic structure. This new structure is more than the sum of previous childhood identifications; rather, it is a configuration that now enables the holder to mediate rather than be mediated by these earlier identifications of childhood. Or, in Jason's words described earlier, "I think identity is present when other people's opinions become something to reflect upon, rather than to live by."

Additional Identity Concepts

Erikson furthermore used the concepts of *identity crisis, foreclosure, negative identity,* and *moratorium* in describing aspects of the identity-formation process. In 1968, he noted that both the terms identity and identity crisis had come to acquire many varied meanings, both in popular and scientific usage, over the 20 years since he had first used the terms with the particular connotations he had intended. By identity crisis, Erikson did not wish to convey a sense of impending disaster as was earlier interpreted, but rather a key turning point in one's identity development. "It [identity crisis] is now being accepted as designating a necessary turning point, a crucial moment when development must move one way or another, marshaling resources of growth, recovery, and further differentiation" (Erikson, 1968, p. 16). It is through such an identity crisis or key turning point that the identity formation process can proceed. At such a turning point, one is propelled to seek answers or resolutions to questions of life's meaning and one's purpose in it. During an identity crisis, one searches to integrate or reintegrate earlier interests, talents, and values into a coherent personality structure that can find suitable forms of social expression and recognition.

Erikson (1968) only briefly mentioned the concept of psychological foreclosure but did so to describe a premature closure of identity. He gave greater attention to the issue of negative identity, a maladaptive identity resolution whereby an individual bases an identity on all the identifications and roles presented to them in their earlier development as being undesirable or even dangerous. Thus, Erikson (1968) described the situation of the daughter of an influential southern preacher found among narcotics addicts in Chicago. In such cases, it is easier to forge an identity based on all that one is not rather than struggle toward some recognition and actualization of genuine personal talents expressed in a meaningful context.

By moratorium, Erikson referred to a period of searching for or exploring meaningful identity commitments. During a psychosocial moratorium, one lives life "suspended." Erikson, indeed, described how his late adolescent work as an artist while he traveled through Europe provided a kind of "passing" identity while he searched for his life's personal and vocational commitments. Psychosocial moratorium to Erikson meant a delay of adult commitments by youth as well as a period of permissiveness by a society to allow young people the exploration time necessary to make deeper and more meaningful psychosocial commitments.

Contemporary Approaches to Identity: An Overview

From Erikson's original writings on identity, theorists have generally followed one of five major avenues in defining its meaning, and different research traditions have followed from these differing understandings of identity. Recently, there has been a growing body of literature that has examined identity from a *historical* point of view. As Erikson has pointed out, a concern with issues of identity has been a rather recent phenomenon in Western, technologically complex societies. Work by Baumeister (1986, 1987), Cushman (1990), and Neubauer (1994) have provided historical perspectives on why issues of individual identity have become a relatively recent problem in those societies that do not prescribe specific adult roles and life philosophies for their youth.

Furthermore, *structural stage* models, following the tradition of Piaget (1968), have generally focused on structurally defined stages of ego development, that is, intrapsychically defined stages of meaning construction that give rise to developmental differences in the ways in which people filter and make sense of their life experiences. Recent theoretical advances in the area of ego development by Jane Loevinger (Hy & Loevinger, 1996; Loevinger, 1976) and Robert Kegan (1982, 1994) exemplify this approach.

At the other end of the spectrum comes a large and rather diverse body of literature that views identity from a *sociocultural* perspective. Changes in identity according to this tradition are viewed as changes in culturally defined roles and status, often in response to an individual's changing biology and social learning. Following the early interactionist writings of Mead (1934), recent writers such as Côté and Levine (2002) and Shotter and Gergen (1989) have, in varied ways, viewed identity as the result of cultural possibilities and limitations available to an individual within a given context.

In addition, identity has been conceptualized through *narrative* analysis. Our identities take form as our life stories evolve, argue narrative psychologists, and we come to live the story as we write it. Contemporary narrative psychologists such as Dan McAdams (1988) attempt to understand identity through the stories people tell about their lives in order to bring many diverse elements together into an integrated whole and to provide some sense of sameness and continuity to their life experiences. Identity, in narrative terms, does not exist until one's story is told.

Finally, *psychosocial* models adopt an intermediate position between structural stage and sociocultural approaches, viewing identity in terms of the interaction between internal structural characteristics and social tasks demanded by a particular society or social reference group. Identity development here has been conceptualized as a progression of psychosocial tasks, exemplified by the psychosocial models of Erikson (1963, 1968) and Levinson (1978, 1996).

Identity in Historical Terms

One approach to identity focuses on changing historical conditions that have precipitated a contemporary concern with identity (e.g., Baumeister, 1987). Erikson (1975) has noted that the very concept of identity bears historical relativity, for identity had become an issue of individual attention just at the exact point in American history when a new generation of immigrants were struggling toward self-definition in a land far removed from that of their ancestors. "From the point of view of an historian, the entire contemporary discourse on identity occurs at a specific moment in Western history and under very specific conditions" (Grotevant & Bosma, 1994, p. 119). Those conditions involve the disintegration of an old social order, with the issues of personal identity that are then aroused.

Baumeister (1986, 1987) has observed that identity for adolescents and adults in medieval (11th–15th centuries) and early modern (15th–17th centuries) historical epochs were clearly defined. "My thesis is that the self has *become* a problem in the course of historical development" (Baumeister, 1987, p. 163). As many Western societies evolved, deep conflicts were often experienced between the individual and the state. Puritanism (early modern era) raised feelings of self-consciousness and the possibility of self-deception. In the Victorian era (approximately 1830–1900), there arose crises for many individuals on issues of both personal identity as well as in the nature of the relationship between the individual and society. By the early 20th century, themes of alienation and of devaluation of selfhood were widespread.

Identity as an issue of concern particularly among adolescents arose at the very time that many European countries and North American states experienced rising industrialization and an accumulation of wealth (early

each successive structure enables a person to have an increasingly complex way of making sense of his or her life experiences. Within structural stage traditions, there have been several different approaches to an understanding of identity. However, what all approaches hold in common is the awareness of a developmental process in which the intrapsychic organizations (ego structures), through which one interprets and makes sense of the world, change in important ways over time. Movement from childhood through adolescence through adulthood is not just a matter of adding more and more information to an already existing structure of meaning making, but rather of changing the basic meaning-making structures themselves. This phenomenon enables the individual to interpret and understand his or her life experiences in vastly different ways over the course of time. These structural stage approaches follow in the tradition of Piaget (1968), who used the term *accommodation* to describe this process of changing the schemata when new information can no longer be assimilated into existing structures of knowledge. Theoretical advances in the area of ego development by Jane Loevinger (Hy & Loevinger, 1996; Loevinger, 1976), Robert Kegan (1982, 1994), Robert Selman (1980), Sharon Parks (1986), and James Fowler (1981) all exemplify this structural stage tradition. For present purposes, only the work of Loevinger and Kegan will be briefly reviewed, because their models more directly address questions related to underlying structures of identity.

Loevinger (1976) has viewed the ego as a "master trait" of personality, which undergoes predictable, hierarchically organized, developmental stage changes over the course of time. Such changes bring radical differences to the ways in which individuals are able to filter and make sense of their life experiences: "The search for coherent meanings in experience is the essence of the ego or of ego functioning. . . . The ego maintains its stability, its identity, and its coherence by selectively gating out observations inconsistent with its current state . . ." (Hy & Loevinger, 1996, p. 4). Through her revised Sentence Completion Test scoring system (Hy & Loevinger, 1996), Loevinger has identified a sequence of such filtering structures (stages of ego organization) that may evolve over the course of childhood, adolescence, and adult development. Current structures are identified as follows: Impulsive, Self-Protective, Conformist, Self-Aware, Conscientious, Individualistic, Autonomous, and Integrated. Through this sequence, children move from a position of egocentrism and being controlled by their impulses through a structural stage of manipulating others for their own purposes to a position of being able to conform to the rules of a larger social system in early adolescence. From mid- to late adolescence and onwards, individuals may move into more differentiated ego structures. However, while earlier ego stage organizations are strongly correlated with age through mid-adolescence, these latter, more mature stages of ego organization are less strongly linked with age beyond mid-adolescence. Thus, one may find any particular late adolescent or adult making meaning of his or her life experiences from any stage of ego development beyond the impulsive level.

Kegan (1982, 1994) has also proposed a hierarchically organized developmental sequence of underlying structures of meaning construction, which enable people to understand their life experiences in increasingly complex ways over the course of time. Kegan provides a strong theoretical rationale for the developmental forces that drive such changes and discusses the process of transition between more stable structures in some detail. He uses the concept of changes in subject-object balances (self-other differentiation) to describe movement from one mode of meaning-making organization to the next. Subject refers to that in which one is psychologically embedded and cannot distance oneself from (that which *is* me); object refers to that which is possible to manipulate or act upon in some way (that which *is not* me). The process of identity development is a process whereby that which once was subject becomes object of a new subjective; that is, "what I am" becomes "what I have" at the next more mature stage of meaning construction. For example, early adolescents are likely to be embedded in (subject to) the opinions of others—they *are* rather than *have* their relationships. By late adolescence, there has often been a developmental shift that enables a youth to reflect on and consider others' opinions but not be subject to them—to *have* rather than *be* embedded in their relationships with others. Kegan has proposed a five-stage sequence of changing subject-object balances: the Impulsive, Imperial, Interpersonal, Institutional, and Interindividual Balances. These balances reflect increasing levels of self-other differentiation over the course of time. See Kroger (2004) for more detailed discussions of both Loevinger's and Kegan's work.

Both Loevinger and Kegan provide important insights into identity by focusing on internal identity structures and how such structures enable one to interpret the content of one's life experiences. However, these models largely neglect the role that certain contents of identity may hold in shaping any given identity structure itself. Some identity contents, in fact, may make structural transitions more difficult and thus operate to maintain the existing structure. Strongly held religious beliefs, for example, experienced *as* self and reinforced by surrounding group sanctions may make it difficult for one to construct meaning in more complex ways about religion. Noam (1992) has argued, furthermore, that certain incidents within an individual's childhood or adolescent biography may reevoke difficult, encapsulated feelings during times of structural transition so as to limit one's possibilities for growth. In addition, the relationship between structural development and mental health has not been adequately explored when identity has been viewed primarily in structural terms.

What aspects of identity change over time according to structural developmental perspectives? Although the contents of identity (one's interests and values through which one defines oneself) may or may not change with time, structural developmental models describe predictable sequences in the ways in which one will construct meaning and filter one's life experiences, at least through the years of mid-adolescence. And what elements of identity remain constant, according to this tradition? Both Loevinger and Kegan indicate that beyond late adolescence, stages of ego development or meaning-making structures may undergo continued development for some individuals but remain static for others. Research stemming from both Loevinger's and Kegan's works are examining conditions likely to facilitate or impede further identity development during adult life. Kegan and Lahey (2001) address how language and social pressures within the workplace may indeed facilitate or impede the way we come to make meaning in our lives.

Measurement of Identity in Structural Stage Approaches

Although there are a number of different structural stage approaches to understanding adolescent and adult identity and ego development, the work of Loevinger and Kegan more directly addresses questions related to underlying structures of ego development, self-other development, and identity; thus only these two measures are described in the following paragraphs.

Loevinger and her colleagues (e.g., Hy & Loevinger, 1996) have worked over many years to develop the Washington University Sentence Completion Test (SCT). The current version of the SCT (Form 81 for men and Form 81 for women) is composed of 36 incomplete sentence stems, which the research participant is requested to complete in any way he or she wishes. The forms for men and women are comparable, with only the gender of certain nouns and pronouns changed. Examples of some items are as follows: "Education . . . "; I feel sorry . . . "; "What gets me into trouble is. . . . " The most recent scoring guide (Hy & Loevinger, 1996) provides guidelines about how to assess each sentence stem according to ego development stage as well as how to give a total protocol rating. Reliability for this instrument has been assessed in terms of internal consistency (Cronbach's alpha = .91; Loevinger & Wessler, 1970) and interrater reliability, which has also been high (Loevinger & Wessler, 1970). Construct validity has been evaluated in a number of ways and has generally been high (for a review, see Manners & Durkin, 2001).

Kegan and his colleagues (Lahey, Souvaine, Kegan, Goodman, & Felix, 1987) have developed a semistructured interview for the purpose of assessing one's current stage of meaning construction. A person is shown a series of 10 cards, each with one of the following key words or phrases: angry, success, anxious or nervous, strong stand or conviction, sad, torn, moved or touched, lost something, change, important to me. These particular words or phrases were carefully chosen because they all contain elements of self-reference and boundary and are likely to pull information regarding the structure of an experience more readily than other key words. The person is then asked to select several cards that evoke memories of a recent experience for further discussion.

Following a description of the experience, the interviewer carefully probes the situation to learn more about *how* the self must be constructed in order to feel the particular boundary violation the individual has described. Questions such as, "What was the best or hardest part of the experience for you?" and "What might have been lost or gained had the experience not taken place?" help the interviewer draw information about how the individual is actually constructing his or her experience according to one of Kegan's (1982, 1994) meaning-making stages. Interviews are tape-recorded and transcribed, structural units are identified, and one's predominant meaning-making stage is determined according to the predominant mode of meaning construction. Lahey and her colleagues (1987) report four studies of inter-rater reliability, one of test-retest reliability, and one of interitem consistency. All forms of reliability have been high, ranging from 82 to 100 percent. Construct validity has been undertaken by examining meaning-making stages in relation to other structural developmental measures; findings have been satisfactory (see Kegan, 1994, for a review).

Sociocultural Approaches to Identity

A third general approach to identity focuses on the role that society plays in providing (or not providing) individual identity alternatives (e.g., Shotter & Gergen, 1989). From this orientation, contexts involve significant relationships wherein language and actions serve as the primary media for the formation of the self, and intrapsychic processes are unnecessary in accounting for the process of self-definition. From Mead's (1934) early interactionist approach to identity, contemporary writers such as Côté (1996; Côté & Levine, 2002), Gergen (1991), and Shotter and Gergen (1989) have, in varied ways, continued to view identity as the result of cultural possibilities and limitations available to the individual within a given context. Mead (1934) proposed that people define themselves according to how they perceive others responding to them. Response from others comes through verbal and gestural communication. Individuals not only become aware of the impact they have on others, but they also use that awareness to determine future communications of the self. Because individuals carry within themselves a whole series of different relationships to different people, Mead (1934) noted that "a multiple personality is in a certain sense normal" (p. 142). Thus, the unity of one's experience of self is merely a reflection of the unity in one's social experience. From Mead's early writings have sprung a number of different theoretical approaches to identity that hold in common the view that an individual's identity is the product of the surrounding social context. As Côté (1996) states, "For many sociologists there is no identity without society, and society steers identity formation while individuals attempt to navigate the passage" (p. 133).

Shotter and Gergen and their associates have examined ways in which personal identities are formed, constrained, and defined by the contexts of their lives (Gergen, 1991; Shotter & Gergen, 1989). Such contexts involve significant relationships with others, in which language and actions serve as the primary agents for the formation of the self. "Persons are largely ascribed identities according to the manner of their embedding within a discourse—in their own or in the discourse of others" (Shotter & Gergen, 1989, p. xi). Cultural texts, or messages from the host culture, thus furnish those who reside within them much information about potentialities as well as limitations for the construction of an identity. Gergen (1991) suggests that communication technologies now demand that people relate to many more individuals and social institutions than ever before, resulting in social saturation. Because, in Gergen's view, identity is the result of social interaction, this multiplicity of relationships results in a self under siege and hence, dilemmas of identity.

Slugoski and Ginsburg (1989) and Yoder (2000) develop these ideas in direct response to Erikson's views on identity. Slugoski and Ginsburg argue that *crisis* and *commitment,* the underpinnings of the identity-formation process according to Erikson, should not be viewed primarily as private, intrapsychic processes, but rather as culturally sanctioned modes of discourse that allow individuals to ascribe to their actions some degree of rationality or meaning. They argue furthermore, that Erikson, in his theory, neglects the many societies wherein youth simply do not have even the possibility of envisioning alternative options for the future.

Yoder (2000) uses the concept of "barriers" to describe sociocultural influences associated with identity exploration and commitment processes that may limit developmental potential. She continues by noting a number of exploration and commitment barrier characteristics that may produce various types of identity resolutions. For example, barriers may reflect sociocultural biases such as stereotypic, negative attitudes toward the elderly or ethnic minority groups. Barriers may reflect social or economic boundaries in one context but not another. And barriers may exist on a continuum, ranging from all inhibiting to those holding minor constraints. Yoder's barriers concept will be discussed further in Chapter 4.

Such sociocultural approaches have provided an important contribution to the understanding of identity by emphasizing the social context and how the feedback and demands by others in society shape the course of one's identity over time. Identity, however, must be viewed as more than a product of social messages alone in order again to explain individual variation within any given social context. The range of identity structures found on measures of identity status (Marcia, Waterman, Matteson, Archer, & Orlofsky, 1993), ego development (Loevinger, 1976), and subject-object balance (Kegan, 1994) testifies to this diversity of response within many contemporary contexts. Smith (1994) has also criticized Gergen's (1991) proposal that social saturation implies a self under siege, bereft of anchors from which to stabilize a view of self and the world. Such a radical position, argues Smith, is unwarranted. Rather, it remains possible to adopt a constructivist, sociocultural position without viewing the self as empty, drifting in the dizzying and disorienting winds of cultural chaos. Indeed, Berzonsky (2005) points to the critical importance of attaining a sense of ego identity or personal standpoint in order to navigate the many social options currently possible within and across many Western contexts. Markus and Nurius (1986) also have noted the difficulties such sociocultural approaches have in describing forces too stable to account for the demands and constraints of moment-to-moment situations.

What aspects of identity change over time, according to sociocultural perspectives? Perhaps most writers working within this framework would argue that as one changes contexts or receives differing messages from new people within the same physical setting, one's identity is likely to undergo change. Because one's identity is primarily a product of social discourse, a change in feedback about oneself from important others will precipitate a change in one's own sense of identity. Stability in one's sense of identity is likely only if social contexts remain unaltered or if one continues to receive nonconflicting messages from significant others about who one is or should be in the world.

Measurement of Identity in Sociocultural Approaches

As noted previously, there are a range of writers and researchers taking a sociocultural perspective on the study of identity. Common to such approaches, however, is a focus on social groups and their overt or covert means of impacting identity choices of those residing within. Sociocultural approaches to identity typically have not developed interviews or other types of measures given directly to individuals within a context to examine identity concerns, but rather have focused both on demographic data, such as population and employment statistics, as well as information regarding political, economic, and social trends to draw conclusions about identity development. Kinnvall (2004) and Rattansi and Phoenix (1997) have both undertaken sociocultural approaches to adolescent and adult identity, and their methods for assessing social trends are presented as examples of sociocultural approaches in the following paragraphs.

Kinnvall examines the impact of economic globalization and its political, social, and economic consequences on Eriksonian ideas regarding identity. She notes that globalization in its widest sense often threatens human security. This ideology has often changed the role of the state from a welfare provider for its inhabitants to that of a market competitor. Furthermore, there have been recent attempts to democratize societies in ways that delegitimize previous forms of governance. In addition, trade liberalization policies have often deprived nations of their main source of income (i.e., taxes), making it more difficult for the state to deal with alleviating poverty. Programs aimed at privatization and increasing global competitiveness have often also resulted in job losses or underemployment. And the ability of many international firms to relocate at short notice has accelerated feelings of insecurity among people in both rich and poor countries alike. Thus modern society has often given people a sense of uprootedness from their original social environments and traditional ways of living. Kinnvall explores the implications of these various social forces upon Erikson's ideas about identity and the importance of biographical continuity to optimal identity development for both adolescents and adults.

Similarly, Rattansi and Phoenix (1997) focus upon the problem of the decontextualization of young people's identities. They, too, note that the rapid social changes of late modernity have disembedded previously "settled" identities. The erosion of older, more settled collective identities through globalization forces leave adolescents and adults currently in the process of searching for identifications with an overwhelming diversity of new social and cultural values and behaviors. The authors argue that the notion of a stable, coherent identity, such as that described by Erikson, is virtually impossible to attain, and that fluid, fragmented identities are perhaps most adaptive for youths attempting to engage with the variety of values presented by their sociocultural contexts. These types of social commentaries, coupled with demographic data, have been common among sociocultural orientations to the study of identity.

Narrative Approaches to Identity

A narrative approach to identity (e.g., McAdams, 1988) suggests that language is a text out of which identities are constructed, justified, and maintained. Narrative approaches to identity can be found among virtually all other approaches to identity; however, it is also considered as an approach within its own right here, for narrative analysis has become an increasingly popular way of examining adolescent and adult identity developments. Biographies are studied as life stories in an attempt to understand how people make sense of their lives and give meaning and coherence to them. Narrative approaches to identity can be regarded as attempts to interrelate internal psychological processes and societal messages and demands. McAdams (1988) argues that we construct stories that serve as the basis of identity; "We create stories, and we live according to narrative assumptions. . . . As the story evolves and our identity takes form, we come to *live* the story as we *write* it. . . . " (p. ix).

McAdams (1996) differentiates the *I* and the *me* in the narrative study of identity. He views the *I* as the process of creating a self through the experience of narrating, whereas the *me* is defined as the product that the *I* constructs. The *I* is the source of experience and evolves over time to more complex levels of meaning construction. The *me* is termed a self-concept by many and is an evolving collection of self-attributions. Personality traits, concerns, and stories are not components of the *I*, but rather *me* elements that have implications for how the *I* works. In seeking to understand identity, McAdams believes that one must look to life stories, the "telling" of the self that synthesizes many *me* elements in such a way as to provide coherence and unity through the passage of time and discrepant experiences. Identity resides in the binding together of the *I* and the *me*. The life story portrays the characteristic ways in which the *I* arranges elements of the *me* into a temporal sequence having a setting, plot, and characters. The life story is thus a psychosocial construction. Five questions guide the examination of a life story: What is a life story in terms of structure and content? What is the function of a life story? How does a life story develop over time? What kinds of individually different life stories are there? What constitutes an optimal life story?

Narrative approaches have become increasingly popular in studies of identity, for such analyses emphasize an understanding of the whole person and how he or she integrates life experiences, rather than the understanding of isolated values, accomplishments, or other personality features. These processes of integration are often difficult to examine through traditional empirical research. At the same time, narrative analysis appears limited by several important considerations. Narrative analyses seek only to understand and interpret an individual life story, rather than looking for important patterns of identity development over a wide range of people. By focusing on a single individual, it is possible to gain insights into processes of identity that might later be empirically tested across broader samples of individuals, but this purpose is not the goal of narrative analysis.

Marcia and Strayer (1996) have criticized the narrative approach to identity for its lack of scientific criteria for analysis. Without a broader framework for organizing and interpreting individual life stories, a narrative approach remains limited in its ability to describe general processes of identity development, they argue. Furthermore, data obtained by narrative analysis is limited by the meaning-making structure of the storyteller. The life story, for example, of an individual making sense from a less complex, hedonistic focus will differ greatly from a narrator using more complex modes of reasoning, capable of integrating multiple perspectives on an issue. The narrative approach has no system for examining the identity structure of the individual narrator in relation to the types of life stories that he or she tells.

What about identity changes, from the perspective of narrative analysis? One's struggle for unity and the sense of an internally coherent identity throughout the inevitable vicissitudes of life forms the basis of one's life story. Some life stories work better than others, and McAdams (1996) points out that within certain cultural contexts, some stories are probably better stories than others. And some stories bring one a greater sense of unity than others. One may reconstruct one's story of the past in order to provide the present *me* with a greater sense of unity or purpose. Thus, one's life story, giving rise to identity, is likely to change over time to bring a greater sense of unity, coherence, and purpose to an individual's existence as he or she meets new life circumstances. Are there any elements of identity that remain constant in this perspective? Certain *me* elements or self-attributions may, in fact, remain stable over time, whereas others will change.

Measurement of Identity in Narrative Approaches

A variety of qualitative methods have been used in narrative approaches to the understanding of identity. Some of these include ethnographic studies (in which the investigator engages in participant observations of and interviews with a particular group of people), to case study methods and biographical studies of single individuals, to grounded theory methods (focusing on deriving some general principles from observations and/or interactions with individuals or small groups of people), to phenomenological methods, whereby the investigator focuses on a single phenomenon to understand an individual's experience of that phenomenon. The general purpose behind the use of qualitative methods is to build a complex, holistic picture of an individual, studied in a naturalistic setting. Ragin (1987) characterizes a key difference between quantitative and qualitative approaches when he notes that quantitative researchers work with a few variables and many cases, while qualitative researchers work with a few cases and many variables.

Josselson, Lieblich, and McAdams (2003) offer keen insights into the study of identity and relationships via narrative methods (among other issues). They provide a collection of chapters that try to elucidate how the researcher is guided by some larger conception of the meaning that the narrator might be trying to make. This larger conception is based on, but not entirely present in, the text itself; rather it depends on our assumptions about the meaning that we bring to this larger picture (Ochberg, 2003). Rather than forming hypotheses to be tested, narrative researchers are guided by questions for exploration. Thus, there are no predeveloped, semistructured interview frameworks—rather there are primary questions guiding the researcher in his or her interview work. The researcher, furthermore, is called upon to examine his or her assumptions and understandings of the interview's thematic content.

While there is no "one right way" to undertake narrative research, those using this method to study identity generally do so by transcribing interviews that are read by at least two people (and often more) in an attempt to find consistent interview themes, but also to examine underlying assumptions of the interviewers themselves as they attempt to make sense of these themes. Thus, narrative approaches challenge the more traditional, positivist approaches to the study of identity that emphasize objectivity and distance in examining large numbers of individuals and attempt to generalize patterns of behavior and development across certain populations. Narrative approaches, rather, focus on small numbers of people to examine an individual's understandings of (often unique) life experiences as well as an interviewer's own assumptions about how who one is influences what one is able to see (Josselson et al., 2003).

Psychosocial Approaches to Identity

A fifth approach seeks to integrate the roles played both by society and an individual's intrapsychic dynamics and biology in developing and maintaining personal identity. Erikson (1963, 1968) and Levinson (1978, 1996) are two of a number of psychosocial theorists who have attempted to interrelate societal demands and individual internal forces of development in their general discussion of identity during adolescent and adult life. As Erikson's work has been presented in an earlier section of this chapter, Levinson's work will be presented here. Examples of measures drawn from both Erikson's (1968) discussions of identity and Levinson's work on life structures will be presented in conclusion.

Levinson (1978) published *The Seasons of a Man's Life,* an extensive study of psychosocial development among men. This volume proposed a predictable, age-linked series of developmental, psychosocial stages that participants traversed in the course of their late adolescent and adult years. Nearly two decades later, Levinson (1996) produced a similar study of psychosocial development among women, *The Seasons of a Woman's Life*. This research again showed amazingly predictable stages of identity changes over the course of adolescence and adulthood (these women, both traditional homemakers and career women, were actually interviewed only slightly later in time than the cohort of men, so possible cohort differences was not a confounding factor). Furthermore, these psychosocial stages were very similar to those of men in terms of their developmental timetables; yet some profound differences did emerge for the two sexes in the division of labor between the domestic and the public occupational arenas. Many homemakers as well as career women interviewed were struggling against traditional definitions of acceptable social roles for women and were working toward greater gender equality. This struggle permeated the psychosocial phases of their lives in a way that was not apparent for men.

A primary concept for Levinson is the individual life structure, the patterning of one's life at any given time. The individual life structure refers to the means by which an individual engages with society. A life structure has three elements: the nature of one's sociocultural world (class, religion, ethnicity, family, friendship networks, occupational structure, and particular social conditions like war, liberation movements, economic depression), one's way of participation in the world, and the aspects of the self that are actualized in the various facets of one's life. The study of a life structure places equal emphasis on all of these elements and their interactions.

For both genders in Levinson's studies, the Early Adult Transition, occurring between about ages 17 and 22, marked the end of childhood and the creation of the basis for Entering the Adult World Life Structure (ages 22 to 28). During this time, the primary task was to evolve and test out a life structure that would provide a workable link between the self and the adult world. A further transition (the Age 30 Transition) was experienced between about ages 28 and 33, as the foundations for the Culminating Life Structure for Early Adulthood were laid (experienced between about ages 33 and 40). Early adulthood concerns of getting established with one's vocational and family concerns were then left behind in the next transition (the Midlife Transition, ages 40 to 45). During this transition, an important new set of developmental tasks arose, when the entire life structure established during early adulthood came into question. Issues such as "What have I done with my life?" predominated and "What do I still really want to do?" came to the fore. Any major transition brings a profound reappraisal of all that has gone before; the midlife transition often involved recognizing illusions that had given form to one's life until that time. The life structure that followed this

Age 40 Transition varied greatly in the degree of satisfaction it brought to participants in both studies. Throughout middle adulthood (about 45 to 60), a similar alternating sequence of structure-building and structure-maintaining eras was proposed for both genders.

While Levinson's model has generated great interest in predictable life transitions, it was developed based on interviews with men and women in specific social and cultural contexts. It would be instructive to undertake similar interviews with men and women in a diversity of social and cultural circumstances to study the relationship between individual life structures and contextual demands. In addition, Levinson's interviews were conducted with samples of adults in their 40s, and the retrospective nature of the data used to describe earlier life phases as well as the inability of the data to predict identity transitions in later adulthood beg for future longitudinal investigations to overcome these difficulties.

Erikson's psychosocial approach to identity development, described earlier in this chapter, has demonstrated wide cultural applicability (Marcia et al., 1993) and has provided a helpful, integrative framework for those working in applied areas. Yet, at the same time, Erikson only briefly alludes to three intrapsychic structural organizations (introjection, identification, identity formation) that seem to shift during childhood and adolescent development; it would be instructive if further research might examine possible new intrapsychic structures that may underlie Erikson's three psychosocial stages of adulthood. In addition, the many and varied meanings Erikson has attributed to the concept of identity itself have made researchers struggle to operationalize definitions amenable to empirical study; such studies have, in turn, often produced conflicting results.

What dimensions of identity change, from a psychosocial perspective? As one ages, societies require individuals to assume different roles in the course of daily living; in addition, an individual's biology, psychological defenses, and cognitive processes all mature so that changes in one's sense of ego identity will undergo phases of formulation and reformulation throughout adolescent and adult life. At the same time, Erikson has argued that a stable sense of self must remain across time and place for optimal identity development.

Measurement of Identity in Psychosocial Approaches

The work of James Marcia (1966, 1967; Marcia et al., 1993) has been central in expanding the conception of identity presented by Erikson (1963, 1968). In Erikson's view, finding a resolution to the fifth psychosocial task of Identity Versus Role Confusion was conceptualized as finding a place on an identity continuum, ranging from high (identity achievement) to low (role confusion). Thus, to Erikson, identity was something you had "more or less of." However, Marcia (1966) proposed four qualitatively different ways of addressing (or not addressing) identity issues of late adolescents. Erikson (1963) had suggested that finding resolutions to work and ideological values were central to the identity formation task of adolescence. Based on the processes of exploration and commitment that Erikson had also described in the identity formation process, Marcia identified four different styles (identity statuses) that youth use to find initial resolutions to Identity Versus Role Confusion: identity achievement, moratorium, foreclosure, and diffusion.

Identity achieved and foreclosed individuals had both made important identity-defining commitments; however, the identity achieved had done so following a time of active exploration and searching, while the foreclosed had made identity-defining decisions primarily on the basis of identifications with important others. Thus, the identity achieved had actively constructed a sense of their own identities, while the foreclosed had a kind of conferred identity, based on the values of significant others and obtained without serious exploration. Moratorium and diffused individuals had not formed strong identity-defining commitments; however, moratoriums were in the process of actively searching and trying to find meaningful resolutions to questions of work roles and ideological values, while diffusions were drifting, unable to engage in the identity formation process.

Marcia (1966; Marcia et al., 1993) developed the Identity Status Interview, initially for use with late adolescents but later adapted for use with both adults and younger adolescents. The interview, lasting about 30 minutes, probes various identity domains important to the participant (e.g., work, political, religious, sexual and sex role values) to identify the primary style (or identity status) by which the individual seems to be going about resolving questions of identity. Interrater reliabilities for the interview (based on percentages of agreement between two or more raters) have generally been high—around 80–85 percent (Marcia et al., 1993). Numerous measures have also been used to help validate the identity statuses (e.g., personality measures of locus of control, anxiety, authoritarianism, defense mechanisms). Status differences in scoring have most frequently been in predicted directions (see Chapters 3 and 4 for reviews). Since Marcia's work, several pencil and paper measures of identity status and identity style have also been developed (e.g., Adams, 1999; Berzonsky, 1992).

Levinson (1978, 1996) also has relied on interview techniques to examine the concept of life structures. Using intensive biographical interviewing and biographical reconstructions, Levinson's goals were to elicit the life stories of his participants, to construct an individual biography of each person in his or her own words, and to learn something from this material about life issues relating to friendship, work, love, marriage, parenthood, and good and bad times. Each interview session lasted one and a half to two hours, and each participant was interviewed over the course of a 2- to 3-month period for a total of 15–20 hours. Researchers met regularly to discuss individual interviews and how themes related to other participants in the project as a whole. However, in using this qualitative method, Levinson has not provided details of any standard semistructured interview format, nor has his work been extensively replicated by others. He has, however, provided interesting insights into both the lives of his participants and themes specific to the groups of men and women that were interviewed.

Key Similarities and Differences Across Identity Models

Table 1.1 summarizes the strengths and limitations of the five general approaches to identity that have been reviewed in this chapter.

Table 1.1   Summary of Strengths and Limitations of Varied Identity Approaches

Identity Approach	Strengths	Limitations
Historical	Acknowledges historical relativity of concern with identity	Difficulty explaining individual differences in identity
Structural Stage	Acknowledges developmental structures in filtering life events	Difficulty explaining mechanisms of how context may impede development
Sociocultural	Addresses how identities are formed, constrained, and defined by context	Difficulty explaining individual differences in identity
Narrative	Focuses on the whole person and how identity elements are integrated via one's life story	Difficulty generalizing identity principles beyond level of individual description
Psychosocial	Addresses biological, psychological, and societal influences on identity	More attention needed to intrapsychic developmental structures

Table 1.2   Summary of Change Perspectives

Identity Approach	Identity Change	Identity Constancy
Historical	With change in historical circumstances	With constancy in historical circumstances
Structural Stage	In predictable developmental sequence through adolescence; in some contents (values, interests)	In some contents (values, interests)
Sociocultural	With contextual change	With contextual constancy
Narrative	With reconstructed life story; with some *me* elements	With some *me* elements
Psychosocial	In psychosocial tasks required by society; in some biological elements; some psychological elements	In some psychological elements; in some biological elements

Table 1.2 summarizes the perspectives on identity change and identity constancy held by the five general approaches to identity reviewed in this volume.

Back to the Beginning

This chapter began with three questions and a quotation from Elaine, a 55-year-old woman returning to university study. In Elaine's words, there is the feeling that she is still the same person she was as a child, though her body has changed and other people's expectations of her have changed. Some psychological processes, however, have remained the same so that Elaine experiences a sense of continuity in who she was, is, and will become. In addition, Elaine finds herself once again searching for new identity-defining directions in life, although she had found directions and goals that were previously satisfying. It may be that internal psychological factors, external conditions, or a combination of the two situations conspired to again raise identity issues for Elaine at midlife. Different theoretical approaches interested in understanding Ellen's identity would view her comments about identity change and stability in different ways.

PART II

Adolescence

Even the raven began in human form, but he cast about, directionless, until he found who he was and what his purpose on this earth was to be.

—Arctic creation myth

My sisters are real feminine. They help a lot. They're a lot more feminine than I am, but that's because I'm younger than they are.

—13-year-old schoolgirl (Archer, 1985, p. 92)

2

Identity in Early Adolescence

- How do the changes of puberty affect identity in early adolescence?
- Does a society's lack of formal puberty rites help or hinder early adolescent identity development?
- Do parents of pubertal adolescents change their ways of relating to their children?

The principal at school recently talked to us about options when we get to high school next year and about how important our decisions are for the courses ahead. He said we should be basing our choices for next year on what we wanted to do when we left school. This all jolted me into thinking about how I'm growing up and really gave me a sense of panic.

—John, 13-year-old schoolboy

Will my body ever start changing? Will my body ever stop changing? Is this normal? Am I normal? Do my friends really like me? Can I ever be in with Dan's crowd? Could boys really like me? Will I ever kiss a girl? What will I look like when I'm older? Why am I suddenly interested in girls? And why are the girls all taller (and seem stronger) than me? What am I going to do when I grow up? How can I ask Mom if I can shave my legs? When can I stop going to mass? Why is God punishing me?

The responses in the previous paragraph were some of the key identity-related questions that emerged when I recently polled a class of 12- to 13-year-old adolescents regarding the kinds of questions they think most about when they consider who they are. Themes of changing biology pervaded their responses, followed by issues of wanting to fit in, to be normal, and to be liked by significant others. Occasionally, concerns for the future and one's work roles and relationships in it also emerged. Sometimes, just sometimes, came more existential questions about the existence of God and the meaning of life and death.

Themes of biology, individual psychology, and social surroundings, the three components Erikson (1968) describes as contributing to one's overall sense of ego identity, can be clearly seen in previous passages. Although many of these young citizens will be emerging from the Eriksonian stage of Industry Versus Inferiority, we can hope with some sense of their own competencies, interests, and abilities, the task of identity formation has yet to begin. I turn now to the world of early adolescence, to offer an overview of some normative biological and psychological structures emerging during this time, as well as some of the key societal demands experienced by young adolescents in many Western, technologically advanced nations. I define early adolescence here in terms of both chronological age and psychosocial tasks—the time from 11 to 14 years, during which the young person is likely to experience many new events. The biological changes of puberty, the move to more complex ways of thinking, redefining the self within the family, developing new forms of relationships with peers, and adapting to the more complex demands of a junior high or middle school system—all raise important identity considerations for the young adolescent.

Intersection of Biological, Psychological, and Societal Influences on Identity in Early Adolescence: An Overview

Certainly some of the most significant identity issues of early adolescence are associated with the biological changes of puberty and their reverberations in psychological processes and societal responses. The word *puberty* (derived from the Latin *pubescere,* meaning to grow hairy) refers to the complex sequence of biological changes whereby one becomes a sexually mature adult, capable of reproducing and assuming the height, weight, body contours, and increased strength and tolerance for the physical activity of adulthood (Bogin, 1994). All adolescents undergo puberty (except those with endocrine disorders that prevent puberty), although pubertal timing can vary greatly from one individual to another (Archibald, Graber, & Brooks-Gunn, 2003).

In appreciating the enormity of change emerging within the biological, psychological, and societal contexts overviewed in the following paragraphs, it is equally important to appreciate the interaction among these spheres and the identity-related readjustments such interactions among systems bring. Young adolescents, for example, are able to reflect upon and attribute meaning to their biological metamorphoses; furthermore, they also receive many identity-related cultural messages about the implications that having an adult anatomy now holds (Paikoff & Brooks-Gunn, 1990). The identity-related difficulties of undergoing multiple transitions within different arenas of development at the same time must also be appreciated when examining the biological, psychological, and social/cultural dimensions of identity separately. For example, experiencing a changing biology at the very time one is likely to be moving from an elementary to a junior high or middle school system may only compound identity readjustments for some.

In the overview of changes in the biology of puberty that follows, the purpose will be to present key features of change affecting identity during early adolescence rather than giving a detailed review of endocrinological activity associated with puberty. Similarly, key psychological issues and societal responses affecting most directly one's sense of identity will be presented, rather than attempting to delineate all major cognitive, social, and psychological features of early adolescent development.

Biological Processes

When does puberty begin? Puberty is not a single process or stage with specific beginning and end points, but rather a continuum of changes that evolve gradually over the course of adolescence. This slow process eventually results in mature reproductive capacity, the development of secondary sex characteristics, and the assumption of adult height and body proportions. Archibald and colleagues (2003) point to five general areas of physical functioning that change over the course of five or six years during pubertal development: (1) the "growth spurt" (acceleration followed by deceleration of skeletal growth); (2) increases in and redistribution of body fat and muscle tissue; (3) changes in circulatory and respiratory systems, bringing newfound abilities in strength and endurance; (4) maturation of secondary sexual characteristics and reproductive organs; and (5) changes in hormonal and endocrine systems, which regulate the timing of pubertal events. These processes are all impacted by genetic factors, nutrition and other environment agents, as well as hormonal factors (Archibald et al., 2003).

The phenomenon of accelerated physical development during only some life stages is quite unusual among mammals. "Most mammals progress from infancy to adulthood seamlessly, without any intervening stages, and while their growth rates are in decline" (Bogin, 1994, p. 31). The enormous physical transformations of early adolescence do hold many psychological reverberations, including the need to integrate such changes into a new sense of self and identity, of who one is, how one relates to, and fits into surrounding social contexts. Not surprising, heightened emotionality with more extreme mood swings (moodiness) do seem to be associated with pubertal transitions among young adolescents (Larson & Richards, 1994). In addition, important changes take place in regions of the brain during early adolescence that process emotions (Spear, 2000). The impact of these biological, behavioral, and other identity-related changes will be more fully discussed in the following section.

Puberty actually begins long before any visible signs of biological change occur. For young girls, this process can begin as early as age 7, and by age 9 and a half for boys. The endocrine system regulates levels of hormones circulating in the body. This system receives messages from the central nervous system (primarily the brain) and operates like a thermostat in controlling the secretion of hormones circulating within the body. Between infancy and puberty, parts of the brain (specifically the pituitary gland, which controls hormone levels generally, and the hypothalamus, which controls the pituitary gland) have acted to inhibit levels of sex hormones circulating in the body. However, about a year before any visible signs of puberty appear, there is a change in the regulating system so that levels of sex hormones circulating within the body rise (Archibald et al., 2003). It is this rise in the circulation of sex hormones that induces the many biological changes of puberty. The reasons for this rise are not well understood, although increasing research evidence suggests that increasing levels of a protein produced by fat cells called "leptin" are associated with pubertal events (Apter & Hermanson, 2002). Earlier research suggested that individuals must reach a "critical weight" and body mass before puberty can occur, and the accumulation of leptin from fat cells is consistent with these earlier observations. However, to date there is no evidence that increases in leptin levels actually *cause* pubertal changes (Archibald et al., 2003). Stress, illness, nutrition, and excessive exercise and excessive thinness can all influence pubertal timing.

The two primary classes of sex hormones are called androgens and estrogens. Testosterone is an androgen that plays a key role in male pubertal development, whereas estradiol is an estrogen that plays a key role in female pubertal development. As testosterone levels increase at puberty for boys, a number of biological changes take place. There is an enlargement in the size of the testicles and penis, accompanied by the first appearance of pubic hair; minor voice changes ensue, followed by the first ejaculation, the peak velocity in the height spurt, more noticeable voice changes, and finally the growth of facial and body hair. As levels of estradiol as well as some androgens rise for girls, breast development occurs first, followed by growth of pubic hair, broadening of the hips, the growth spurt, and the onset of menstruation (Rabin & Chrousos, 1991). Noteworthy is the fact that girls experience their growth spurt before becoming capable of reproduction, although for boys the reverse is true. Additionally, the onset of the skeletal growth spurt occurs about two years earlier for girls than boys (Archibald et al., 2003).

This ordering of pubertal events for the two genders has been viewed from an adaptive, evolutionary perspective, which may hold important identity implications. Boys become fertile long before their bodies assume full adult stature and proportions, generally around 13.4 years of age (Muller, Nielsen, & Skakkebaek, 1989). However, very few teenage men become fathers. In the United States, several surveys have reported that about two-thirds of sexually active school-age mothers have partners who were at least 20 years old (Miller, Bayley, Christensen, Leavitt, & Coyl, 2003). Bogin (1994) notes that one reason for the lag between sperm production and fatherhood may be that the sperm of young adolescent males may not have the motility or endurance to reach an egg cell in the female's fallopian tubes. However, a more probable reason, Bogin believes, is that the average 13.4-year-old boy is likely to be only in the beginning of his growth spurt and not yet physically mature in appearance (or psychosocially ready for fatherhood) and hence not perceived as an adult by any potential mates. Bogin (1994) describes the evolutionary value of this human pattern of early adolescent pubertal development:

> In summary, the argument for the evolution and value of human adolescence is this. Girls best learn their adult social roles while they are infertile but perceived by adults as mature, whereas boys best learn their adult social roles while they are sexually mature but not yet perceived as such by adults. Without the adolescent growth spurt this unique style of social and cultural learning could not occur. (p. 33)

Although the gender-specific sequence of biological change is uniform, the timing and tempo of pubertal change varies enormously from one individual to the next (and until recently, from one generation to the next). Within any group of early adolescents, there are likely to be some who have completed the entire sequence of pubertal changes, whereas others have not yet begun any visible transformations. Classroom photographs of those in the 11- to 14-year-old age range are likely to present a vivid visual illustration of the enormous variation in individual developmental timetables of puberty. Recent research comparing identical twins (genetically identical) and adolescents who are not identical twins indicates the timing and tempo of pubertal maturation to be largely inherited (Dick, Rose, Pulkkinen, & Kapiro, 2001). Within the United States, research has suggested strong ethnic differences in both the timing and rate of pubertal maturation that is not a result of socioeconomic status, weight, or residential area. For example, African American girls mature earlier than Mexican American females, who, in turn, mature earlier than white American girls (Chumlea et al., 2003). There are many identity related issues involving being early, "on time," or late in one's biological development at puberty relative to one's peers, and these issues are discussed in some detail in a subsequent section of this chapter.

Psychological Issues

My sisters are real feminine. They help me a lot. They're a lot more feminine than I am but that's because I'm younger than they are.

—13-year-old schoolgirl (Archer, 1985, p. 92)

With the advent of puberty and the transition into early adolescence, childhood "proper" comes to an end. Erikson (1963) has stressed that with this new phase of adolescence, all the "sameness and continuity" of earlier years are brought into question. Both the rapidity of bodily growth as well as increasing genital maturity bring new questions of identity at the time of early adolescence. Crises of earlier years are raised again for some, and Erikson has stressed the need for a moratorium period to integrate identity elements from past childhood stages into the present. The demand for an enlarged sense of identity to encompass the physiological changes of puberty is also encouraged by new demands of society.

Erikson does not detail identity-related tasks specific to *early* adolescence, but rather outlines identity-related tasks of adolescence more generally—many of which are more relevant to mid- and late adolescence. In fact, Kegan (1982) has drawn attention to this theoretical gap in Erikson's writings:

I believe Erikson misses a stage between "industry" and "identity." His identity stage—with its orientation to the self alone, "Who am I?" time, achievement, ideology, self-certainty, and so on—captures something of late adolescence or early adulthood, but it does not really address the period of connection, inclusion, and highly invested mutuality which comes between the more independence-oriented periods of latency and [late adolescent] identity formation. (p. 87)

Thus, Kegan describes an Affiliation Versus Abandonment stage, additional to Erikson's eight-stage sequence of psychosocial tasks, as representing the key psychosocial conflict of early adolescence. From the introductory statements by 12- to 13-year-olds that appeared at the beginning of this chapter, concern with being liked and accepted by the group was an important identity issue for many.

Identity concerns with affiliation and abandonment during early adolescence have also appeared in many studies of relationships during adolescence (see Kegan, 1982, 1994, for examples). In 1983, I approached groups of 6th-, 8th-, 10th-, and 12th-grade students in both New Zealand and the United States (California) to compare attitudes toward self and others (Kroger, 1983). Students completed sentence stems dealing with many relationship items, including feelings toward friendships in small and large groups. Toward large groups, at least two-thirds of youths from all age levels in the United States and New Zealand expressed little tolerance for a peer who was not part of the crowd.

- **11-year-old girl:** If someone is not part of the group, they pose a threat to our privacy.
- **11-year-old boy:** If someone is not part of the group, they are probably really thick.
- **13-year-old boy:** If someone is not part of the group, they are outcasts and no one likes them.
- **16-year-old boy:** If someone is not part of the group, they must be highly and totally boring people to be with. (Kroger, 1983, p. 3)

Thus, themes of affiliation and abandonment, of being accepted or left behind by others, appear to be prevalent identity concerns among many early adolescents. It may be that the need for affiliation, completion, being recognized and supported by the family and, later, the group is essential to the process of one's identity formation.

Marcia (1983) has built further upon Erikson's writings and discussed some identity-related psychosocial tasks specific to early adolescence. He has noted that early adolescence is a period of disorganization—and that such disorganization characterizes early adolescence whether it is navigated smoothly or not. Marcia has proceeded to outline key identity-defining tasks of early adolescence, including the necessity of beginning to "free" oneself from the dictates of the "internalized parent." This internalized parent refers to prohibitions and aspirations from one's parents, which have been taken into the self through childhood and upon which one has built a sense of self-esteem. This internalization of parental standards was adaptive in childhood, for it enabled the child to function more autonomously without the parent needing to be physically present. However, the continued, unreflective, and rigid adherence to standards from internalized parents is not adaptive to the many demands presented by adult life, at least in Western, technologically advanced societies. Other writers such as Blos (1979) and Levine, Green, and Millon (1986) have also pointed to the early adolescent task of beginning to disengage from the internalized parents and starting to seek extrafamial outlets for emotional and sexual energy, until now bound up within the family triangle. Certainly research on adolescents and their families has pointed to increased levels of conflict at the time of puberty and physical maturation, likely to reflect growing desires for autonomy on the part of young adolescents (e.g., Collins & Laursen, 2004).

Thus, there are many necessary but formidable psychological tasks for the early adolescent. Finding one's way in the transition to a new school system and adjusting to new teachers, peers, and organizational systems more generally present important challenges. Beginning to differentiate one's own interests, needs, attitudes, and attributions from those of one's parents and significant others is an initial undertaking. Integrating newfound bodily changes and sexual desires into a sense of personal identity, different from but related to all previous identifications, is a further challenge. And beginning to channel these new capacities into socially available outlets using culturally appropriate forms of expression is yet a further demand required of young adolescents across many cultural contexts.

Societal Influences

When does adolescence begin? Transitions into both adolescence and adulthood are often marked in different ways around the world. In many preindustrial societies, puberty rites are often a hallmark of early adolescence. Schlegel and Barry (1980) have defined such rites of passage "as some social recognition, in ceremonial form, of the transition from childhood into either adolescence or full adulthood" (p. 698). Puberty rites generally involve a separation of the adolescent from society, preparation or instruction from an elder, a transition in status, and a welcoming back into society with acknowledgment of the adolescent's changed status (Delaney, 1996). Oftentimes, puberty ceremonies occur for groups of people, and strong bonds may occur as a result of this special ceremonial time together.

Different puberty rituals often exist for the two genders. Rites of passage for males often include circumcision, tests of physical endurance, tattooing, and/or segregation in bachelor huts. These ceremonies generally occur when the youth is considered strong enough to undergo the elaborate proceedings. For females, such puberty rites generally occur at the time of the first menstrual period and include such rituals as cleansing, beautification, and/or segregation in menstrual huts (Muuss, 1980). In Navajo communities today, a pubertal ceremony for adolescent girls called the Kinaaldá is celebrated at the time of puberty (Markstrom, in press). Rituals such as the Kinaaldá ceremony clearly delineate a change in status from child to adolescent or adult. Such rites of passage commonly hold three elements: a phase that separates individuals from their previous social roles/identities, takes them through a time of transition to a new identity, and incorporates them into a new role or status. Markstrom and Iborra (2003) illustrate how the ritual aspects of this rite of passage are critical to the identity formation of young Navajo girls. Rites of passage, in general, inform not only adolescents themselves of varied social expectations that will accompany their new status but also the community of a change that is now important for them to recognize in their interactions with the novice adult.

Most Western, technologically advanced nations today, however, have no such clear delineation between childhood and adolescent or adult status. Rather, a period of "dual ambivalence" occurs—ambivalence on the part of both society and adolescents themselves regarding role expectations for youth. In the United States, various states grant adult rights and responsibilities to adolescents at somewhat different ages, but such rights invariably are granted over a number of years. One can commonly obtain a driver's license at age 15 or 16, at the same time one can legally be permitted to work and leave school. However, it is not until age 18 that one can vote and not until age 21 in many states that one is permitted to purchase alcoholic beverages. Additionally, various institutions of society enable participation in various adult activities less formally but also over a long period of time. Thus, early adolescents often take part in leisure and consumer activities (witness the advertising aimed at early adolescents in any teen magazine), while participation in various forms of political and community activities is generally not encouraged until mid- to late adolescence; social support for moving away from home and entering occupational training is generally not given until mid- to late adolescence (Chisholm & Hurrelmann, 1995). Some adolescent observers have argued that where no clear-cut puberty rites are provided by a culture to delineate adult status, adolescents, themselves, will devise various rituals and "trials by ordeal" with functions similar to those of the puberty rituals in many preindustrial societies. And, indeed, the "hazing," tattooing, dieting, dress, and beautification rituals found within many contemporary adolescent peer groups do show strong similarities to puberty rituals of many preindustrial societies.

Elkind (1981) has argued that clear social markers providing societal recognition of a young person's developmental level are essential to adequately recognize the special needs of adolescents. And, no doubt, many living in contemporary Western cultures have longed for some kind of social clarity that differentiates childhood from adolescent or adult status. Marcia (1983), however, has argued that the contemporary lack of societal or culturally sanctioned rites of passage are, in fact, the ideal conditions for ego growth and identity development among adolescents: "By not imposing a particular organization on a temporarily disorganized ego at early adolescence, we make self-definition possible. . . . [However] all of us are aware that our unstructured form of adolescence with its attendant chaos and anxiety has its casualties" (p. 218). Piaget (1972) has indicated that a certain degree of lack of structure, ambiguity, conflict, and provision for hands-on exploratory experience within the child's learning environment is necessary to stimulate cognitive growth and development. Similar conditions are likely to facilitate the process of identity development among young adolescents, if social support during this process is forthcoming.

For young adolescents, shifting expectations within and across various agencies of socialization are taking place. Families, friends, schools, providers of odd jobs, places of worship, and facilities for recreation and community service generally do have different informal expectations of early adolescents than they do of children. Tolerance for the formerly egocentric modes of reasoning and behaving during childhood gradually are replaced with societal expectations of cooperation and coordinating one's viewpoints and activities with those of other people. Special privileges are granted to adolescents, such as being able to drive a car, that are not granted to children. In some countries, such as New Zealand, a special judicial system operates for young offenders. Within such systems of juvenile justice, efforts are often made to avoid providing a label, such as "delinquent" or "criminal," that youths in search of an identity might be only too willing to accept and fulfill. The special status of adolescence thus brings numerous changes in responses from a variety of social institutions, and entry into adolescence is most commonly considered a time of instruction for future adult rights and responsibilities.

Societal responses to an adolescent's physical changes during puberty provide critical input to identity development during early adolescence. In a recent Norwegian study, some 55 percent of girls and 60 percent of boys reported that other people had started to behave differently toward them since theirs bodies had begun changing; these perceptions were not correlated with the actual degree of their pubertal change (Alsaker, 1995). Most (about 85 percent) of these young adolescents said that they liked this behavior change on the part of others, whereas the remaining 15 percent of the sample said they found others' responses difficult to handle. A more detailed discussion of the role of societal response to pubertal change and its impact on identity development appears in the following section.

Socialization factors such as relational and institutional responses to early adolescent characteristics and behaviors are implicated in many hormone-behavioral associations affecting identity as well. Brooks-Gunn and Warren (1989) point out that, in fact, social factors may account for more variance than do the physiological processes themselves. Paikoff and Brooks-Gunn (1990) suggest that pubertal changes and societal events may act in concert. If a social change occurs at a certain point during puberty, its impact may have a stronger effect than if the social change had occurred either before pubertal changes had begun or after they had been completed. The researchers give the example of a social event such as a family move, which might occur at the same time as a hormonal change that may increase a pubertal adolescent's excitability or arousability. The event itself may elicit a stronger impact on adolescent identity development due to the young person's heightened state of physiological arousal than the event would have elicited had it occurred before or following pubertal change. Thus, institutional and relational responses to an early adolescent's changing biology, appearance, psychological needs, and cognitive capacities play a vital role in helping answer the questions of who I am and what I can become in the rapidly approaching world of adult life.

Section Summary and Implications

Pubertal processes produce a predictable sequence of changes for both genders, which may have an adaptive evolutionary value. There is evidence that the timing and tempo of puberty are genetically controlled, though subject also to influences of nutrition, health status, and additional environmental factors.

Erikson does not detail psychological identity-related tasks specific to early adolescence, though themes of Affiliation Versus Abandonment and intrapsychic disorganization have dominated research and theory on early adolescent identity concerns.

Most Western nations have no clear delineation of status between childhood and adult status; whereas Elkind believes it is essential for societies to provide clear social markers in recognition of early adolescence, Marcia believes lack of clear social guidelines actually facilitates identity development.

Coming to Terms With Pubertal Change: Identity Implications

Because I was very tall at 13 and my last name was Green, all the boys called me things like "Green bean" or "String bean." Even now that I'm married, I still am so very self-conscious of my height around men.

—Young adult woman, looking back

From the sometimes bewildering array of changes in physical features and appearance that puberty brings, how do adolescents come to terms with their changed physiques? Furthermore, how do such changes affect their senses of identity—of who they are as gendered people, of how they will relate to others, and of what they can do and be in the world?

Pubertal adolescents are very preoccupied with their physical changes and appearances (McCabe & Riccardelli, 2003). Research has also shown that biological changes of puberty generally are viewed positively by boys and negatively by girls (Dorn, Crockett, & Petersen, 1988; Phillips, 2003). For boys, there are the advantages of increased size, increased muscle mass, and physical strength, whereas girls see only increases in their body weight and in fat deposits at the time of puberty. And such weight and fat increases bring greater body dissatisfaction, probably because of conflict with the North American and European cultural ideals of slimness and an elongated body shape (Petersen & Leffert, 1995; Phillips, 2003). Studies of pubertal changes have examined the psychological impact of the height and weight spurts and the development of secondary sexual characteristics for both boys and girls.

Unfortunately, little is known about the experience of pubertal changes other than the menarche for girls. Brooks-Gunn and Warren (1988) undertook research to learn more about the psychological impact of very early noticeable signs of puberty for young girls, because menarche is a relatively late event in the pubertal sequence of changes among girls. They predicted that the onset of breast development (an event publicly noticeable) but not pubic hair growth (an event not publicly noticeable) would be associated with a better body image, more positive peer relationships, greater salience of reproductively linked sex roles, and superior adjustment, as measured by self-report inventories. These predictions were generally supported. The study also found that height, relative to classmates, was linked to superior adjustment and career importance. Thus, physical changes that can be observed by others seem to have an impact on one's sense of self more than other forms of pubertal changes. The authors conclude by speculating that breast development, but not pubic hair development, is imbued with cultural meaning and that such information influences how pubertal girls alter their own sense of identity at this time.

From the previous discussion, however, one should not conclude that unobservable physical changes of puberty do not alter one's self-definition at puberty. Menarche, an event unobservable by others, has attracted much research attention in terms of its associations with changing early adolescent self-definitions. It may be that pubertal events laden with cultural meaning, rather than public observability, have the most impact on identity redefinition among young adolescent girls.

How does menarche affect identity for young girls in early adolescence? Menarche, and its associations with changing self-definition for young adolescent girls, has received much research attention. In one investigation, Brooks-Gunn and Ruble (1982) found a wide range in responses of girls to menarche; however, most responses were quite mild. In fact, menarche was frequently described as a little exciting, a little upsetting, or a little surprising. In interviews with a subsample of their larger investigation, Brooks-Gunn and Ruble obtained more detailed information about the girls' experience of menarche. The most frequently occurring response was positive—that menarche was a signal of their maturity. Other positive responses were ones associated with their new reproductive capacities and being more like their friends. Negative responses were centered on the hassles (of having to carry around supplies) and physical discomfort. Brooks-Gunn and her associates also found that the specific information a young woman receives about menarche from parents, teachers, friends, and health advisors all affect the way in which menarche is experienced (Brooks-Gunn & Paikoff, 1993). Another critical factor is the timing of menarche in the life of the adolescent girl, which is discussed later in this chapter.

Do specific pubertal events affect identity for young boys in early adolescence? Studies addressing the effects of specific pubertal changes among boys have been infrequent. One event that has received some attention is boys' reactions to their first ejaculation, which did not appear to be associated with undue anxiety or embarrassment (Gaddis & Brooks-Gunn, 1985). Boys, however, did not discuss their first ejaculation with friends or their parents, unlike girls, who tended to discuss their first menstrual cycle with parents and friends immediately after the event had occurred, the researchers found. Much more information is needed on the impact of specific pubertal events for boys, such as the voice change and increases in acne and body hair, to understand the identity-related significance of puberty for them.

Puberty holds important implications for body image and self-esteem, and much research has examined the relationship between self-esteem, physical attractiveness, and pubertal change. The vast majority of Caucasian adolescent girls are dissatisfied with their bodies and would like to be thinner (Gardner, Friedman, & Jackson, 1999). This body dissatisfaction and feeling overweight spills over into dissatisfaction with one's self and lowered self-esteem. From a large, longitudinal study of over 600 adolescents in the United States, Simmons and Blyth (1987) found consistent gender differences in both body image and self-esteem among early and mid-adolescents. Girls were consistently less satisfied with their weight and body type than boys, from Grade 6 through Grade 10. At each grade level, girls had lower senses of self-esteem than boys and a greater degree of self-consciousness. In general, boys had a more positive body image than girls. Other research indicates girls tend to be most satisfied with their bodies when they perceived themselves to be slightly underweight, whereas boys felt best about their bodies when they were of average weight and worst about their bodies when they were under- or overweight (Brooks-Gunn, 1991; Gardner, Friedman, & Jackson, 1999).

However, a growing number of studies have pointed to some important ethnic differences in terms of how early adolescent girls view their body weights (e.g., Parker, Nichter, Nichter, Vuckovic, Sims, & Ritenbaugh, 1995; Rosenblum & Lewis, 1999). Whereas 9 out of 10 junior high and high school Caucasian girls were found to be dissatisfied with their body weight, 7 out of 10 African American girls were satisfied (Parker et al., 1995). Furthermore from this study, the majority of African American girls sampled felt it was better to be a little overweight than underweight—a marked contrast to statements by the Caucasian American girls.

Are pubertal changes associated with personality changes during early adolescence? In Spain, Canals, Vigil-Colet, Chico, and Marti-Henneberg (2005) studied some 578 school children aged 10 and 11 years old at one-year intervals over five years. They obtained medical examination reports (rather than self-report) measures of pubertal development, alongside measures of personality from the Junior Eysenck Personality Questionnaire. Results showed that few dimensions of personality were stable for either boys or girls over the course of early adolescence. Age 13 was critical for an increase in depressive disorders among girls. Furthermore, with increasing age, there was an increase in extroversion, sincerity, antisocial behavior, and psychotic behavior for both genders. However, there was no effect of stage of pubertal development on personality dimensions. The question of why personality factors during early adolescence are so unstable is in need of further study. Biological factors other than puberty and particular social factors may be responsible.

Do pubertal changes affect one's social relationships? Bulcroft (1991) examined the effects of physical changes associated with puberty on peer and parent relationships for early and middle adolescent Caucasian boys. As anticipated, greater physical maturity among the boys was associated with increased peer status and greater independence from parents. Furthermore, the effects of pubertal changes on these relationships appear stronger in early adolescence. When parents did not grant greater independence to physically changing adolescents, the parent-adolescent relationship was negatively affected. This research also suggested that parents alter their expectations for teenagers and give greater independence to their offspring on the basis of physical appearance alone.

Additionally, several studies have pointed to a "distancing" effect of puberty on parent-adolescent relationships among those living in two-parent families. As puberty progresses for both boys and girls, conflicts intensify and reported distancing occurs, particularly between the adolescent and his or her mother (e.g., Ogletree, Jones, & Coyl, 2002; Paikoff & Brooks-Gunn, 1990). In addition to increases in conflict (complaining and expressions of anger), there has been a decrease in positive exchanges (such as support, smiling, laughter) (e.g., Holmbeck & Hill, 1991). Allison and Schultz (2004) also found considerable variation in both the frequency and intensity of conflicts across specific issues; conflicts between mothers and daughters often dealt with issues involved in traditional gender role stereotypes. To date, however, the reason for the increase in conflict is not generally well understood. It may result from hormonal changes of puberty among adolescents, change in their physical appearances, role strains in desire for greater autonomy, or a combination of all of these factors.

Timing of Pubertal Change: Identity Implications

> I can remember being a bridesmaid in my sister's wedding. I was overly endowed even then, at age 14. My own sense of joy and beauty on that day, however, came to a screeching halt when I had to dance in front of everyone with the groom's 14-year-old brother, half my size and twice my awkwardness. The cruelty of it all!
>
> —Late adolescent woman, looking back

The timing of pubertal change holds important implications for early adolescent identity development. Being an early, on time, or late maturer in relation to one's peers affects one's sense of self-esteem and identity. Brooks-Gunn

(1991) has found that most timing effects seem to be related to early, not late physical maturation. Among boys, early maturers seem to hold a more positive body image, whereas among girls, the late maturers feel more positive regarding their bodies and more physically attractive than early maturers. (Early maturing girls tend to be shorter and heavier than their late maturing counterparts, and because thinness is generally a socially desired state by girls throughout adolescence, this phenomenon may explain the higher self-esteem found among late maturing girls.) Alsaker (1990) tested a Norwegian sample of adolescent girls to see whether body weight might actually explain the relationship between perceived early maturation and low self-esteem; with the exception of the youngest sixth-grade subjects, timing effects could largely be explained by being overweight relative to population norms. In addition, a higher incidence of eating-related problems has been found among early maturing girls when compared with their on time and late maturing counterparts (Brooks-Gunn, 1991).

Early maturing girls may be particularly vulnerable to a range of adjustment difficulties. For example, early pubertal maturation has been linked with depression, not only during adolescence, but across the life span among Caucasian Americans (Archibald et al., 2003). However, this pubertal timing effect was not found among African American or Hispanic girls. Stattin and Magnusson (1990) found that it was early maturing girls in Sweden who associated with older boys and who were most likely to engage in problem behaviors such as early sexual behaviors and pregnancy following early pubertal development. Reasons that early maturing girls have an especially difficult time are not entirely clear, however. Context may actually determine whether or not being an "off-time" maturer is important (Archibald et al., 2003).

Is there a direct relationship between pubertal timing and an identity crisis? Berzonsky and Lombardo (1983) directly investigated the relationship between pubertal maturation timing and identity development. The researchers used retrospective self-report data from late adolescent men and women to study whether or not there was any relationship between personal decision-making identity crises and pubertal timing. They reasoned that early maturing boys and late maturing girls were less apt to have experienced a personal decision-making identity crisis than late maturing males and early maturing girls. (From previous research, early maturing males tend to be more successful athletically and socially and more apt to possess the socially desirable mesomorphic physiques, whereas late maturing females are more apt to possess the socially desired ectomorphic body types and have a higher sense of self-esteem.) The study found that those males who had experienced an identity crisis did, in fact, report a relatively late pubertal onset, whereas females who had experienced an identity crisis reported an earlier pubertal onset compared with noncrisis peers. Although self-report data must be viewed cautiously, those who fit the prevailing socially desirable body build norms (i.e., the early maturing males and late maturing females) may be less likely to have experienced a personal identity decision-making crisis than those who do not have such socially desirable physical characteristics. The experience of being "different" in relation to one's peers may precipitate a crisis of personal identity.

Identity and Sexuality

> *Clouds of muddy carnal concupiscence filled the air. The bubbling impulses of puberty befogged and obscured my heart so that it could not see the difference between love's serenity and lust's darkness. Confusion of the two things boiled within me.*
>
> —Augustinus, *Confessions* (1991, p. 24)

A key developmental task of early adolescence is beginning to come to terms with a new sense of sexual identity, which the biological changes of puberty bring (Erikson, 1968). Although recognition of oneself as a boy or girl has occurred well before the time a child reaches the preschool years, it is during the years of adolescence that newfound feelings of sexual interest and awareness must be integrated into one's sense of identity. Researchers studying gender differences in personality have differentiated the following three elements of one's sexual self:

1. *Sexual (or gender) identity,* or one's feelings of being male, female, androgynous, or undifferentiated

2. *Sex (or gender) role,* or the way in which one expresses one's biological gender in society according to social norms and stereotypes

3. *Sexual orientation,* or the object(s) of one's sexual interest; one may be homosexual, heterosexual, bisexual, or asexual in one's sexual orientation

Sexual identity has generally been differentiated from sexual behavior, as sexual behavior has been shown to be more varied than sexual identity (Petersen et al., 1995).

Unfortunately, little research has addressed developmental changes in one's sense of sexual identity in the transition through puberty. Buzwell and Rosenthal (1996) noted that this lack of research is surprising, given the critical importance of sexuality in adolescent identity development. Indeed, even more recently, Brooks-Gunn and Graber (1999) argued that physical changes during adolescence, in combination with their meanings to adolescents themselves, their girlfriends and boyfriends, their parents, teachers, and societies in general become incorporated into their identities. However, the emergence of an adult body is commonly not addressed in discussions of adolescent identity. At the same time, identity has generally been left out of discussions of adolescent sexuality.

Although current researchers have recently begun examining issues of sexual identity from the perspective of sexual minority adolescents (e.g., gay and lesbian youths; see, for example, Savin-Williams, 2001), little is known about the development of a sense of sexual identity among adolescents more generally.

How do early adolescents change in their awareness of gender roles? A number of studies have explored changes in early adolescent awarenesses of gender roles. Hill and Lynch (1983) first elaborated the gender intensification hypothesis—that early adolescence is the time when gender roles become increasingly differentiated for boys and girls. Galambos, Almeida, and Petersen (1990) undertook a longitudinal investigation of young adolescent girls and boys (mean age 11.6 years, sixth grade) to see if young adolescents would experience an intensification of gender-related expectations, with increased socialization pressures to conform to traditional male and female sex roles. Masculine roles have traditionally stressed instrumental behaviors, whereas feminine roles have emphasized expressive behaviors. The researchers argued that puberty, with the physiological changes it brings, may act as a signal to parents, teachers, and peers that the adolescent is approaching adulthood and should begin to act in ways that society regards as appropriate for male and female adults. Thus, the investigators hypothesized that differences in masculinity, femininity, and general sex role attitudes would intensify across the sixth, seventh, and eighth grades (between ages 11 and 13 years) and that pubertal timing would play a role in this intensification. Their analyses showed that sex differences in masculinity and sex role attitudes increased across grades, but there were no sex differences in femininity. Their study also showed that pubertal timing was not associated with this gender divergence.

Results of further research on the gender intensification hypothesis have produced mixed results. For example, Simmons and Blyth (1987) failed to find gender divergence between boys and girls during early adolescence in terms of their plans for future work and education. However, Crouter, Manke, and McHale (1995) did find evidence of gender intensification during early adolescence to be associated with some aspects of family socialization (that is, an adolescent's involvement in dyadic activities with the same-sex parent) but not others (parents maintaining traditional sex roles in the home). In a more recent cross-sectional study in Norway, Wichstrøm (1999) examined rates of depression among early adolescents and the gender intensification hypothesis. He found that greater incidences of depression among young adolescent girls was linked to increased importance of feminine sex role identification; this depressed mode was not associated with masculinity or school change.

From a further cross-national study of care-based moral reasoning among Canadian and Norwegian early adolescents, Canadian girls scored significantly higher on an ethics of care moral reasoning interview than boys as well as generating more relational, real-life dilemmas (Skoe et al., 1999). No such differences were found among Norwegian girls. Additionally more Canadian than Norwegian girls demonstrated conventions of goodness and caring for others on the interview, an embodiment of "traditional" female sex role values. Norway has been far more equalitarian in its gender role expectations for men and women, and this difference may be reflected in study results. Thus, the gender intensification hypothesis may be a product of societies that sharply differentiate male and female sex role values.

The issue of gender intensification is complex; certainly, children in every society learn expected role behaviors for boys and girls and develop a sense of basic gender identity and roles most appropriate for men and women. Perhaps a statement by Huston and Alvarez (1990) best illustrates possible reasons for such mixed results:

> Early adolescents are often intensely concerned with "sex appropriate" attributes, but what they absorb about femininity and masculinity can vary widely, depending on the ideas conveyed by various socialization agents during the particular slice of historical time when they pass through this period. (p. 175)

Contexts Affecting Early Adolescent Identity Development

Early adolescence, with the many biological changes it brings, is also a time when many young adolescents report changed relationships with parents, peers, teachers, and others with whom they interact regularly. Many of these relational changes raise identity-related issues for young adolescents and herald a time of disequilibrium in their relationships with others. A general systems approach has recently been taken in attempting to understand the ecology of adolescence in various contexts (e.g., Granic, Dishion, & Hollenstein, 2003). This approach looks at the interaction among biological maturation, relationships, and the social and historical contexts in which these interactions are embedded. Thus, biological maturation itself has been associated with change in family and peer relationships that many young adolescents report. In addition, schools, neighborhoods, places of community service, and cultural norms all interact in multiple ways during the identity-formation process of early adolescence.

This research has focused on central issues of socialization both within the family (connection, regulation, and autonomy) and across the multiple contexts of family, peers, school, and community (e.g., Barber & Olsen, 1997; Eccles, Early, Fraser, Belansky, & McCarthy, 1997). Results have demonstrated that parents, first, and peers, second, appear to be the contexts of primary influence for early adolescent identity development, although all contexts and social networks contribute influential socialization experiences. The same research has also demonstrated that as the quality of conditions within the family for optimal identity development decreases, the impact of other socialization contexts increases. Congruence across parenting style, teaching style, and school atmosphere has also been an important factor associated with early adolescent school achievement and positive identity development (Paulson, Marchant, & Rothlisberg, 1998).

The Family

Recent researches on adolescents and their families have increasingly focused on the reciprocal socialization processes involved (e.g., Grotevant, 1998; Patterson & Fisher, 2002). This approach examines not only how parental behaviors impact adolescents, but also how adolescent behavior impacts parents and siblings. For example, a nine-year longitudinal study by Kim, Conger, Lorenz, and Elder (2001) found that negative feelings of both adolescents and their parents had a reciprocal relationship over time. The more negative adolescents felt about their parents, the more negative the parents felt about their adolescents.

For early adolescents, the biological changes of puberty do seem to bring both discontinuous shifts in some personality factors as well as reorganization in parent-child relationships. How the family system adapts and restructures itself will depend upon previously established patterns of relationships and the willingness of all participants to adapt to changed adolescent circumstances (Granic et al., 2003). Pubertal changes, alongside cognitive maturation during early adolescence, bring marked changes to the family system as a whole. As noted earlier in this chapter, conflicts between early adolescents and their parents do often increase around the time of puberty, but begin decreasing thereafter (e.g., Allison & Schultz, 2004; Ogletree, Jones, & Coyl, 2002; Paikoff & Brooks-Gunn, 1990). This distancing may be observed through such adolescent behaviors as increased desires for privacy and diminished physical affection; however, this distancing phenomenon is generally temporary and does not reflect a serious breech in family relationships. Conflicts often involve disagreements regarding chores, dress, and other daily life issues. However, such conflicts are likely to take some toll on parents, though they also generally stay involved and loving (Granic et al., 2003). By late adolescence, relationships between parents and youths are often again more intimate and less conflicted. These rising levels of conflict among family members during early adolescence are best understood in the context of the adolescent's growing need for autonomy (Granic et al., 2003).

A good deal of research exists on the relationship between parental practices and adolescent identity development. Generally, an authoritative (in which warmth and nurturance are coupled with firm control) rather than an authoritarian or permissive parental style of childrearing has been associated with greater self-reliance, social responsibility, and achievement motivation in later childhood and adolescence (Baumrind, 1991). Research has consistently found that for young, mid-, and late adolescents, the quest for autonomy is best facilitated within the context of close relationships with both mothers and fathers (e.g., Grotevant & Cooper, 1986). The importance of family experience in offering supportive connection while encouraging autonomy and regulating behavior has been strongly linked with positive mental health issues among early adolescents (Barber & Olsen, 1997). Psychological well-being among early adolescents has been concurrently linked with positive paternal and maternal attachment (Kenny, Lomax, Brabeck, & Fife, 1998).

Both satisfaction and dissatisfaction with specific areas of family functioning have been associated more directly to identity development among early adolescents (Papini, Sebby, & Clark, 1989). Identity exploration among early adolescents was highest in families where mothers generally approved of their child's behavior but were dissatisfied with the affective quality of their relationship with the adolescent. In addition, identity exploration among adolescents was highest in families in which the mother reported high frequencies of conflict with the adolescent. Identity exploration among early adolescents was also highest in families in which the father and the adolescent were most dissatisfied with one another's behavior and with the affective quality of the relationship; however, adolescent identity exploration was linked to low levels of father-adolescent conflict. Studies linking styles of parent-adolescent relationships to adolescent identity formation have most frequently been conducted with mid- to late adolescents and thus are discussed further in the next two chapters.

Friendships and the Peer Group

My parents let me spend a lot of time with my friends, and that's been really important. We experience so many new things together and can talk about them all. It makes life so much easier this way.

—12-year-old schoolgirl

For young adolescents, friendships and peer groups provide a further important context for later identity development. Relations with peers established during childhood undergo important transitions in the move to early adolescence. The same-sex peer groups of the middle childhood years begin from loose associations with peer groups of the opposite sex (Brown & Klute, 2003). It is that very sense of self, established within the family, that enables early adolescents to begin expanding relationships outside of it. In contrast to school-aged children, who tend to choose friends on the basis of common activities, this criterion for friendship during early adolescence is enlarged so that friends are also likely to share interests, values, and beliefs—in general, to be supportive and understanding (Youniss & Smollar, 1985).

As the young person enters a period of intrapsychic disorganization, friends and peer groups provide a reference for testing new identity-related skills; social support in the form of approval from peers is a strong predictor of global self-worth among young adolescents (Harter, 1990). The quality and stability of early adolescent friendships are also strongly linked to self-esteem; when friendships become unstable, early adolescents of both genders feel less satisfied with their own appearance and performance during the year (Keefe & Berndt, 1996). Several investigations have pointed to the strong relationship between adolescent problem behavior and involvement in a peer group that places little value on constructive behaviors (e.g., Barber & Olsen, 1997).

Brown and Klute's (2003) overview of 30 years of research about young adolescents' friendships has produced the following findings: Young adolescents are likely to select as friends those who are similar to the self in terms of gender and interests. Most early adolescents have at least one close friend, though the stability of these relationships is not high (six months or less). In multiethnic contexts, there is also a preference for same race friends. Equality and reciprocity are mandates in friendships. And, girls display more intimacy in their friendships than boys. Furthermore, young adolescent friends generally report similar levels of friendship motivation, with girls reporting greater self-determined friendship motivation than boys (Richard & Schneider, 2005). And one of the strongest correlates of behaviors is the behavior of a close friend; friends do influence young adolescents, particularly in the assumption of risky behaviors. Those who have examined, for example, early pubertal development among girls have found that early sexual activity is strongly influenced by the behavior of friends (Cavanagh, 2004).

With regard to the larger peer group, early adolescence often marks a general shift from the small group interactions of childhood to larger, interaction-based groups called *cliques* (Brown & Klute, 2003). In early adolescence, cliques are generally single-sex, though the leader of one clique may begin to interact with an opposite-sex leader of another clique. In addition to cliques, those moving toward mid-adolescence in many communities may also begin to become associated with larger groups called *crowds* (Brown & Klute, 2003). Crowds are clusters of cliques, with individuals sharing similar basic interests among their members. Crowds are identified by a label that often reflects an area of residence, ethnic or socioeconomic background, peer status, or members' abilities or interests. Most crowds have norms that define a distinctive lifestyle, and membership is determined by reputation. Many of the early adolescent's peer relations are continuations of childhood associations as well as extensions of more formal interests, such as being in a religious youth group or sports club. Hodges, Boivin, Vitaro, and Bukowski (1999) have found that those with limited success making friends during childhood are likely to continue struggling with relationships throughout adolescence; those without friends also are good targets for bullies, and it becomes difficult for a young adolescent to break out of this pattern of isolation and peer rejection.

Broader Community Contexts

The roles of contexts beyond the family and peer group for early adolescent identity development are now being explored in systematic ways. Studies of school climate and structure on early adolescent identity have been undertaken (e.g., the impact of single-sex versus coeducational schools on psychological adjustment at puberty; Caspi, 1995). However, discussions of the impact of broader social contexts on identity development for early adolescents have only recently been undertaken (e.g., Barber & Olsen, 1997; Eccles et al., 1997; Sampson, 1997). Such studies point to the potentially regulating effects that broader contexts such as neighborhood and community have for early adolescent social control. They furthermore point to the problematic socialization experiences many early adolescents have in the school environment, particularly in terms of positive connections with teachers, and a school's ability to adequately regulate behavior. However, because such research with early adolescents is in its infancy, more general comments on early adolescent identity development and broader social contexts are presented here.

Newman and Newman (2001) offer thoughts on the role of group affiliations and social networks for identity development during early adolescence. They point out the critical role that group identifications play in the process of individual identity development: "Especially in early adolescence, young people seek connections, supportive relationships, and an understanding of groups and communities, all of which help them take the risks that eventually give rise to an articulated sense of personal meaning [and identity]" (Newman & Newman, 2001, p. 516). The capacity to invest in and to commit oneself to various social networks during early adolescence provides the foundations and supports necessary for later individual identity exploration and commitment. Most adolescents will experience feelings of both belongingness to and alienation from particular social networks at the same time. Resolution of this group identity versus alienation crisis serves as a prelude to the later Identity Versus Role Confusion crisis. Resolution to this early adolescent task will have implications for one's ability to feel a sense of both identity and belonging to smaller groups and to larger social networks in later life.

Adams and Marshall (1996) also present a theoretical model for the discussion of broader contexts on adolescent identity formation more generally. They note that all societies provide institutions and settings in which early adolescents (and all adolescents) can learn to imitate roles and identify with others, the foundations of the identity-formation process. They argue that social contexts that provide a baseline of values for the maintenance and promotion of the self as well as others are the conditions for optimal identity formation. An expectation of high cohesion and conformity by a social group or institution may facilitate identification and imitation but limit later identity formation. The authors note at the same time that any contextual influence is likely to be mediated through both intra- and interpersonal processes. Specifying exactly what such processes are and how they apply during early adolescence are questions that await future generations of researchers.

Section Summary and Implications

Increasing physical maturity during early adolescence brings a restructuring of family relationships; conflicts on minor issues often begin in early phases of puberty and subside after the changes of puberty stabilize.

A style of authoritative parenting has been associated with both self-reliance as well as social responsibility among early adolescents.

One of the strongest correlates of a young adolescent's behavior is the behavior of his or her close friends.

Research on identity implications for early adolescents of broader social contexts, such as the school, neighborhood, and community, has just begun. However, having a sense of multiple group identities provides a base for the later adolescent task of Identity Versus Role Confusion.

Back to the Beginning

This chapter began with three critical questions about identity in early adolescence and a quotation from John, a 13-year-old boy who suddenly realizes that he is growing up and must begin to think about what he wants to be in the future. John's "jolt" comes when his school principal points out that John must soon make some important, identity-defining decisions. John's plight is characteristic of many early adolescents, not only undergoing the physical changes of growing up but also of beginning to experience changes in social expectations, expectations for developing a sense of identity-defining, personally meaningful psychosocial roles and values that fit.

Answers to Chapter Questions

◈ **How do changes of puberty affect identity in early adolescence?**

Early adolescents must begin to integrate a new sense of sexual identity into their sense of self. Being an early maturing girl or late maturing boy (different from one's peers in terms of physical maturity) is more likely to be associated with an identity crisis.

◈ **Does society's lack of formal puberty rites help or hinder early adolescent identity development?**

This issue is controversial; however, identity research suggests identity development is best facilitated through a lack of predefined social roles for adolescents. Supportive parental and peer relationships, however, are vital to adaptive outcomes.

◈ **Do parents of pubertal adolescents change in relating to their children?**

Yes. Family conflict over minor issues often begins with early signs of pubertal change and subsides when the pubertal apex has passed. When parents have not granted greater independence to physically changing adolescents, the parent-adolescent relationship has been negatively affected.

High school was a time when everyone was trying new things out, from clothes to haircuts, and from new ideas to alcohol and drugs. In fact, it was during this time that lots of my peers tried drugs, and I think the fact that everyone kept an eye out for everyone else helped us all get through this time without really going off the rails. In fact, I believe that if the group of friends you have are really close, it makes the transition through adolescence that much smoother.

—19-year-old female, looking back

3

Identity in Mid-Adolescence

> - How does a sense of ego identity begin to form?
> - How does vocational identity development occur?
> - In what way does community service affect ideological identity formation during mid-adolescence?

In high school, I've explored being an intellectual to a class clown to a rebellious delinquent. And I've found advantages and disadvantages to all these personality types. But I also found a person I didn't have to try to work hard to be—and this was the beginning of my own self-identity.

—Bill, 17-year-old high school junior

Do boys find me attractive? Who is interested in me? Am I popular? How can I make Shane H., the gorgeous boy in my math class, fall madly in love with me? What do I want to do when I leave high school? Where will my friends all go after high school? How can I become a great writer and dancer? Will I do OK at the university? How do I want to be treated? What do I value? What am I like? Why are people prejudiced against me because I am different? What is justice? How much control do I really have in my life? How much control should my parents have over my life now? Why does society expect things from me that are not what *I* want?

These were questions raised by a class of high school students, aged 15 to 17 years old, when asked to anonymously note the kinds of questions they were thinking about now when they considered who they were. From their responses, changing biology played a less significant role in issues related to identity than did interest in the opposite sex, the peer group and the need to fit in, societal expectations, and thoughts about their futures. Questions of justice and of values also entered in, as some respondents considered themselves in relation to larger issues of morality.

The Eriksonian themes of biology, individual psychology, and social surroundings as ingredients of ego identity appear now in a somewhat different proportional mix compared with those responses of the younger (11- to 14-year-old) age group discussed in the preceding chapter. By age 15 to16, the rate of biological change for both genders is declining, and changing physique no longer appears as a preoccupation in defining oneself. Biology and the physiological capacities of the individual, nevertheless, remain a cornerstone not only of one's sense of gender identity but also of the more general capabilities of individuals themselves. Many of these teenagers will, by now, begin the identity formation process described by Erikson (1968) and will be struggling to find some optimal balance between Identity Versus Role Confusion. I now enter the normative world of mid-adolescence and review some of the biological and psychological structures commonly present, as well as some of the key societal demands placed on those mid-adolescents living in Western, technologically advanced nations. I define mid-adolescence in terms of both chronological age and psychosocial tasks—the time from 15- to 17-years-old when most can begin to make peace with the biological transformations of puberty and to move further toward more complex ways of thinking. In addition, mid-adolescents continue renegotiating family relationships and focus attention more fully on the peer group and the beginnings of one-to-one love relationships, experimenting with expressions of sexuality, considering potential vocations, and moving toward greater participation in community roles.

Intersection of Biological, Psychological, and Societal Influences on Identity in Mid-Adolescence: An Overview

Following the years of rapid physical and cognitive changes of puberty, mid-adolescence, for most, is marked by a time of adjusting to and consolidating these transformations into a revised sense of identity. No longer are bodily changes the source of great apprehension or anxiety; rather, most mid-adolescents can now take such changes for granted. Whereas much early adolescent energy has been directed toward the family and renegotiating one's place in it, much mid-adolescent energy is more often directed outward toward peer groups and negotiating places therein. Tentative experimentations with a budding sense of personal identity, including sexual and sex role identity, are important dimensions in the lives of many mid-adolescents.

At the same time, it must be noted that for some late maturers, observable pubertal changes will be just beginning in the 15- to 17-year-old age span. Although the enormous individual variability in pubertal timing observable in any junior high or middle school will not be as evident within a high school classroom, there will, nevertheless, be some variation in attaining one's full adult stature and secondary sex characteristics. As a result, there will also be variation in the timing of one's reworking a sense of sexual identity and interest in sex role explorations. Much individual variability is also apparent in the desire to begin thinking about and planning for one's future and developing a set of meaningful values that will at least carry one into late adolescence and early adult life. For some mid-adolescents, however, these tasks will be delayed or arrested for many years to come. Again, an appreciation of the interaction among biological, psychological, and societal systems is important to bear in mind, as these arenas are described individually in the following sections.

Biological Processes

By mid-adolescence, most, though not all, teens can begin to take their changed biology for granted. The average mid-adolescent boy or girl will have nearly attained his or her full adult height. According to Tanner (1991), an average 14-year-old girl and 16-year-old boy have already reached about 98 percent of their total adult heights. Any further noticeable increases in height stop at about age 18 for women and age 20 for men. And it is the beginning of sexual maturation that hastens the end of one's physical growth spurt in height. Thus, the later growth spurt in boys results in their greater leg length compared with girls. Adult males are, on average, about 10 percent taller than adult females; later-maturing boys have a longer period of time to grow taller before the development of sexual maturation brings a halt to their growth spurts. Similarly, early maturing girls are likely to be shorter in stature than their late-maturing female counterparts as a result of this same link between the growth spurt and sexual maturation (Tanner, 1991). At the same time, height and weight following the growth spurt are strongly correlated with height and weight before puberty. Thus, if one is tall relative to same sex peers prior to puberty, one is also likely to be taller than one's peers following puberty.

Through the years of mid-adolescence, there will generally be some increases in weight as well as in muscle strength and endurance. By about age 14, boys will surpass girls in both height and weight. Susman and Rogol (2004) found that some 50 percent of one's adult body weight is generally gained during adolescence. Weight increases during adolescence are more affected by factors such as one's diet and exercise than are height increases, however. Muscles continue to develop not only in size but also in strength. In fact, the size of muscle cells generally continues to increase until the late 20s.

The consolidation of the biological changes of puberty, including new-found muscular coordination, strength, and endurance during mid-adolescence, does hold some important identity implications. Newly developed physical skills involving strength and endurance for mid-adolescent males, in particular, may lead some into dangerous or reckless physical acts that can have serious consequences. Although increased risk taking likely results from multiple causes—including reasoning ability, peer pressure, and testing new biological capacities—increased levels of physical endurance and muscular strength play an important role through the years of mid-adolescence (Arnett, 1992). Ultimately, however, one must consider multiple levels of factors, such as an individual's temperament before puberty, presence of early behavior problems, and timing and rate of physical maturation during puberty, within the contexts of peer group, family, classroom dynamics, and school and community contexts to appreciate links between postpubertal, biological consolidation, and identity-related behaviors (Archibald, Graber, & Brooks-Gunn, 2003).

Psychological Issues

> I really began to think about my own identity over the past two years. I've had little responsibility other than schoolwork and a weekend job. I'm young enough to feel like an adult, yet I'm not expected to act like one. I'm taking this time to really experiment with friendships, family relations, and my personality.
>
> —17-year-old female high school student

The time of mid-adolescence is likely to capture the true beginnings of Erikson's (1968) identity formation process. Preceding this phase, one's sense of identity has been primarily formed through identifications with significant others. As Erikson points out, identity and identification have common roots, for they both involve making use of significant others in the service of composing a self. Personality qualities, values, physical features, and characteristics of important others are emulated via the process of identification, as the primary school-aged child and young adolescent assume these attributes in the service of organizing a functioning self (Marcia et al., 1993). Mid-adolescence, for many, begins with the development of new identifications "no longer characterized by the playfulness of childhood" (Erikson, 1968, p. 155). The task now begins in earnest of considering choices and decisions from one's previous identifications that may lead to long-term commitments in the rapidly approaching world of adult life. Erikson regards much of mid- and late adolescence as a psychosocial moratorium, when role experimentation with a workable adult identity can begin in earnest. This moratorium is spent in the service of synthesizing all previous identifications of childhood and early adolescence into a new identity structure that is uniquely one's own.

Experimentations with meaningful vocational directions, a set of sustaining values, and a more consolidated sense of sexual and sex role identity enable one to integrate elements that fit into one's budding sense of identity during mid-adolescence. In Erikson's (1968) view, however, "it is the inability to settle on an occupational identity that most disturbs young people" (p. 132). A sense of vocational direction requires the assessment of one's skills, interests, and talents, as well as channels for expression. Mid-adolescence is often marked by serious considerations and assessments of one's abilities and goals in preparing for further education or work after high school (Nurmi, Poole, & Kalakoski, 1994; Vondracek & Porfeli, 2003). Exploring meaningful life philosophies, social values, religious or spiritual orientations, and values regarding important relationships are also important to the lives of many mid-adolescents (Furrow, King, & White, 2004; Markstrom-Adams & Smith, 1996). Peer support and the mirroring of one's values in combination with supportive relationships with one's parents serve essential functions in the process of self-definition. Similarly, exploring the implications of one's adult physique through expressions of sexuality and gender roles is common in mid-adolescence. Many mid-adolescent "love" relationships, however, are not really a sexual matter or an experience of true intimacy, but rather an effort to define one's own identity through the clarifying eyes and ears of a trusted other (Erikson, 1968).

A new form of relationship with one's family also begins to emerge, as friendships and peer groups become the primary focus of relational energy for many mid-adolescents and changes in identity occur (Akers, Jones, & Coyl, 1998; Reis & Youniss, 2004). As increasing intrapsychic differentiation of one's own values and goals from those of one's parents proceeds, the peer group assumes functions it has not held before. For example, to protect against the loss of a fragile sense of identity, some mid-adolescents may attempt totalistic identifications with social groups that cruelly exclude others who are different according to some physical or psychological attribute (Erikson, 1968). Responses from a study I conducted in the 1980s examined changing relational attitudes toward different significant others by early, mid-, and late adolescents in three Western nations. Some mid-adolescent responses to items dealing with parents (as follows) illustrate this shift of energy:

- **15-year-old girl:** *When a girl is with her parents,* she feels embarrassed if anyone sees her.
- **15-year-old boy:** *When a boy is with his parents,* he tries to avoid his friends. (Kroger, 1983, p. 4)

The most popular model used to research identity development from mid-adolescence through middle adulthood, based on Erikson's writings, has been the identity status model developed by Marcia (1966; Marcia, Waterman, Matteson, Archer, & Orlofsky, 1993). This model, originally developed for use with late adolescents, has also been used in studies of identity formation among mid-adolescents as well as adults. Because this model is important for understanding some of the research presented later in this and subsequent chapters, it is briefly described here.

Marcia expanded Erikson's (1963) original bipolar task of Identity Versus Role Confusion by proposing that adolescents may adopt one of several different styles of approach to making key identity-defining decisions, such as those involving vocational directions, alongside values regarding political, religious, sexual and sex role values, and family/career priorities. Marcia used the variables of exploration and commitment to operationalize these differing styles or identity statuses as follows:

- *Identity achieved*—One who has undergone a period of exploration prior to making identity-defining values and commitments.
- *Moratorium*—One who is in the process of exploring various identity-defining values and commitments.
- *Foreclosure*—One who has adopted identity-defining values and commitments without exploration. Such commitments are based primarily on those of parents and significant others.
- *Diffusion*—One who is unable or unwilling to make identity-defining commitments. There may or may not have been a period of prior exploration.

These identity statuses have been able to be reliably evaluated and empirically validated, and their antecedents, consequences, and developmental patterns through adolescence and adult life have been examined. The arenas of vocational direction, political and religious values, and forms of sexual expression and sex role identity are often discussed when determining identity status and identity development among adolescent and adult participants in Western contexts.

During mid-adolescence, identity status research has pointed to similarities for the two genders in patterns of identity development (Archer, 1982; Kroger, 1997). Although a significant increase in the identity-achieved status by grade was found by Archer during the years of early and middle adolescence, the majority of identity-related decisions at all grade levels appeared rather unsophisticated. Flum (1994) identified styles of identity formation during early and mid-adolescence that may be precursors to the identity statuses. Flum's diffusion, foreclosure, and moratorium styles each reflected coherent patterns of attitudes and emotions relevant to the lives of young adolescents. A further evolutionary style of identity formation was identified among a group of mid-adolescents who had seemingly resolved at least some identity issues on their own terms but had not experienced any intense period of identity confusion. These studies of identity formation among high school students suggest that it may not be until later adolescence, when society's demands to take a place in the real world occur, that identity issues are ultimately addressed by many youth.

Mid-adolescents do develop a greater level of cognitive complexity. Possibilities for imagining alternative futures arise through more developed and organized uses of formal operational logic (Piaget, 1972). Some mid-adolescents may be entering Piaget's stage of full formal operations. As such, they are able to understand the operations involved in propositional logic, hypothetical reasoning, combinatorial logic, control of variables, constructing a ratio, and probabilistic reasoning (among the many skills of formal operational reasoning). Propositional logic involves the ability to generate hypotheses or statements, given certain conditions. Combinatorial logic involves the ability to generate all possible combinations of a given number of individual variables. Control of variables involves the ability to test the likely cause of a relationship between two factors by examining each possible causal factor and its effect on the variable in question while holding other possible causal factors constant. Probabilistic reasoning involves the ability to understand the concept of probability—that a phenomenon has a certain likelihood of occurring, but that the occurrence is not always likely to happen. Early adolescents are just beginning to understand some of these operations but are not able to apply them consistently or to articulate proof in their reasoning. The skills mentioned in this paragraph are critical to the cognitive operations involved in the identity formation process.

Identity formation requires, for example, that individuals be able to imagine alternative futures for themselves (hypothetical reasoning) and to formulate possible future scenarios if various pathways are taken (propositional and probabilistic reasoning and combinatorial logic). They also must be able to consider what the necessary steps are to be able to actualize such futures and what kind of future is most appropriate for them (propositional reasoning, control of variables, combinatorial logic). Such cognitive skills generally begin to appear in early adolescence, but it is often not before mid-adolescence that such skills begin to consolidate. Identity formation requires the flexible, abstract thinking skills and reality testing that only full formal operations can bring. Research has generally demonstrated positive correlations between many of these formal operational skills and degree of identity attained (Marcia et al., 1993). However, the use of formal operational reasoning in no way guarantees one's ability to achieve a sense of identity. Research with high school students suggests that one's ability to make future-oriented decisions based on rational rather than experiential information may be a further important cognitive prerequisite to attaining identity achievement (Klaczynski, Fauth, & Swanger, 1998).

Societal Influences

Identities are formed through the mutual regulation of society with individual biology and psychology; thus, the range of variation in the identities that will be sanctioned and fostered lies in the hands of the culture itself. Social institutions within a culture provide the general framework in which identity takes shape and is allowed expression. In turn, these social institutions are dependent upon the energies of their youthful members for shaping their future directions as well as retaining connections with the past.

Many societies or cultures institutionalize some kind of moratorium process for their youth. Such provisions by Western cultures appear in work-study programs offered through many high schools, work apprenticeship programs, youth divisions in many political groups, and opportunities for work in a number of voluntary community programs. In preindustrialized cultures, other opportunities to learn the skills that are valued in a culture are also provided. Such institutionalized moratoria provide opportunities for participation and exploration; however, they may also provide the foundations for more lasting identity-defining commitments.

Major features of societies and cultures have changed over the last centuries; these features, in turn, have altered the nature of identity as individuals have sought to adapt themselves to such new conditions (Baumeister & Muraven, 1996). One form of change that has taken place in many Western societies is the degree to which society dictates the roles each person will play as an adult in that society. This enormous loosening of societal guidelines has meant that mid- and late adolescents living in many contemporary Western contexts have enormous choice—a necessary condition, according to Erikson's model, for the identity formation process to unfold. At the same time, this greater latitude for identity development in many Western nations has coincided with more pluralistic diversity in their values evolving from the loss of main value bases. Baumeister and Muraven (1996) point out that these contemporary social conditions place a great burden on mid- and late adolescents, who must find ways to make their lives meaningful alongside those of others, who may have opted for quite different value bases to give shape to their lives.

Zeldin and Price (1995) show that many social policies aimed at mid-adolescents focus specifically on trying to "fix" adolescents by preventing problem behaviors and/or correcting perceived deficits. Far less attention has been given to promoting optimal identity development, the authors point out. They also note a growing awareness among policymakers, however, that avoiding trouble is only part of the picture of adaptive functioning for mid-adolescents. Most societies and their socializing agents are clear about what they wish their mid-adolescents to avoid (e.g., drugs and alcohol, delinquency, teenage pregnancy); however, they are less clear about what they wish their adolescents to achieve.

Over the past five years, attention has begun to turn toward factors associated with positive youth development. Danish, Taylor, and Fazio (2003), for example, stress that youth development ought not to be viewed as a happenstance matter. They call for more intentional designs to promote optimal development in community facilities where youths may gather. Such facilities should place strong emphases on providing continuity, predictability, and tradition, the researchers argue. Such goals are often a far cry from those of the settings where many mid-adolescents congregate. For example, shopping malls are a common hangout for many during mid-adolescence. Kim, Kim, and Kang (2003) actually examined motivations among teens for visiting shopping malls in the United States. These researchers continue by suggesting ways in which educators might make use of such shopping mall contexts to fill social, economic, and diversion needs that the malls seem to meet for many mid-adolescents.

Research involving mid-adolescents and social contexts has generally focused on features of the family, peer group, and school. However, as Zeldin and Price (1995) note, there are numerous additional contexts that serve youth, such as national and grassroots youth organizations, community and religious organizations, as well as public sector institutions, such as museums, parks, and other recreation facilities. All may play an important role in the lives of many mid-adolescents. The impact of such organized contexts on the identity formation process of mid-adolescents has only recently begun to be examined. Flanagan (2004) points to the connection to broader goals that such organizations provide. In addition, opportunities for the exploration of alternative values, roles, and relationships also arise for mid-adolescents in many of these arenas. With such features, Flanagan (2004) notes that many organizations for mid-adolescents also promote a sense of institutional and community membership—a connection to a broader social arena. All of these circumstances provide the conditions necessary for fostering optimal identity development. Certainly Werner and Smith's (2001) long-term study of children at risk vividly illustrates the vital role that many such community organizations may play in the lives of many at risk adolescents who overcame the odds to lead satisfying and productive lives during their adulthood years.

Section Summary and Implications

Most mid-adolescents are generally more comfortable with the biological changes of puberty. Identity issues other than accommodating to one's changed physique often come to the forefront for mid-adolescents.

Marcia has empirically validated four styles (identity statuses) that adolescents use to make identity-defining decisions: identity achievement, moratorium, foreclosure, and diffusion. These statuses are not static resolutions, but rather an attempt to capture an individual's primary mode of addressing identity-defining decisions. The identity statuses may change considerably over the course of mid- and late adolescence.

Zeldin and Price have noted that although most societies are quite clear about what they wish their mid-adolescents to avoid, they are not often clear about what they wish mid-adolescents to achieve. Many social policies aim to fix or prevent problem behaviors among mid-adolescents, but research is now focusing upon ways to promote optimal identity development among teens.

Identity and Sexuality

I remember at age 15 feeling scared, really scared but at the same time excited to know that now I was really a woman, with all the new meanings that held.

—22-year-old woman, looking back

Although the foundations of gender identity are developed in early childhood, the task of clearly defining oneself as male or female and integrating one's emerging sexual identity with one's sense of personal identity is an important task of mid-adolescence. "Adolescents cannot simply add new sexual feelings to an old self. They must revise that self so that what they add fits. . . . [Adolescents] cannot simply see themselves as children and simply add sexual feelings and behavior to this self-image" (Cobb, 1995, p. 129). Becoming sexual means becoming an adult; the integration of one's sexuality into one's emerging sense of adult identity means leaving the knowns of childhood behind and risking an unknown future in expressing one's gendered self. This may prove to be a monumental task for some mid- to late adolescents.

As was noted in the last chapter, research on the development and integration of sexuality into the sense of personal identity has been scarce. Sexual identity refers to the person's internal sense of being male or female, which is expressed in personality and behavior. And whereas numerous studies linking various sexual behaviors with age and other variables have been undertaken, how an adult sense of a sexual identity is formed has received little research attention.

Graber, Brooks-Gunn, and Galen (1998) found that the process of developing a concept of oneself as a sexual being begins when adolescents recognize feelings of sexual arousal and seek outlets for sexual expression. Graber and colleagues (1998) describe several dimensions of one's sexual identity. Issues of sexual self-esteem, sexual self-efficacy or mastery, and sexual self-image seem to lie at the core of sexual identity. As one's sense of identity as a male or female becomes integrated into one's more general sense of identity, Buzwell and Rosenthal (1996) have identified styles by which sexual identity may be expressed: sexually naive, sexually unassured, sexually competent, sexually adventurous, and sexually driven. The latter styles were more likely to be associated with sexual risk-taking behavior than other styles.

Research by Breakwell and Millward (1997) highlights differences in the ways in which sexual self-concept may be structured for males and females. Among males, the emotional dimensions of sexuality were distinguished from its relationship aspects in Breakwell and Millward's research, whereas these two elements were integrated in females' sexual self-concepts. In addition, having a sense of control over when and where intercourse took place was central to the ways in which adolescent women construed their sexual self-concept, whereas for men this issue was not central to their sense of sexual identity. There were no gender differences in terms of sexual responsiveness and desire. Furthermore, the greater the concern shown by males for the relationship dimensions of sexuality, the less likely it was that sex or being sexually attractive was a central focus in their lives. It was less likely that these males would engage in risky sexual behaviors that would endanger their health. Among women, sexual self-concepts incorporated a complex blending of traditional notions of feminine receptivity with assertiveness and entitlement, taking initiative in encounters, and ownership of their sexuality. Breakwell and Millward suggest that a sense of responsibility in having safer sex is being reworked into an identity in which having a sense of sexual freedom was central for these mid- to late adolescent women.

Identity and Vocation

Erikson (1968) has noted that finding a meaningful sense of vocational direction is what most disturbs young people. Certainly, this statement has been supported by the many writers and theorists who have examined the process of vocational decision making during mid- and late adolescent development (e.g., Vondracek & Porfeli, 2003). And this concern with finding a meaningful vocational direction has certainly punctuated the identity-related concerns of early, mid-, and late adolescents whose questions begin each of the chapters about adolescence in this volume. The process of finding a vocational direction that can meaningfully express elements of one's identity is a formidable task. And certainly, few decisions have such wide-ranging implications on many elements of one's future. One's general level of life satisfaction, circle of friends and intimates, style of parenting, income level and standard of living, place of residence, use of leisure, and general level of health all are outcomes of finding a suitable vocational niche among the opportunities and constraints found in one's social context.

How does a sense of vocational identity begin to develop? Ginzberg (1972) views vocational decision making as an adaptive process that unfolds over three stages during childhood and adolescence: fantasy, tentative, and realistic. The *fantasy* stage lasts throughout childhood. During this time, children imagine themselves in an array of roles, from those of real figures seen in everyday life to those of cultural heroes to those of the imaginary characters seen on television or in comics. The *tentative* stage captures the years of early and mid-adolescence, when one's thoughts about a vocation begin to reflect one's own interests. During mid-adolescence, young people also begin to consider more carefully their abilities as well as what they value. How much value they place on such issues as education, money, social service, working alone or with others, job security, opportunities for development, and having free time will now enter into their pool of potential employment possibilities. Mid- and late adolescents enter the *realistic* stage when they actually begin to explore their tentative choices. This process might include taking courses in a given area at school or trying out different types of jobs after school. Ginzberg (1972) discusses how adolescents then begin to crystallize or pull together the many factors that will bear on a career choice—the training required, opportunities that exist for employment in this line of work, their own interests and abilities as they work toward a vocational decision. Ultimately and ideally, late adolescents will develop a given area of vocational interest. Ginzberg's model of vocational development has met a number of criticisms. For example, some contexts do not provide meaningful vocational opportunities for adolescents, and individuals will vary in the rate and timing of vocational development. Nevertheless, Ginzberg's model has provided a useful framework regarding the process by which realistic vocational choices are made.

Many high school students in the United States as well as some other industrialized nations now have part-time jobs. In the United States, the average high school sophomore now works about 15 hours per week in paid employment; the average number of working hours per week increases to around 20 for high school seniors (Mortimer, 2003). About three-fourths of high school juniors hold part-time jobs during the school year; this figure presents a marked contrast to many European countries, in which paid employment for high school teens in formal work settings is relatively rare (Flammer & Schaffner, 2003). However, many European teens do work in government-sponsored apprenticeship programs for non-college-bound youth.

One might imagine that such work experiences during adolescence would be beneficial, teaching such things as responsibility and the value of money as well as providing skills training. Within many European apprenticeship programs, in which on-the-job training is often directly related to one's future vocation, such experiences are, indeed, very valuable. However, within the United States, part-time work experiences for high school students are most commonly available in industries such as fast-food restaurants or retail sales that will have little in common with a teen's eventual vocational choice. Furthermore, the work required in such settings often involves repetitive, boring tasks and does not help teens develop special skills or provide opportunities for interaction and cooperation with coworkers and supervisors. Many young people in such jobs work alone with no additional personnel or customers immediately available. Mortimer (2003) notes the limited positive, long-term impact that part-time employment during high school may have on youths' future vocational development. And the demands of part-time employment may considerably reduce the time available for study as well as engendering a sense of cynicism toward working environments among teens (Greenberger & Steinberg, 1986). However, Vondracek and Porfeli (2003) do point to positive consequences of more limited part-time employment experiences for teens within the United States. They stress the need for evaluating the quality, meaning, and context of the teen work experience in order to fully understand the implications of such work for future identity development. It would seem that an important focus for future applied research would be on how best to facilitate the school to work transition for *both* college-bound and non-college-bound youths.

Some writers have directly examined the relationship between identity development and vocational decision making. Skorikov and Vondracek (1998) used Marcia's identity status approach with high school students in the United States and found the area of vocation to be the one of greatest salience. There were far higher percentages of moratorium and achieved adolescents within the vocational identity domain than in identity domains of religion, lifestyle, or political values. Wallace-Broscious, Serafica, and Osipow (1994) found identity status to be a stronger predictor of career maturity than one's self-concept; those higher in identity exploration and commitment showed greater career maturity than those who simply felt positive about themselves. Researchers have also found that high school students who explore a variety of career possibilities make career choices more in line with their own personality needs than adolescents who do not explore options as broadly (Grotevant, Cooper, & Kramer, 1986). It thus appears important to encourage adolescents to explore a wide variety of options in their vocational identity decision making. Appreciating the need for differential interventions on the basis of one's identity status is also likely to be of greatest value in facilitating vocational identity development (Raskin, 1989). Differentiating different dimensions of career indecision may also hold important implications for intervention (Vondracek, Hostetler, Schulenberg, & Shimizu, 1990).

Identity and Meaningful Values

> *When I was fourteen, I took some food and stickers without paying for them. This is something I am not proud of now. But this was an exploration of mine. I was trying to be cool. I soon realized that I didn't want to take something without paying for it. I knew it was wrong, and I didn't like the feeling it gave me. After this incident, I began to think about my values and what was important to me.*

> —17-year-old high school female

Considerations of morality and the development of meaningful values also play an important role in the identity-formation process among mid-adolescents. With the ability to think more abstractly, using some of the advanced reasoning strategies available to formal operational thinkers, many mid-adolescents begin to consider more existential questions of values, morality, and the meaning that their lives hold. Keating (1996; Keating & Sasse, 1996) has suggested five basic characteristics that distinguish mid- and late adolescent thinking from that of childhood: thinking about possibilities, thinking ahead, thinking through hypotheses, thinking about thought, and thinking beyond conventional limits. All of these features are critical to the way in which mid-adolescents begin to develop meaningful life philosophies, including those related to political, social, and religious values described in the following paragraphs.

Erikson (1968) has stressed that adolescents need ideological guidelines to bring some sense of meaning and order into their lives. At the same time, he emphasized that such ideological guidelines need to have a quality of transcendence—in other words, they must transcend family values and give young people a sense of connection to their broader social and cultural contexts. Adams (1985) noted the importance of political ideology to late adolescent identity and the need for adolescents to have the opportunity to explore many realities, challenges, and perspectives. He pointed out, however, that political thoughts, participation, attitudes, or actions are far from central in the lives of most early and mid-adolescents. He also pointed to the relative lack of research on how commitment to a general political ideology and social value system evolves. Within the past several decades, however, research has indicated ways in which community service by mid-adolescents can provide opportunities for identity development by stimulating the process of reflection on a society's political organization and general moral order; this work will be discussed in the concluding section of this chapter.

Models to address steps in the development of moral reasoning during adolescence have been proposed by Kohlberg (1969, 1984) and Gilligan (1982). These models also provide valuable guidelines regarding the formation of a sense of ideological values during the adolescent identity-formation process. In the late 1950s, Lawrence Kohlberg became interested in extending work that Piaget had begun in order to examine the development of moral reasoning. Initially interviewing a sample of boys regarding situations involving a moral conflict, Kohlberg came to describe a hierarchical sequence of developmental stages (six stages divided into three levels) that he believed reflected changes in the ground on which moral decisions are based.

At the *preconventional level* of childhood according to Kohlberg (1969), reasoning is based upon self interest; the Stage 1 child considers his or her interests alone in trying to avoid punishment for transgressions, whereas the Stage 2 child may manipulate others toward his or her own self interests. At some point toward the end of the primary school years, most children begin to shift to the *conventional level* of moral reasoning, whereby the conventions of some larger social order are the sole basis upon which moral decisions are made. At Stage 3, "right" moral decisions involve upholding the expectations of one's family or other immediate social groups, whereas at Stage 4, the focus shifts to the larger social structure. In this latter phase, right moral decisions involve upholding the laws of society. It is conventional-level reasoning that most commonly characterizes the moral development of mid-adolescents. At the *postconventional level,* moral decision making is based on principles of democratic decision making. No longer are laws upheld merely for their own sake, but rather they are considered in relation to moral principles; it is recognized that moral principles and laws may sometimes be in conflict. At Stage 5, individuals base moral decisions on a socially agreed-upon contract orientation to moral problems, which remains flexible and open to change according to circumstances. Reasoning at Stage 6 is very rare but involves decision making according to self-chosen principles of life, justice, and fairness for all.

Mid-adolescents are most commonly reasoning from a conventional orientation; indeed, only about 10 percent move into the postconventional level by young adulthood (Kohlberg, 1984). Moral reasoning appears to develop at a time of readiness; development may be stimulated by exposure to the next more advanced form of moral decision making. How moral reasoning develops has been further explored recently by Walker, Gustavson, and Hennig (2001). These researchers found that people move from periods of consolidation into times of transition (where reasoning from two adjacent states is present) to new stages of consolidation at more complex stages of development.

Concerned that Kohlberg's justice-based dilemmas did not adequately capture the concerns of women, Gilligan (1982) proposed a three-level system that assessed moral dilemmas involving issues of care; dilemmas involving a real-life decision among women contemplating an abortion were also used to assess reasoning. In Gilligan's Level 1, *individual survival,* moral reasoning is based on the needs of the self alone; the needs of others are not seriously considered. In Level 2, *self-sacrifice,* the needs of the self are sacrificed in order to meet the needs of others, while at Level 3, *nonviolence,* a balance is found so that both one's own needs and those of others are taken into consideration in moral decision making. Again, Level 2 (self-sacrifice) is most frequently found among mid-adolescents.

Research supporting Gilligan's initial claim of a male bias in the justice-based nature of Kohlberg's original dilemmas has been mixed. Extensive comparisons of stages attained by both boys and girls and men and women, using dilemmas from both Kohlberg and Gilligan, have generally failed to find significant gender differences in responses (e.g., Walker, 1984, 1986). Kohlberg and Gilligan have, however, provided models of the development of moral reasoning based on an ethic of justice and an ethic of care, respectively. Skoe (1998) has developed an interview measure that is currently being used to assess moral reasoning in terms of an ethic of care. Skoe's work has spawned much interest in the reasoning processes used by adolescents as well as adults in the course of forming a meaningful sense of interpersonal identity and making decisions about conflicting relational demands.

Literature on the roles of religious identity and prosocial behavior in identity development has been rapidly increasing over the past 10 years. Garbarino (1999) notes that religion would seem an important antidote to the experience of meaninglessness; religion may serve as a buffer against risky behaviors for some troubled youths. And, indeed, youth participating in religious communities have been more likely to report a sense of purpose in their lives and a general life philosophy than those not in such environments (Markstrom, 1999). In addition to these functions, religion may also help to promote prosocial behavior, as individuals consider issues that transcend their own immediate interests and consider the common good (Markstrom, 1999). Youths for whom religion is salient have indeed been more involved in community service than youths not concerned with religious issues (Youniss, McLellan, & Yates, 1999).

Furrow, King, and White (2004) undertook a study of more than 800 high school students in the Los Angeles area to directly examine the relationship between religious identity with personal meaning as well as prosocial concerns. The researchers administered standardized, self-report measures of how an individual behaves in response to perceived meanings and a prosocial behavior inventory, along with self-descriptions of religious identity. The researchers found a positive relationship between religious self-understanding, personal meaning, and prosocial concerns; youth indicating a strong religious identity were more likely to have a meaning framework that added direction and purpose to their lives than nonreligious youths.

Additionally, Hunsberger, Pratt, and Pancer (2001) investigated links between high school and university students' efforts to deal with religious issues and identity development. They found that the identity achieved sought out both belief-confirming as well as belief-threatening consultation in dealing with their religious doubts. Moratoriums showed modest levels of religious doubting, in contrast to foreclosed individuals, who were both more religiously committed as well as less doubtful of their religious beliefs. The foreclosed were also unlikely to seek out belief-threatening consultations with others. Diffuse individuals were uncommitted in terms of religious beliefs, held many doubts, and avoided any kind of consultation about religion. The researchers also found identity achievement to be positively related to personal adjustment and diffusion to be negatively related to personal adjustment. Findings from the two studies on the relationship between religion and identity illustrate the resources that meaningful spirituality can provide to the identity formation process during adolescence.

Contexts Affecting Mid-Adolescent Identity Development

The impact of contextual factors on adolescent identity development is complex. And although individual contexts most commonly affecting the identity-formation process of mid-adolescents are addressed in the following sections, their interactive effects must be appreciated. Researchers are now beginning to appreciate and investigate the relationship between an adolescent and his or her social contexts in terms of dynamic systems. Thus, while adolescents are impacted by their contexts, so, too, are contexts impacted by the development of adolescents themselves.

The family, peer groups, and school and neighborhood community activities are the primary groups affecting and being affected by adolescents' identity development. One might consider the family and peer group to be most directly involved in an adolescent's socialization. However, community organizations such as 4-H Clubs, the YMCA, YWCA, and church organizations have provided invaluable sources of connection and regulation for those desiring connection to a larger social order. In addition, such community groups have also provided alternative sources of connection among adolescents who have experienced many physical and emotional risk factors during childhood (Werner & Smith, 2001). Current research is now examining issues of connection, autonomy, and regulation across multiple contexts as well as in terms of dynamic systems (e.g., Granic, Dishion, & Hollenstein, 2003).

The Family

While I was in high school, my parents encouraged me to try a variety of experiences, suggesting hobbies or leisure activities to try. Once my mom even signed me up for guitar lessons without consulting me after I had been experimenting on my sister's guitar. I was angry at first, but she gave me the option to pull out immediately if I didn't like it. But I did and continued the lessons for years to come. My parents never pushed me into something

*that I didn't want to do, but they gave me the opportunity to
experience a wide range of things. This really helped me to discover what I enjoyed and to pull together aspects of my identity.*

—18-year-old male university student, looking back

The relationship between differing styles of family communication and
identity development among mid- and late adolescents has been widely
researched. As noted in Chapter 2, results have generally found that adolescents in families that encourage individuality and connectedness are more
likely to explore various identity alternatives prior to commitment; those
adolescents in families discouraging individuation are less likely to explore
identity alternatives (Grotevant, 1998; Grotevant & Cooper, 1986). A
related observational study of mid-adolescent ego development and various
styles of family communication also found that adolescents with high levels
of ego development came from families where there was respectful sharing
of perspectives, as well as presentation of challenges in the context of support (Hauser, Powers, Noam, Jacobson, Weiss, & Follansbee, 1984). From
these researches, however, it is not possible to determine the direction of
cause; it may be that adolescents in differing identity statuses or levels of ego
development evoke differing parental behaviors or that differing styles of
parenting facilitate or arrest adolescent identity development. The dynamic
systems approach to researching issues of adolescent-family relationships
proposed by Granic and colleagues (2003) may be valuable in understanding the developmental nature of parent-adolescent relationships.

In Belgium, Beyers, Goossens, Vansant, and Moors (2003) have attempted
to further clarify the concept of adolescent autonomy in parent-adolescent
relationships. They point out that some early measures of autonomy actually
seemed to be measuring detachment from parents, and high scores were
associated with negative developmental processes. Thus, they undertook an
investigation into mid- and late adolescents' reports of relationships with
their parents. They proposed that connectedness, separation, detachment,
and agency are factors most likely to capture associations among a broad set
of measures of adolescent autonomy and family relationships. Their results
indicate the importance of differentiating these dimensions of autonomy
when examining parent-adolescent relationships.

Additional family factors also appear related to mid-adolescent identity
development. A New Zealand study found that the quality of a mid-
adolescent's affect toward both their mothers and fathers has a significant
and meaningful effect on the overall sense of self-esteem and coping (including exploration) abilities (Paterson, Pryor, & Field, 1995). In Germany,
Zimmerman and Becker-Stoll (2002) directly examined the relationships

between identity achievement and diffusion statuses and the stability of attachment representations by a group of many mid-adolescents that were followed over a two-year period. Results indicated high stability of attachment representations during this time, with secure attachment associated with identity achieved individuals and dismissing attachment associated with diffuse individuals.

Thus, mid-adolescent identity exploration and commitment appear positively related to a secure attachment representation and a type of family interaction style that encourages individuality within a supportive context. Research on family structure and adolescent individuation does need replication and longitudinal study, but the quality of the adolescent's affection toward both parents appears strongly related to the course that future forms of autonomy and connection will take in the young person's life.

Friendships and the Peer Group

High school was a time when everyone was trying new things out, from clothes to haircuts, and from new ideas to alcohol and drugs. In fact, it was during this time that lots of my peers tried drugs, and I think the fact that everyone kept an eye out for everyone else helped us all get through this time without really going off the rails. In fact, I believe that if the group of friends you have are all really close, it makes the transition through adolescence that much smoother.

—19-year-old female, looking back

Friendships and interactions with larger peer groups serve important functions in mid-adolescent identity development. During mid-adolescence, youths begin to shift away from parental control and authority and become more intensely involved with friends and peer groups (Jackson, 1993). Although this shift of focus certainly does not imply that parents no longer make a significant contribution to their adolescent's development, it does mean that subtle intrapsychic changes are taking place as mid-adolescents begin to individuate, to renegotiate both external and intrapsychic ties with parents, and assume more responsibility for their own decisions and life courses (Silverberg & Gondoli, 1996). In doing so, feedback from friendships and the peer group provides not only support but also a mirror for the self as different behaviors are tried and different possibilities for self-definition are tested.

Friendships and peer groups serve somewhat different functions to mid-adolescent identity development. Friendships provide mid-adolescents with confidants and experiences of closeness with both same- and opposite-sex companions. Among mid-adolescents, mutually identified best friends have shown similarities in terms of identity status, as well as many behaviors, attitudes, and goals related to ego identity (Akers, Jones, & Coyl, 1998). Similarities among best friends have been greatest in the specific identity domains in which identity status was assessed, rather than in the overall global identity status rating. Thus, a confidant similar in identity status may facilitate identity development as one undergoes a renegotiation of relationships with parents. And conversely, persistent conflict with friends has been associated with detrimental identity changes over mid-adolescence (Reis & Youniss, 2004). Interestingly, Noack and Buhl (2004) found that as German adolescents experience greater closeness with friends, there is also an increase of reciprocity and egalitarian exchanges with parents during both mid- and late adolescent age spans.

Across the years of mid-adolescence, the functions of friendships and peer groups change in facilitating identity formation. Whereas peer groups of early adolescents generally consist of same-sex friends, the peer groups of mid-adolescents generally move to loose associations of heterosexual cliques. The peer group of mid-adolescence thus provides a meeting ground and experimental arena for forming bonds with a single partner (Brown & Klute, 2003). The peer group for mid-adolescents also helps facilitate awareness of one's sexual and sex-role identity and provides important confirmation of self-esteem (Silbereisen & Noack, 1990). In terms of experiences with intimacy, however, romantic idealization has been higher among early and mid-adolescents, compared with older youths (Montgomery, 2005).

Although Erikson (1968) has conceptualized the task of intimacy primarily as a task of young adulthood following identity consolidation during late adolescence, Allison and Sabatelli (1988) argue that intimacy needs to be viewed as an evolving phenomenon, which both contributes to and emerges from ongoing individuation and identity development during adolescence. Where families have been unable to tolerate adolescent individuation, however, adolescents may either withhold themselves from close friend and peer relationships or, alternatively, throw themselves into narcissistic involvements with peers in opposition to parental wishes. In either case, more mature forms of mutuality with peers are unlikely to evolve without some form of psychotherapeutic intervention or fortunate life circumstances.

The School

The church-affiliated high school I attended was intent on creating boys with a certain type of identity. It had rules like you couldn't have hair down below your collar or you couldn't wear jewelry. We spent most of our time trying to buck the system at school. That school just took away so many options for trying new things . . . it really hindered rather than helped me to grow.

—19-year-old male, looking back

Like families and peer groups, schools are a further context in which mid-adolescents spend a significant period of time. Many vital dimensions of adult life are critically dependent on the kinds of decisions that mid-adolescents make in the context of the school environment, as well as the kinds of experiences they have there. What subjects to take, what vocational directions to pursue, what extracurricular activities to join, and what friends does one seek? All of these issues require important decisions of mid-adolescents involved in the identity formation process. And factors such as the general school structure and climate, alongside interactions with teachers and peers will all provide social and emotional experiences with possible long-term implications for identity. The outcomes of one's mid-adolescent decisions and experiences in school will thus help to set the foundations for vocational, ideological, and relational pathways into adult life.

However, despite the critical role that schools play in adolescent identity development, research on the impact of schools in relation to this process has been scant. As Eccles and Roeser (2003) note, developmental researchers interested in adolescents have focused primarily on the family and peer group as facilitators of identity development, and educational researchers have attempted to understand the impact of schools on scholastic and intellectual rather than socioemotional outcomes. The schools will affect and be affected by adolescent development at a variety of levels. A few dimensions of the school environment, however, have been explored in relation to mid-adolescent identity outcomes.

The general structure and emotional climate of schools have been the focus of several investigations into mid-adolescent identity development. In France, for example, Lannegrand-Willems and Bosma (2006) examined mid-adolescent identity exploration and commitment in three high school contexts. They undertook a short-term (6-month) longitudinal study of mid-adolescents' identity and exploration and commitment processes in one school drawing primarily from students of higher socioeconomic backgrounds, another school drawing students from primarily middle-class groups, and a third school drawing students from lower socioeconomic backgrounds. Results showed that the impact of the school context on identity became stronger during the school year in all three schools; however, the more favorable the socioeconomic background of students in the school settings, the higher were their levels of identity exploration and commitment. Students of lower socioeconomic backgrounds often tended to detach themselves from the school context.

In England, Roker and Banks (1993) found some school structures more likely to facilitate identity development than others. Using Marcia's identity status approach, the researchers explored the identity formation process of mid-adolescent girls attending both private and state-supported schools. Though girls in both school settings were comparable in age and family background, a significantly greater proportion of private school girls were foreclosed in their identity-defining decisions, particularly regarding politics. By contrast, those girls attending state schools were much more likely to be moratorium or diffuse in their political decision making and achieved or moratorium in their occupational directions. The authors suggest the relatively homogeneous environment of the private school, where pupils were exposed to few competing ideological viewpoints and pressured to make career plans at an early age, was likely to be associated with foreclosed identity development. The state-supported schools, on the other hand, provided girls with exposure to many differing political views and belief systems, a condition more likely to support identity exploration and future commitment.

Dryer (1994) has outlined ways in which educational environments and curricula might be structured to best facilitate adolescent identity development in the high schools. Identity formation can be encouraged by providing adolescents with educational environments that stimulate exploration and commitment. More specifically, an identity-enhancing curriculum should promote student exploration, responsible choice, and self-determination, according to Dryer. It should also stimulate role-playing and social interaction across generations, as well as an appreciation of how the past is related to the present. Finally, it should enhance student self-acceptance and provide teens with positive feedback from teachers and counselors. Dryer also points out that a curriculum based on the psychosocial needs of young people has been sadly missing in recommendations of reports regarding the educational agenda for U.S. schools. Identity theory offers the potential for many important applications in the high school arena.

The Community

The percentage of high school seniors participating in volunteer work in their communities is becoming common in the United States, more so than in many European countries. In fact, community service is sometimes required by certain high school districts in the United States. Flanagan (2004) argues that community-based organizations and neighborhood opportunities for volunteer service provide structured outlets for leisure and opportunities for youths to work toward common goals, in which the status of all members is equal. Additionally, volunteerism provides teens with the opportunity to develop social trust with reference to a wider group of people than one's immediate family and peer group. Apart from attending a school in which community service is a requirement, the two best predictors of community service among high school students are having parents who are actively involved in volunteer community work and being involved in religious organizations (Flanagan, 2004). Thus, the community is a further context in which many mid-adolescents are spending significant periods of time; such venues offer further opportunities for promoting identity development.

Over the past decade, research has been undertaken into ways in which school-based community service may promote adolescent identity formation (e.g., Blyth & Leffert, 1995; McIntosch, Metz, & Youniss, 2005; Yates & Youniss, 1996). In the early stages of this work, Yates and Youniss (1996) undertook longitudinal work that assessed the impact of a mandatory, school-based service program on the development of ideological identity. (This program required adolescents to work four times in a soup kitchen as part of a year-long course on social justice.) Yates and Youniss analyzed essays that the students wrote at two points during the year-long course and found a developmental progression of views, moving from statements dealing more with concrete, immediate issues to those raising broader reflections on justice and responsibility. These authors concluded that community service during high school helped to foster greater political-moral interest, as well as a sense of ideological identity; the kinds of service experiences that may stimulate mid-adolescents in the development of values meaningful to their identities are in need of further research, however.

McIntosh and colleagues (2005) have examined the role that community service activities play in the process of identity clarification during the high school years. The authors hypothesized that community service involvements would provide youths with opportunities to develop ideological commitments that could give meaning and direction to their lives. The researchers hypothesized that over the high school years, identity during mid-adolescence would depend more on community and school-based activities than family and peer group involvements alone. This hypothesis was based on Erikson's (1968) writings, suggesting the base for identity development expands to larger social contexts. The authors also examined other factors such as personality features, demographic factors, and peer group affiliations that would also be important to identity formation during high school. Their results showed that community service and volunteerism, alongside peer group affiliation and personality factors, are indeed associated with identity clarification during the high school years.

Blyth and Leffert (1995) have undertaken research more generally on the impact of growing up in different kinds of communities. They examined 112 different communities as experienced by 9th to 12th graders in public schools. The researchers focused on three community health types, which were defined in terms of levels of problem behaviors by youth. The authors found that healthier communities tended to be smaller, less densely populated, with fewer female-headed households. Vulnerable youths benefited from living in healthier communities. The types of benefits such youths gained were less related to increases in self-esteem but more related to internalizing community norms for acceptable behavior. Although the direct study of identity development was not a part of this investigation, one might suspect that adolescents who felt more connected to and supported by their communities of residence were likely to experience fewer identity-related problem behaviors as well.

Section Summary and Implications

Numerous research findings show a strong relationship between an adolescent's identity status or level of ego development and parental communication behaviors. Adolescents who have explored identity-defining options and have higher levels of ego development have parents who respectfully encourage autonomy within a supportive context.

Parents and peers contribute to different aspects of mid-adolescent identity development. Peers enable one to experiment with different expressions of self, and they may act as a mirror as different behaviors are tested. The peer group for mid-adolescents helps facilitate sexual and sex role identity.

Preliminary evidence shows that schools providing a homogeneous environment may give little opportunity for student exploration of differing alternatives and discourage more mature forms of identity development.

Community service by high school students facilitates political-social awareness and identity development.

Back to the Beginning

At the beginning of this chapter, three questions propelled us into the study of identity development during mid-adolescence, along with Bill's remarks. Bill is a 17-year-old high school junior, exploring a wide variety of roles, from class clown to rebellious delinquent. He finds advantages and disadvantages to all of these personality types. However, Bill also finds something far more important through his explorations—a person that he does not have to work hard to be, his own identity. It is this identity search that often begins among mid-adolescents.

Answers to Chapter Questions

◈ **How does a sense of ego identity begin to form?**

Experiences in a broad range of social contexts, from the family to the peer group, from the school to broader community agencies, that provide opportunities for the exploration of genuinely meaningful values, roles, and life goals are most likely to facilitate the identity formation process.

◈ **How does vocational identity development occur?**

Ginzberg suggests vocational identity occurs through fantasy, tentative, and realistic stages in considering vocational directions. Mid-adolescents are most likely engaged in tentative and realistic explorations of future vocational roles.

◈ **In what way does community service impact on ideological identity formation during mid-adolescence?**

High school students taking part in community service programs have developed higher levels of political-social awareness than nonparticipants. Volunteerism during high school is linked with opportunities for identity clarification as well as a broader foundation for establishing meaningful directions to one's life.

University has been probably one of the biggest influences in my personality development. I think that's because you meet so many different people at university and you are subsequently presented with so many more options.

—21-year-old male, looking back

4

Identity in Late Adolescence

- How does one's identity develop over late adolescence?
- What is the relationship of identity to intimacy development in late adolescence?
- Do men and women differ in the types of identity-related values they hold?

I think I am now in transition between adolescence and adulthood. I feel more independent, and I don't need to defy my parents anymore. I have a more responsible, mature attitude towards boys and relationships, and I support myself financially. But I still don't feel as though I have found my identity. I don't have a definite career in mind, and I feel lost in society, as though I have to conform to society's expectations.

—Jeanne, 20-year-old university student

Who am I *really*, and what will happen to me? What do *I*, not my parents, but *I* really believe in? So much responsibility lies out there for me—can I really do it? What if I don't make it through school? Do I really want a long-term relationship? Do I really want *this* relationship?

Could I really handle being a parent? Will I be able to earn enough to take care of a family? How can I really make a contribution to life and to other people? What will make me happy? How can I feel a sense of completeness in my life? Why is there so much evil in the world?

These issues were foremost in the minds of groups of late adolescent university students and youths working in the community whom I have interviewed in studies of identity conducted over the past few years. Again, individuals were asked what kinds of questions they considered when thinking about who they are as people—about their own identities. These responses convey the awesomeness of real responsibilities that lie ahead in adult life, the hesitancy regarding one's capacity to cope, the hope for finding some way of meaningful living, and the fear of failure.

The Eriksonian biological, psychological, and societal dimensions of ego identity reappear in the previous statements. Questions of one's capability as a parent, both in the biological and psychological senses, commonly occurred alongside concerns with intimacy and what a long-term relationship commitment to a partner would mean. Concerns with values, morality, and ideals also were strong, as were questions of knowing which path was right. Many of these late adolescents were in Erikson's identity-formation process itself. They were sifting and synthesizing significant identifications of their childhoods into a new identity structure and sense of self while at the same time trying to find ways they could meaningfully express themselves in and be recognized by a larger social context. I step now into the world of late adolescence to overview some of the normative biological, psychological, and societal issues contributing to ego identity, and then I turn to examine key identity dimensions in greater detail. I define late adolescence here both in terms of chronological age and psychosocial tasks—from age 18 to 22 years, during which young people are likely to actualize many identity-defining decisions. Finding a vocational path and an intimate relationship with a partner, forming new ways of relating to one's family of origin, and developing a set of meaningful values that will at least carry them into early adult life are among the many psychosocial tasks of late adolescence.

Intersection of Biological, Psychological, and Societal Influences on Identity in Late Adolescence: An Overview

During the years of late adolescence, the immense challenge of entering adulthood, with its many new arenas of responsibility, looms large. By the late teens, one's physical sense of identity has stabilized. Late adolescents have become aware of the strengths and limitations of their physical features and abilities, of that which can be changed and that which must be accepted and taken as given. The majority of late adolescents have begun to search for comfortable expressions of their sexuality and gender roles. Qualities valued in friendships and intimate relations are also important concerns for many, and broader personal and social values also become matters evoking greater attention. With further consolidations of growth in the biological sphere, it is perhaps the psychological and societal arenas that dominate the identity-formation process of late adolescence. Identity work now takes on a new urgency, for soon life in the adult world must be entered "for real" and "will I actually survive there" becomes an issue of vital importance.

Again, however, the interaction of one's biological features with psychological processes and societal expectations and demands must be appreciated in understanding the identity-formation process of late adolescence. In many societies, being an individual of a certain gender about to assume adult roles brings strong expectations of what is considered acceptable behavior. Although the rigidity of previously defined gender roles has been changing greatly in many Western cultures over recent decades, many stereotypic attitudes in certain segments of society still prevail such that some women will still experience gender discrimination in the workplace (Anthis, 2002).

Differential rates of pay still remain for many men and women in identical positions in the United States; this phenomenon is one way in which employers express gender role expectations and stereotypes (U.S. Bureau of the Census, 2003). The psychological challenge of differentiating from one's parents and establishing new close relationships are given added impetus by the expectation within many societies that one will assume greater self-responsibility upon entering adult life.

Biological Processes

Whereas clearly visible signs of puberty mark the beginning of adolescence, few such clearly observable physical signs herald its conclusion. By late adolescence, the growth rate has decelerated significantly, and sexual maturation has generally been completed by most. Observable changes in height generally stop for women by about age 18 and for men by about age 20 (Tanner, 1991). The body has now assumed its adult contours and proportions, with a substantial contributor to weight gain coming from the increased musculature of the body. Average ages for attaining full adult height are certainly different from those at the turn of the century, when men continued to grow until about the age of 26 years (Roche, 1979). Throughout the years of mid-adolescence, there has been a steady improvement in physical strength, skill, and endurance for both genders. Pubertal changes, however, leave the two genders with somewhat different physical capabilities by the time of late adolescence.

Prior to puberty, there are virtually no gender differences in muscle mass, bone mass, and body fat; however, by late adolescence, males have about one and a half times the lean muscle mass and bone mass of females, and postpubertal girls have about twice the body fat of postpubertal boys (Grumbach & Styne, 1998). Following puberty, gender differences in skills and endurance appear and persist throughout adult life. Late adolescent males, for example, have greater speed and coordination in body movements than women, whereas women have greater finger dexterity and fine motor coordination than men. Women's greater body fat ratio, coupled with a lighter bone structure, will give women an advantage over men in physical activity requiring stamina. However, the additional muscle tissue of males makes tasks requiring upper body strength (such a lifting heavy objects) much easier for them than for women (Thomas & French, 1985). Numerous physical differences that have become established for the two genders during puberty do have widespread implications for identity development in late adolescence and beyond.

Late adolescence is one of the physically healthiest phases of the life span, with relatively few incidences of chronic illnesses, hospital stays, and fewer days at home sick in bed, compared with other life stages; however, depression, asthma, or skeletal disorders (such as arthritis) do affect one in five adolescents (Ozer, Macdonald, & Irwin, 2002).

Psychological Issues

Adulthood suggests mortgages and responsibility, which I'm trying to avoid at all costs!

—19-year-old male teacher trainee

Perhaps two of the most important identity-related psychological developments of late adolescence are the second separation-individuation process and the capacity for new forms of intimacy; these two developments are closely related dimensions of psychological functioning. Peter Blos (1967) first drew attention to the separation-individuation transition of adolescence, which involves the capacity to assume increasing responsibility for those matters that previously had been left to others. Blos was also the first psychoanalytic writer to discuss the intrapsychic mechanisms giving rise to this newfound, albeit rather frightening capacity captured in the fears of the quote from the teacher trainee.

Current research and theory point to late adolescence as a time of major advances in the second separation-individuation process; such issues will be described more fully in a later section of this chapter. The separation-individuation process of late adolescence involves the development of a more autonomous sense of self through reworking internalized ties to representations of one's parents. The growth of a more autonomous sense of self also involves the development of new forms of relationships with others, including one's parents. The second separation-individuation process involves intrapsychic restructuring so that youths become more capable of evaluating, deciding, and taking responsibility for issues in their own lives, on their own terms. Not all cultures encourage this process among late adolescents, but Western cultures generally do (Marcia, 1993). However, not all adolescents within Western contexts undergo such intrapsychic restructuring.

For Erikson (1968), late adolescence sees the identity-formation process generally well under way, as decisions regarding suitable social roles and values are tentatively made, and comfortable social niches are gradually found by many. An identity based on previous identifications with important others gives way for many to an identity based on a more personal assessment of one's own skills, strengths, interests, and talents. One needs to earn an income, and so decisions regarding one's vocational directions become a priority. However, one also needs to establish a meaningful life philosophy, spiritual and/or social values, form of sexual expression, and sex-role orientation to have some kind of direction and overarching life structure for entering young adulthood. And as these identity issues begin to find resolution, issues of intimacy come to the fore.

Erikson (1963) has described the psychosocial task of Intimacy Versus Isolation as primarily a task of young adulthood; one's capacity for different types of intimacy is certainly contingent on one's resolution to identity issues (Orlofsky, Marcia, & Lesser, 1973). Intimacy during late adolescence includes both close friendships and romantic involvements. Intimacy has been defined as "the intersection of two identities. . . . In a truly intimate relationship, each partner preserves a sense of separateness and has the ability to retain his or her unique qualities" (Whitbourne, 2005, p. 45). One's ability to enter into such relationships is based on the assuredness and stability of one's own sense of identity. If this sense has not been attained, closeness with another brings the threat that one's own identity will dissolve or be lost, and in such situations, relationships may be more superficial or distant. One must also find ways to express one's sexuality comfortably and openly with a loved partner and thus make a deeply involved commitment to another, even when it may involve some degree of self-sacrifice or compromise (Erikson, 1968).

Cognitive developments also occur during late adolescence. Many late adolescents have now moved into Piaget's (1972) stage of full formal operations, where such abilities as the use of propositional logic, combinatorial reasoning, and the ability to understand ratios and to hypothesize about the future become reliably used in approaching problems. Although Piaget, in his later writings, believed formal operational thought to be achieved between about 15 and 20 years old, many developmental psychologists now find considerable variation in when these operations actually are attained. Markovits and Valcon (1990), for example, find that it is not until late adolescence that formal operational thinking may become consolidated. It is important to be aware that many late adolescents may not be using formal operational logic at all, however, or using it inconsistently.

Both exposure to and experience with problems requiring formal operational logic appear crucial to its development (Whitbourne, 1996a); identity issues pressing for resolution during late adolescence would seem ideal for the stimulation of these new cognitive operations. However, the precise nature of the relationship between formal operational skills and ego identity during mid- and late adolescence has not been clear (see Kroger, 2004, for a review). Boyes and Chandler (1992) have suggested that the shift to formal operational thought carries with it many unsettling consequences, as young people shift from a sense of certainty regarding truth and objective knowledge to an appreciation that there is no objective reality and that reality is, rather, a social construction. During this transition, youth may become either dogmatic or skeptical before becoming more rational in their means of coping with doubt. Boyes and Chandler have linked these developmental advances in cognition to developmental shifts in the identity-formation process, as young people move from a diffuse or foreclosed identity status through moratorium to an identity achievement position.

Societal Influences

> I realized I had an identity when I started to feel like I actually belonged in society. This happened after four years of living and working in [names city], when I returned to [names another city] where I was born and grew up. This return gave me a feeling of having found a place in society, a place where I felt comfortable. I now know the career path I want to pursue and how to achieve it. I know myself, and I like who I am. I do have questions, though, about the meaning of life and why I exist.
>
> —21-one-year-old female, working full time

Society plays a critical role in the identity-formation process of late adolescence, for it is at this time that broader social institutions prepare to receive and confirm (or not) the late adolescent as a fledgling member of a larger collective order. It is clear from the young woman's statement, the feeling of actually belonging to such a community actively confirms her own sense of identity. The role of society both to "recognize and be recognized by" late adolescents cannot be underestimated in the identity-formation process of youth. For late adolescents, the transition from the established norms and social networks of the school, which has given a structure and framework to one's life since earliest childhood, to a frameless, postschool world of unknown futures with multiple possibilities is a daunting one. Finding a place in the broader social arena where "I can feel comfortable and confirmed" is a difficult task. All of one's earlier identity consolidations—coming to terms with one's sexuality, discovering one's interests, capabilities, and limitations—are prominent in finding a societal framework for one's existence beyond secondary school.

Baumeister and Muraven (1996) have proposed that the relationship of identity to the broader social order be considered in terms of adaptation: "More precisely, individual identity is an adaptation to a social context" (p. 405). Individuals must find satisfaction of their own biological and psychological needs within some context, and so, Baumeister argues, people modify their identities according to what will best help them live in a particular context. Different societies and cultures demand different forms of adaptation on the part of the individual. As has been noted in Chapter 2, some cultures discourage identity decision making on the part of teenagers by actively prescribing or conferring particular adult roles for them; in fact, identity in such societies or cultures is a nonissue for their more youthful members. "I just wasn't even given a chance to think about my identity, what I wanted to do for work, who I wanted to marry—my life was just already laid out for me," complained one young woman of an ethnic minority group in a research interview I conducted in New Zealand. But adaptation to most arenas within contemporary Western social contexts requires some identity questioning by late adolescents in order to enter a satisfying young adult life.

What are the experiences of late adolescents who retain their identity structures of childhood in contexts that demand identity related decisions? In university settings, which provide exposure to many new ideas, ideals, and values, foreclosed late adolescents appear to develop specific strategies in order not to be overwhelmed by the anxiety created by the demands of the social surroundings. Slugoski, Marcia, and Koopman (1984) studied late adolescent male foreclosures in interaction with peers of differing identity statuses. They found foreclosures most likely either to acquiesce or to become antagonistic in their interactions with peers. Through both strategies, these foreclosed youths managed to deflect the impact of dissonant information that might raise the need for reexamination of their own identity structures.

Côté and Levine (2002) detail the concept of adaptation to social contexts through use of the term, "identity capital." Identity capital describes the personal resources that an individual brings to various social contexts. Their term, identity capital, refers to two types of individual assets: *tangible* and *intangible*. An individual's tangible assets are those that are socially visible, that serve as "passports" into other social and institutional spheres. Examples of tangible assets would be one's academic credentials or group memberships. Intangible identity capital resources refer to individual personality characteristics and cognitive abilities used to negotiate various obstacles and opportunities within a certain context. Thus identity capital refers to investments that people make in who they are. Optimal identity adaptation is based on the wise use of one's tangible and intangible resources in the "identity markets" of late modern communities.

Section Summary and Implications

Few visible signs of biological change mark the end of adolescence. However, important gender differences in muscular strength, height, weight, and physical endurance emerge, which do have widespread implications for late adolescent identity development.

Two important psychological changes of late adolescence are the second separation-individuation process and the development of new forms of intimacy. Adolescents generally rework internalized ties to parents that enable them to experience new forms of intimacy in a relationship outside the family.

Society both recognizes and becomes recognized by late adolescents finding their ways into adult life. This process of mutual regulation, in Erikson's view, is central to the identity-formation process. Côté and Levine (2002) elaborate how individuals adapt to social contexts through their use of "identity capital."

The Second Separation-Individuation Process and Identity Formation

Erikson's (1968) identity-formation process of adolescence has intrapsychic underpinnings. Erikson described identity formation as moving from an identity based on identifications with important others to a new structure more uniquely one's own; this new structure is based on a synthesis of all these earlier identifications into a new whole, greater than the sum of its parts. Recent research and theory development has attempted to explore this intrapsychic movement in greater detail. Initially, Peter Blos described adolescence as a second individuation process. He drew upon the earlier work of psychoanalyst Margaret Mahler and her studies of infants to discuss general intrapsychic changes of adolescents.

Mahler (1963) and her colleagues had conducted a series of videotaped observations of normal infants and their mothers in interaction to chart how an independent sense of self develops through the first three years of life. Mahler and colleagues described an initial *autistic* state, in which the infant has little awareness of boundaries between self and the outside world. A gradual growing awareness of the primary caretaker over the first three to four weeks of life heralds the beginning of *symbiosis*. During this time, the primary caretaker is perceived merely as an extension of the infant's self, for the infant behaves as though infant and caretaker were one person. It is from this base that four subphases of separation individuation evolve.

The separation-individuation process itself begins with what Mahler calls *differentiation,* when the 5- to 10-month-old infant begins to experience the primary caretaker and others as separate from the self. Furthermore, the child tentatively begins to explore the world while at the same time remaining in close proximity to the primary caretaker. During the ensuing *practicing* subphase, a time of increased exploration occurs between about 10 and 15 months. As long as the trusted caretaker remains in close proximity, the child's explorations of the world generally are very active. But such exuberant explorations soon come to a halt between about 15 and 22 months in the *rapprochement* subphase. For the toddler, the full implications of physical and psychological separateness begin to dawn. The recognition that "I am separate from my main caretaker and am not omnipotent" creates a great sense of loss, and seemingly regressive attempts to reinvolve the primary caretaker in previous symbiotic roles often follow. The toddler's conflict between both a desire for fusion with the primary caretaker and a more differentiated sense of self can be abetted by the father (or important other) in encouraging more autonomous behavior. Ultimately, the child realizes that there can be no return to the fusion of earlier times in the final, open-ended subphase of *libidinal object constancy,* which generally occurs during the third year of life. During this final subphase, a child will optimally attain a sense of physical individuality and the ability to retain an image of the main caretaker that can function in the caretaker's absence. A critique of Mahler's work can be found in Kroger (2004).

Blos drew upon Mahler's work and suggested that adolescence, itself, involves a second separation-individuation process, although he did not attempt to detail the specific movements involved. However, later theorists and researchers have not only undertaken this task but have also found the time of late adolescence to be the most active phase of intrapsychic restructuring during the second separation-individuation process. Josselson (1980) began and I (Kroger, 2004) have continued to map possible parallels between specific separation-individuation subphases of infancy and those of the second separation-individuation process of adolescence. Note that whereas one important infant outcome of separation individuation is the ability to internalize (or carry within oneself) an image of the main caretaker, an important outcome of the second separation-individuation process of adolescence is to relinquish the power held by this internalized representation. In this way, one is able to function more autonomously.

Numerous studies have examined intrapsychic features of the second separation-individuation process in relation to ego identity status (see Chapter 3 for a discussion of Marcia's four identity statuses). Indeed, late adolescents in the foreclosure identity status appear to have an intrapsychic organization wherein the representation of self and primary caretaker is not differentiated but rather fused in a symbiotic relationship (Cramer, 2001; Josselson, 1996; Kroger, 1995; Papini, Micka, & Barnett, 1989). Late adolescents in the moratorium status have shown parallels to differentiating, practicing, and rapprochement separation-individuation subphases of infancy, as these late adolescents go through a process of differentiating themselves from important others whom they have internalized. Josselson (1982), Orlofsky and Frank (1986), and Kroger (1990) all conducted studies of early memories in relation to ego identity status and found many moratoriums eager to explore the world, although sometimes anxious about doing so. Identity-achieved adolescents had obtained a more stable sense of self, consolidated sense of identity, and greater security in attachment patterns. On the other hand, identity-diffusions often had difficulty in internalizing a stable caretaker to serve as a foundation for the later adolescent separation-individuation process.

Other researchers have examined additional features of the separation-individuation process of late adolescence. Secure parental attachments have been consistently linked with healthy levels of adolescent separation individuation and positive adjustment (Kennedy, 1999; Mattanah, Hancock, & Brand, 2004; Scharf, Mayseless, & Kivenson-Baron, 2004). In addition, parental separation anxiety has been studied in relation to adolescent identity development (Bartle-Haring, Brucker, & Hock, 2002). A mother's sense of providing a secure base so her adolescent could explore identity options was linked with her late adolescent son or daughter's identity achievement during college. A father's comfort with providing a secure base, however, was not linked with his adolescent's identity development. However, father's anxiety about distancing was linked with higher foreclosure scores for daughters, but lower foreclosure scores for sons.

Several investigations have also provided links between intrapsychic differentiation, more generally, and identity development. Johnson, Buboltz, and Seeman (2003) found that higher levels of identity achievement predicted higher levels of scoring on the "I Position" scale; this scale reflects a clearly defined sense of self. Higher levels of moratorium predicted higher levels of Emotional Reactivity scale scores. Higher levels of foreclosure predicted lower levels of Total Differentiation scale scores as well as higher levels of Fusion with Others scale scores. Higher levels of diffusion predicted lower levels of Emotional Reactivity and higher levels of Emotional Cutoff scale scores. Quintana and Lapsley (1990) also found adolescents' movements toward intrapsychic individuation related to advanced identity development; they additionally found that parental control restricts successful individuation. Perosa, Perosa, and Tam (1996) found late adolescent female foreclosures had failed to develop a sense of competence in their ability to direct their own lives and had overinvolved relationships with their mothers. In addition, Fullinwider-Bush and Jacobvitz (1993) noted that overinvolved or estranged relations between father and daughter were associated with moratorium and diffusion identity statuses. Considered together, all studies suggest clear links between the second separation-individuation process, type of parental attachment, and pattern of identity development during late adolescence.

The Beginnings of Intimacy

It wasn't until I found myself in an intimate relationship with my present partner that I realized that I hadn't had a really intimate relationship before. Although there were other people, nothing ever lasted and nothing was fulfilling or right. I feel this was because I had not yet discovered myself, I had not found my own identity. Before making the commitment to my present partner, though, I knew that I had found myself. I knew who I was and what I wanted to do with my life, where I wanted to go. I am now really happy to be the person I have become.

—20-year-old female university student

This young woman's statement about her present feelings of intimacy reflects precisely the point made by Erikson (1968) in his discussion of the need for a secure sense of identity before genuine intimacy can form. He states, "It is only when identity formation is well on its way that true intimacy—which is really a counterpointing as well as a fusing of identities—is possible" (Erikson, 1968, p. 135). At the same time, however, Erikson (1963, 1968) also suggested that there were gender differences in the ways in which men and women resolve these two psychosocial stages. He noted that whereas issues of identity needed to be resolved before genuine intimacy could be experienced among men, women might keep their identities more open and less committed until the task of finding a life partner is resolved. The nature of the relationship between identity and intimacy development during late adolescence has been the focus of much research and controversy in the intervening years.

In 1973, Orlofsky, Marcia, and Lesser developed the Intimacy Status Interview, which assessed the style by which one engages in relationships with close friends and romantic partners to understand more about the relationship between identity and intimacy. An individual's style of relating to significant others is determined by the degree to which depth, mutuality, and respect for the integrity of the self and others are expressed in describing close relationships during the Intimacy Status Interview. Following its development, the Intimacy Status Interview was modified (Levitz-Jones & Orlofsky, 1985) so that the following general relational styles are now possible to assess:

• *Intimate*—One who has made a commitment to a partner in a relationship characterized by a high degree of depth and mutuality, openness, and caring. Conflicts can be resolved in constructive ways, and sexuality can be comfortably expressed in a romantic relationship.

• *Preintimate*—One who has a high likelihood for achieving intimacy but who does not yet have a long-term, committed partnership involving a sexual relationship. Friendships here are characterized by many qualities expressive of intimacy, including the ability to communicate openly and mutually and to take an equal role in decision making regarding shared activities.

• *Pseudointimate*—One who has established a long-term, sexual commitment to a partner but whose relationship is superficial, lacking open communication and deep emotional involvement. Personal concerns are not shared, and relationships are treated as conveniences.

• *Stereotypic*—One who has friends and dating relationships, but has not established a long-term sexual commitment to a partner. Friendships are superficial and again lacking in open communication and deep emotional involvement. The emphasis in the relationship is on what can be obtained from others.

• *Isolate*—One who has no close relationships with peers and for whom relationships with acquaintances are more formal and stereotyped. This individual is withdrawn, often lacking in social skills.

• *Merger (Committed)*—One who has established a long-term sexual relationship with a partner but in a style that is characterized by enmeshment, dependency, and unrealistic perceptions of others. This individual attempts to gain a sense of self through the relationship, finding it difficult to pursue interests and activities apart from friends or the partner.

• *Merger (Uncommitted)*—One who has not established a long-term, sexual relationship with a partner, but whose friendships are characterized by a high degree of dependency and enmeshment. Relationships are experienced as an extension of the self.

These styles of intimacy have been associated with various personality features (Orlofsky, 1976) as well as differing ways in which late adolescents actually view their partners (Levitz-Jones & Orlofsky, 1985; Orlofsky, 1978). For example, subjects in an intimate or preintimate status have a greater degree of knowledge and understanding of their partners compared to those in other intimacy status groupings. Women in the merger and low intimacy status groupings have shown more separation-individuation disorders than women in intimate and preintimate intimacy statuses.

It must be noted, before turning to examine the relationship between identity and intimacy, that one's intimacy status has generally been based on the capacity to commit oneself to a heterosexual relationship. Those experiencing intimacy in close friendships without sexual involvements or in relationships with alternative forms of sexual involvement need also to be examined in future research to understand the relation between identity and intimacy more fully. Craig-Bray, Adams, and Dobson (1988) point out that identity formation as it influences intimacy may first be observed in the context of same-sex friendships and only later (with the transition to young adulthood) in the context of heterosexual relationships.

Research into associations between identity and intimacy for both late adolescent men and women has produced mixed findings. Those who have been more advanced in terms of identity statuses have also generally been more advanced in terms of their intimacy status development (e.g., Dyk & Adams, 1990; Kacerguis & Adams, 1980; Marcia, 1976; Orlofsky et al., 1973; Tesch & Whitbourne, 1982). However, a recent meta-analysis of studies dealing with the relationship between intimacy and identity status has shown that a more mature style of intimacy is not conditional upon attaining a more mature identity status for some women; correlations between identity and intimacy among men were significantly higher than the correlations between identity and intimacy among women (Årseth, Kroger, Martinussen, & Marcia, 2005). For some women, identity and intimacy development seem to codevelop, and such women may be defining themselves through their relationships with others.

Some work has found that sex-role orientation actually mediates the association between identity and intimacy, although some contradictory results have again appeared (Dyk & Adams, 1987). It seems that women who have a more feminine sex-role orientation also have a fused identity/intimacy association, whereas women with a more masculine sex-role orientation seem to develop a sense of identity prior to experiencing genuine intimacy in relationship. Men, regardless of sex-role orientation, generally develop a sense of identity prior to intimacy. Schiedel and Marcia (1985) have suggested that women may have two patterns of identity development: One pattern is followed by those women who focus on occupational and ideological identity concerns and achieve a sense of identity by age 20, and the other by women who follow a homemaking track and do not form a self-constructed identity until later in their 20s or early 30s, when family routines have become more established.

Predictors of intimacy in late adolescence and young adulthood have also been examined (Montgomery, 2005; Seiffge-Krenke, Shulman, & Klessinger, 2001). Using cross-sectional methods, Montgomery (2005) found that for both male and female college students, greater intimacy was associated with higher scores on a measure of psychosocial identity, as well as more committed beliefs and less self-consciousness. Women, however, scored significantly higher than men on the measure of intimacy. From Krenke and colleagues' (2001) longitudinal work in Germany, boys reported stronger pressure to develop an independent identity than girls at age 15; however, no gender differences on any of the three components of romantic relationships (closeness and connectedness, sexual attraction, and ambivalent emotions) were found at age 20. In addition, low developmental pressure to establish a separate identity was related to high attraction in romantic relationships. The authors interpret this finding as supporting Erikson's (1968) suggestion that individuals with a firmly established identity can experience a sense of merging with an opposite-sex partner in a sexual relationship without fearing the loss of one's own boundaries.

Understanding the relationship between identity and intimacy development in late adolescence is complex. Future work exploring the role of sex-role orientation for the development of identity and intimacy in late adolescence is warranted. In addition, one must be cautious in comparing findings across studies where different measures of identity and intimacy have often been used. It is important that any general conclusions are based upon studies conceptualizing identity and intimacy in similar ways.

Section Summary and Implications

Erikson has indicated that genuine intimacy can be experienced only when identity formation is well on its way. However, results from a recent meta-analysis of the identity status and intimacy literature indicate the correlations between these two variables are significantly higher for men than women; identity and intimacy may codevelop among women.

The Intimacy Status Interview has been developed by Orlofsky, Lesser, and Marcia to define the following styles of an intimate relationship: intimate, preintimate, pseudointimate, stereotypic, and isolated. Those in intimate and preintimate relationships share a greater degree of knowledge and under-standing of their partners as separate individuals than those adopting other styles of intimacy. Merger intimacy statuses were developed later.

One's sex-role orientation may mediate the association between identity and intimacy. Women with a more feminine sex-role orientation deal with iden-tity and intimacy issues simultaneously, whereas women with a more mas-culine sex-role orientation develop a sense of identity prior to intimacy. Men, regardless of sex-role orientation, generally develop a sense of identity prior to intimacy.

Actualizing Vocational Directions

Studies regarding the importance of vocational decision making for late ado-lescents have certainly supported Erikson's (1968) proposition that it is the issue of vocation that most concerns young people. When asked to rate iden-tity domains of central importance to their lives, for example, late adolescent students have consistently indicated the area of vocation to be that which is most preoccupying (e.g., Kroger, 1986). Thus, one's sense of identity in Erikson's terms is strongly related to one's vocational choices; choice of vocational direction in late adolescence will set up the initial framework for the way in which one's early adult years will be structured.

What factors influence vocational decision making? Among the many factors impacting on one's vocational decision making are psychological characteristics, such as one's own interests and talents, familial influences, and socioeconomic and other situational factors, such as the availability of employment, one's social class, or the possibility of sex discrimination in the workplace. Researchers have recently been focusing on such factors as the role of self-concept, identity status, attachment patterns, as well as situational variables in relation to career development and identity formation.

Mortimer, Zimmer-Gembeck, Holmes, and Shanahan (2002) drew upon qualitative interview data collected as a part of the Youth Development Study in the United States to learn more about the process of how youths make decisions about long-term vocational commitments. This project was longitudinal in design and drew upon the reports of 1,000 individuals as they transited to early adulthood and engaged themselves in paid employment. The study pointed to a diverse set of trajectories of vocational development and a variety of vocational themes that were important to study participants. Most themes indicated that vocational decision making is a dynamic process that cross-sectional research could not address. Many youths felt that their high school expectations about adulthood had not been met; many reported delays in meeting vocational goals they expected. There were a variety of responses to this common experience of delay, with contextual cues aiding or obscuring vocational decision making. Other youths were uncertain about their future plans and lived on a day-to-day basis, hoping that "clarity will happen." For some, a strong turning point occurred, in which a vocational direction crystallized, while others reported a slow process of growing awareness of a preferred vocational direction. The authors point to the need for social policies to assist youths in the unstructured process of shifting from school to work contexts.

The identity-formation process and career development are strongly linked. Variability in the ways by which late adolescents explore and commit to an ego identity have been associated with the ways by which career exploration and occupational commitment are undertaken (e.g., Blustein, Devinis, & Kidney, 1989; Flum & Blustein, 2000; Vondracek, 1992). Blustein and colleagues suggest that the relationships between identity status and aspects of career development such as self-efficacy beliefs, self-concept crystallization, and career maturity might usefully be examined to learn more about the role of identity in vocational decision making. Vondracek, in turn, calls for an articulation of the ways in which earlier psychosocial stages in Erikson's scheme affect vocational identity development. And indeed, Hartung, Porfeli, and Vondracek (2005) have recently published an important review attempting to link researches into childhood vocational development with what is known about adolescent and adult vocational development. In this way, Hartung and colleagues hope to suggest directions for future research that could embed the study of vocational development within a life span developmental framework rather than as a phenomenon to be studied only in isolated age groups.

How does the process of actualizing career directions proceed from those earlier phases of vocational decision making noted in early and mid-adolescence? The entire concept of career choice in relation to late adolescent identity formation is in need of rethinking (Blustein & Noumair, 1996; Flum & Blustein, 2000). The emergence of a global marketplace, with a rapidly changing technology and continual restructuring of employment opportunities, has changed the way contemporary late adolescents must address career-related (and hence identity-related) issues. Blustein and Noumair (1996) point out that many organizations have a less hierarchical structure than in the past and that many middle-level managers have been dismissed or transferred. A noticeable sense of uncertainty has appeared in the labor market, and it thus seems important to both the vocational decision-making process and identity development itself that career decisions be regarded more flexibly than in the past. Although an individual used to be able to assume that his or her general line of work was unlikely to change dramatically over the course of adulthood, such assumptions can no longer be made. The current economic conditions of many Western, technologically advanced societies call for much flexibility in one's sense of vocational identity achievement.

Flum and Blustein (2000) developed a model for the future study of vocational exploration that draws upon the ego identity and human motivation literature in conjunction with an appreciation of historical and sociocultural circumstances. They suggest that an awareness of the ego identity literature would aid in recognizing different developmental pathways to vocational decision making, while the human motivation literature would contribute an understanding of processes that precipitate an approach or avoidance attitude toward vocational exploration. And a consideration of the social milieu that provides the framework for both intra- and interpersonal dimensions of identity exploration would provide a third critical element to any research agenda attempting to tap the complexity of vocational exploration and decision making.

Identity, Meaningful Values, and Personality

Late adolescence has been noted by many researchers, theorists, as well as parents as the time of great psychological advances in the identity-formation process described by Erikson (1968). Building on the cornerstones of preliminary decisions to the question of "Who am I really?" late adolescents are now faced with constructing an identity architecture for psychosocial commitments to see them into early adulthood. Many late adolescents will bring with them increasing abilities to reason abstractly and consider issues from a more autonomous perspective, which, in turn, affects the kinds of considerations they are able to give to their quest for meaningful values and contributions to society. Many dimensions of personality seem associated with steps in and ultimate resolutions to the identity-formation process. How do late adolescents proceed with their searches for meaningful values to live by and roles to engage in? Are there gender differences in the ways by which young men and women consider questions of morality? What personality factors are associated with different steps in the identity-formation process? Is it possible to predict developmental arrest? It is with late adolescents that the greatest amount of research addressing these questions has been undertaken. To date, over 600 published articles and doctoral dissertations have empirically explored Marcia's identity statuses in relation to other variables (Kroger, Martinussen, & Marcia, 2006). Thus, only a few of the many identity-related findings can be presented here.

Investigations have shown identity-achieved individuals to use more adaptive defense mechanisms (adaptive narcissism, internal locus of control) and to have high levels of ego development, personal autonomy, and self esteem (Berzonsky & Adams, 1999; Cramer, 1995, 2001; Hamer & Bruch, 1994; Marcia, 1966, 1967). They also use more planned, rational decision-making strategies than other identity statuses (Blustein & Phillips, 1990). Those in the moratorium status have been shown to be high in anxiety and to use denial, projection, and identification to help control their anxiety; they have also shown high levels of openness to experience (Cramer, 1995; Marcia, 1966, 1967; Tesch & Cameron, 1987). The more self-exploration that students had engaged in (both moratorium and achieved identity statuses), the more prepared they were to undertake tasks in a self-directed manner (Berzonsky & Kuk, 2000). Foreclosure adolescents have consistently shown high levels of authoritarianism, low levels of autonomy, and use of an external locus of control; they also make use of defensive narcissism to bolster self-esteem, and both genders strongly identify with their father and mother (Cramer, 2001; Clancy & Dollinger, 1993; Cramer, 1995; Marcia, 1966, 1967). Late adolescents who are diffuse have shown low levels of parent identification, self-esteem, personal autonomy, and ego development, and they use an external locus of control; they also have been shown to be shyer than those in other identity statuses (Cramer, 2001; Ginsburg & Orlofsky, 1981; Hamer & Bruch, 1994; Marcia, 1966, 1967).

Recent work in Belgium has been attempting to refine and expand Marcia's identity status paradigm by elaborating commitment and exploration processes that contribute to identity development among late adolescents (Luyckx, Goossens, Soenens, Beyers, & Vansteenkiste, 2005). These researchers measured exploration in breadth and depth as well as commitment making and identification with commitment in a longitudinal study of university students, assessed four times over two years. Identity statuses in this study were derived empirically through cluster analysis. Among the many results obtained in this study was empirical support for Marcia's four identity statuses plus a fifth carefree diffusion status. Carefree diffusions (scoring moderately on commitment making and low on exploration in breadth and depth) were as adjusted as those in the high commitment clusters (achievements and foreclosures), while those in the more traditional diffusion cluster, (low on commitment making and identification with commitment, low on exploration in depth, and moderate on exploration on breadth) were not well adjusted. Elaboration of exploration and commitment processes described by Marcia suggests an interesting way of making some important intraidentity status distinctions in the identity-formation process of late adolescence that may have important implications for intervention.

A number of studies have investigated the relationship between identity formation and the development of meaningful moral values. Those studies have examined that relationship in each of Marcia's (1966) identity statuses with respect to Kohlberg's (1984) stages of moral reasoning. (Both Marcia and Kohlberg models have been described in Chapter 3.) Researchers have consistently found that both men and women who have achieved a sense of identity use postconventional levels of moral reasoning, whereas those in less mature (foreclosure and diffusion statuses) use less mature forms of moral reasoning (conventional or preconventional). Moratorium individuals have been less consistent in the level of moral reasoning used across studies (Podd, 1972; Rowe & Marcia, 1980; Skoe & Diessner, 1994).

Skoe and her colleagues (Skoe, Cumberland, Eisenberg, Hansen, & Perry, 2002; Skoe & Marcia, 1991; Skoe, Pratt, Matthews, & Curror, 1996) have developed a care-based model of moral reasoning, based on Gilligan's (1982) earlier theory. They have examined the structure of care-based moral reasoning from adolescence through later adulthood through development of an "ethic of care" (ECI) interview. The interview presents different moral dilemmas involving issues of care; three general levels from which individuals reason about issues of care have been documented from this interview: Level 1 issues of care resolved primarily in terms of the self; Level 2 issues of care resolved primarily in terms of needs of the other; and Level 3 issues of care resolved taking into account both needs of the self and needs of the other. Skoe and Marcia (1991) found a similar relationship between identity status and moral reasoning for both men and women; those in more mature identity statuses reasoned at more mature levels on the ECI. However, the relationship between identity and ethic of care was significantly higher for women than men. It may be that the care ethic is more important to women than men in terms of their identity development.

Patterns of identity-status movement have been examined over the years of late adolescence. Again, longitudinal research has consistently shown an increase of individuals in moratorium and identity-achieved positions by the end of late adolescence, accompanied by decreases of individuals in foreclosure and diffusion statuses (e.g., Cramer, 1998; Fitch & Adams, 1983; Kroger, 1988; Waterman, Geary, & Waterman, 1974; Waterman & Goldman, 1976). It is noteworthy, however, that by the close of late adolescence, large percentages of the participants (approximately half) in all longitudinal studies of identity-status development had not attained a more mature identity position. Why is identity achievement so elusive? This issue will be discussed more fully in Chapter 6, alongside issues likely to precipitate identity exploration.

Contexts Affecting Late Adolescent Identity Development

Research focusing on the interactions between late adolescents and their social contexts has begun to be undertaken. Parental styles of communication and interaction in relation to adolescent identity development have been investigated in a number of studies; however, the roles of peers, educational, and work settings—working particularly in combination—remain relatively unexamined in the study of late adolescent identity formation. In addition, the vast majority of researches into late adolescent identity formation have utilized samples of those attending colleges or universities. Research with early and mid-adolescents in junior and senior high school systems have been able to examine more diverse groups of teenagers present in those educational settings; a move to examine the process of identity development for more diverse groups of late adolescents remains an important direction for future research.

In attempting to understand the relationship between late adolescent identity development and social contexts, Yoder (2000) has proposed a general model of ways in which various contextual barriers may interact with late adolescent and young adult identity-exploration and commitment processes and impact upon internal psychological functioning. The predominant mood of any historical epoch is closely linked with contextual options vital to the late adolescent identity-formation process. Yoder's concept of barriers refers to external limitations imposed by the sociocultural environments, reflecting sociocultural biases; barriers provide contextual boundaries and qualify the nature and process of each of Marcia's (1966; Marcia et al., 1993) identity statuses, described in Chapter 3. By applying the notion of barrier, as well as the complementary notion of opportunity, to each identity status, Yoder (2000) argues that researchers could thereby consistently identify the intersection between the individually driven and the contextually driven ego identity-formation process. In this way, intervention systems could be targeted to individuals or groups of adolescents in ways to most effectively assist them in reaching their aims.

The Family

Among late adolescents, renegotiating relationships with parents and other family members has generally occurred during the identity-formation process. Whereas observational studies of families in interaction have been undertaken with mid-adolescents, it is primarily self-report research that has been used with late adolescent university students and their parents to understand more about parenting styles and their relation to identity formation. Such limitations must be kept in mind when considering research results described in the following paragraphs. Establishing a sense of identity can certainly be linked with certain styles of family interaction and communication as well as attachment style, and existing self-report research does reveal findings similar to those derived from the observational studies described in Chapter 3.

From studies using an identity-status framework, an emphasis on individuality and connectedness has been characteristic of those families having identity achieved and moratorium late adolescent sons and/or daughters (Campbell, Adams, & Dobson, 1984; Kennedy, 1999; Willemsen & Waterman, 1991). At the same time, strong emotional attachment coupled with a lower level of support for autonomy characterized the family dynamics of foreclosure youths in these studies. Foreclosed adolescents have reported their families to be very close and child-centered; among adolescent women, when a mother is too close, overinvolved, and protective of her daughter, the daughter mirrors the mother's values rather than exploring many possible identity-related roles and values for herself (Perosa, Perosa, & Tam, 1996). Little conflict has characterized the family environment of late adolescent foreclosures (Perosa et al., 1996; Willemsen & Waterman, 1991). Diffused youth have reported the least emotional attachment to parents, coupled with limited independence. Some evidence has pointed to sex differences in the relations between parent-adolescent relationships and the identity-formation process. For example, Schultheiss and Blustein (1994) found parental attachment to play a more important role in the identity-formation process for women than men. Weinmann and Newcombe (1990) furthermore found love felt toward mothers and perceived love from mothers but not fathers to be related to those in committed identity statuses (foreclosure and achievement) during late adolescence.

One recent study has focused on intergenerational family systems and identity development among women (Perosa, Perosa, & Tam, 2002). Scores on Intergenerational Intimacy, Autonomy versus Fusion, Intergenerational

Intimidation, and Intergenerational Individuation scales contributed unique variance to the four ego identity statuses. The ability of family members to have open communication, conflict expression and resolution, and clear boundaries in the absence of intergenerational alliances facilitates the identity-formation process of late adolescence (Perosa et al., 2002). Identity achieved women reported feeling a balance between separateness and connectedness with their parents, and that parents did not triangulate them into their disputes but rather responded to their needs for autonomy by developing a mutual relationship with them. Moratoriums reported fearing their parents and modifying behavior to meet parents' expectations, possibly reflecting their own anxieties over differentiation from parental values. Foreclosure women reported a high degree of dependency on parents for approval in decision making and not feeling pressured by parents to change. Diffuse adolescents reported a highly undifferentiated family system in which they were not encouraged to take steps toward defining their own identities. This study gives deeper insights into the intergenerational dynamics among family members that were associated with each ego identity status.

Additional models have focused on the role played by attachment in fostering psychological adaptation during late adolescence. In a meta-analytic review, Rice (1990) defined attachment as the desire to seek proximity and attachment behavior as the means by which proximity is achieved. Predictions derived from attachment studies of infant development are now being applied to later adolescents in studying the identity-formation process. Kobak and Sceery (1988) asked late adolescents to describe their relationships with parents and how such relationships had changed over time, among other issues. Attachment styles were later assessed as secure (positive relationships remembered and easily integrated into overall view of relationship), dismissing (devaluing attachment relationships), or preoccupied (enmeshing relationships remembered and there was difficulty in integrating them). The secure group, in contrast to the dismissing group scored higher on measures of social competence, assertion, and dating competence. Security of attachment to parents has also characterized those in the achieved identity status (Kroger, 2004); security of attachment has also predicted higher levels of identity development and college adjustment among freshman college students (Kennedy, 1999; Lapsley, Rice, & Fitzgerald, 1990).

The Peer Group

The development of intimate relationships during late adolescence has been reviewed in a preceding section, so comments will be made here with regard to friendships in late adolescence. Over the past 15 years, the study of adolescent peer relationships has moved from a focus on the role peers play in helping adolescents disengage from parents and reassess parental values to a focus on the transformation of attachment bonds that takes place with various members of the adolescent's social spheres. Through an atmosphere of continued connectedness, late adolescents renegotiate old forms of attachment bonds with peers and develop new forms of closeness (Cooper, 1994; Rice & Mulkeen, 1995). These studies suggest that identity should not be defined solely in terms of autonomy and self-reliance, but also in term of being able to maintain a distinctive sense of self while remaining close to others (Cooper, 1994).

Transformations in parent-child relationships over the course of adolescence seem to co-occur with changes in the functions of peer relationships. How do connections with the peer group change over the years of adolescence, and what function does the peer group have for late adolescents undergoing the identity-formation process? In general, peer relationships increase in importance and level of intimacy over the course of adolescence (Cooper & Cooper, 1992). A number of studies have found that closeness with friends of the same gender grows stronger as both boys and girls get older, although girls report a higher degree of closeness to friends than boys (Furman & Buhrmeister, 1992; Rice & Mulkeen, 1995). It must be noted that researchers still have little information about the meaning and degree of intimacy experienced with peers for non-Caucasian adolescents. Also, over the course of adolescence, the importance of membership in a particular clique or crowd dissipates as late adolescents move into paired relationships. Brown and Klute (2003) report an age-related decline in the importance of belonging to a larger crowd over the adolescent years. They suggest that crowds offer reassurance to early adolescents in their demand for conformity but frustrate late adolescents in their desire to express their own attitudes and interests. Further research is needed into the functions of peer groups and friendships for the identity-formation process among late adolescents.

Educational and Work Settings

University has been probably one of the biggest influences in my personality development. I think that's because you meet so many different people at university and you are subsequently presented with so many more options.

—21-year-old male, looking back

Institutional contexts for late adolescents, such as the world of work or tertiary education, provide important settings for examining, exploring, developing, and later consolidating competencies and values. It is perhaps useful to address the ways in which such institutional contexts can best meet and support the young person's own identity needs. Context quality and the provision of stable institutional supports during late adolescence are of primary importance, regardless of economic resources available. Comments here will focus on the development of identity within tertiary and other vocational settings during late adolescence.

The limited research that has addressed the relationship between various types of tertiary environments and identity development directly has found that different university departments do attract students of differing identity statuses (Adams & Fitch, 1983; Costa & Campos, 1990). Adams and Fitch (1983) found that university departments that were less practical or community oriented (and more academic and scholastic in their emphases) were likely to attract males in committed identity statuses (achievement and foreclosure). Similarly, departments that emphasized scholastic accomplishment as well as academic propriety and that deemphasized practical or social awareness were attractive to females in more committed identity statuses. Costa and Campos (1990) found significant differences in identity-status distributions across university faculties, with both men and women who were identity-achieved predominating in law and the arts and both male and female foreclosed individuals more numerous in economics and medicine.

Comments have recently been made about the role of colleges as a transition to adulthood and their ability to facilitate psychosocial development more generally (Montgomery & Côté, 2003). These authors note that in the United States, colleges have become part of the late adolescent transition into adulthood for increasing numbers of youths, though fewer than 50 percent obtain a college degree. Thus, there are many other contexts that will significantly impact the identity-formation process among late adolescents. Furthermore, there are few longitudinal studies of the impact of the tertiary educational experience on long-term identity development. However, among researches examining the psychosocial impact of the college experience, findings suggest that it is important to go to college and finish it for those who wish to be stimulated in terms of occupational and personal development. At the same time, college can be a mixed experience, also providing many challenges and stresses. Social integration may be the most crucial ingredient for college students to deal with the stresses and enjoy the opportunities for growth and development.

Few studies have also been undertaken with late adolescents that directly examine the relationship between identity development and varied vocational settings. Munro and Adams (1977) and Morash (1980) both found more identity-achieved individuals among late adolescents who were working compared with those attending college, and they attributed pressures to make life decisions generated by the working environment to be responsible for this phenomenon. However, Archer and Waterman (1988) found college students to be more advanced in identity development than those working or combining college with work when controlling for age, socioeconomic, and geographic effects.

A more extensive qualitative study in Norway by Danielsen, Lorem, and Kroger (2000) examined patterns of identity formation among groups of youths who were unemployed, employed, and students, ages 18 to 24 years. Very different styles of identity decision making characterized individuals in these three groups. Employed youths, who had made early educational decisions to attend a trade school for their vocational qualifications, generally spent little time exploring not only vocational but also relational life options prior to forming commitments. University students, by contrast, were actively exploring not only vocational but also ideological, relationship, and lifestyle issues. Unemployed youths with a broader educational background were often taking time out to consider their futures and engage in a moratorium process, whereas the unemployed with narrower educational backgrounds were primarily foreclosed or diffuse in identity. Interestingly, all three groups of youths indicated work to be of primary importance to their sense of identity.

Section Summary and Implications

Among studies adopting an identity-status approach, individuality and connectedness have been stressed by families of late adolescent identity-achieved and moratorium individuals. Strong emotional attachment coupled with lower levels of support for autonomy have characterized family dynamics of foreclosure youth, whereas little emotional attachment has featured in families of identity-diffuse late adolescents.

Age-related declines in the importance of belonging to a larger peer group have appeared over the years of adolescence. More intimate styles of relating to selected significant others generally characterize peer relationships of late adolescence.

Little is known about the process of identity formation among late adolescents outside of tertiary educational contexts. Within such contexts, research suggests that students may be attracted to various academic departments on the basis of their initial identity status.

Back to the Beginning

This chapter opened with three questions about identity development during late adolescence, followed by 20-year-old Jeanne's comments on being in transition between adolescence and adulthood. Jeanne noted that she felt more independent now, both financially and interpersonally. But she still did not feel she had found her own identity. What issues, then, would contribute to Jeanne feeling a firmer sense of her own identity? She mentions finding a suitable vocational role and developing a stronger sense of herself that does not merely conform to society's expectations. This chapter has focused on both intrapsychic and social processes Jeanne describes that contribute to the identity-formation process as well as the development of more mature forms of intimacy during late adolescence.

Answers to Chapter Questions

◈ **How does one's identity develop over late adolescence?**

Intrapsychic changes of the second individuation process of adolescence enable youths to relinquish the power of internalized parents and begin more autonomous decision making regarding issues of personal identity.

◈ **What is the relationship of identity to intimacy development in late adolescence?**

Erikson believes identity issues must be resolved before more mature forms of intimacy can develop. Some research suggests, however, that identity and intimacy may codevelop for women.

◈ **Do men and women differ in the types of identity-related values they hold?**

Women may be more concerned about issues of care than justice in considering moral dilemmas.

My first year of high school was a particularly bad time. I am adopted, and I spent a lot of time thinking and feeling confused about who I was and that I didn't belong to my family.

—17-year-old male high school senior

5

Selected Identity
Issues of Adolescence

- How does knowledge of one's adoption impact identity?
- Does immigration change one's sense of identity?
- Is a sense of one's ethnic identity critical to one's ego identity?

*I believe that for minority youths, the need to discover their ethnic
identity is a crucial prerequisite for discovering and developing
their personal identity.*

—Sophia, 19-year-old university student

This chapter examines some selected identity issues that may affect the
identity-formation process among significant numbers of adolescents.
It is only recently that research in the areas of adoption, ethnicity, unemployment, and residential relocation has been undertaken in relation to questions
of adolescent identity. Most of these general issues in some way involve
being different from many of one's peers. And although no two individuals

who experience any one of the previous issues are likely to cope in the same way, this chapter will attempt to examine ways in which adolescents come to integrate (or not) a particular feature of "differentness" into their sense of ego identity. There are, of course, many additional issues faced by some adolescents that have an enormous impact on their identity development; however, space prohibits a full discussion of all such circumstances.

Furthermore, some adolescents will experience multiple levels of differentness or a combination of the selected identity issues previously cited. As Grotevant (1997b) has noted, the identity-formation process becomes increasingly complex as layers of differentness or special issues are added. Although the various sections of this chapter will address selected individual identity issues affecting some adolescents, it must be remembered that some adolescents face multiple levels of differentness.

Research on how adolescents come to integrate multiple levels of differentness into a sense of ego identity has been even more limited. For example, in Norway and Sweden, the majority of adolescents who have been adopted as infants and young children by Norwegian and Swedish parents come from outside of Europe, and in the United States, some parents will adopt children differing in ethnic origin. The adolescent identity-formation process for such individuals becomes even more complex, as both ethnic origin and adopted status must be integrated into a sense of one's identity. How these adolescents undergo the identity-formation process, adjusting to and integrating such varied levels of differentness, remains an open question in need of research.

Some of the areas previously mentioned are aspects of identity about which one has little choice. Previous chapters have focused on identity and decision making with regard to issues of vocation, ideological and relationship values, sex role values and forms of sexual expression—areas that allow considerable scope for choice in many Western, technologically advanced nations. As Grotevant (1993) points out, however, issues such as being adopted, being a member of an ethnic minority group, (arguably) being an immigrant, and/or being unemployed have an enormous impact on one's sense of identity yet may remain beyond one's power of choice. The variables of exploration and commitment have been useful in identifying different styles or approaches taken by adolescents to dealing with questions of psychosocial identity discussed in previous chapters, but are these variables useful in considering how nonchosen aspects of identity become integrated into one's personality? Grotevant (1993) argues that although one does not choose one's adoptive status, one does have considerable choice in how one comes to terms with being adopted. A similar argument could also be made for other nonchosen elements of one's identity—one does have considerable choice in how one comes to terms with nonchosen circumstances affecting identity. This chapter will turn now to look at selected issues impacting the identity-formation process for special groups of adolescents.

Identity and Adoption

My first year of high school was a particularly bad time. I am adopted and I spent a lot of time thinking and feeling confused about who I was and that I didn't belong to my family. In my junior year, I spent more time out of class than in class and my grades reflected this. At one point that year, I left home for a month and went to stay at a friend's place. I remember around this time my attitude was really negative, and I seemed not to care about anything at all. All of this came as a bit of a shock to my parents, and they contacted the school counselor. All of this just confirmed to me that I was "mixed up" and not particularly nice to be around.

—17-year-old male high school senior

A number of factors may impact on the identity-formation process for adolescent adoptees. One involves the type of adoption procedure itself that is used in becoming a member of an adoptive family and the degree of openness children receive about their birth parents. Within the United States, there has been a good deal of controversy surrounding various adoption procedures and the effects such procedures may have on the adopted child. Wrobel, Ayers-Lopez, Grotevant, McRoy, and Friedrick (1996) have described the shifting continuum of adoption practices within the United States. This continuum has moved from complete confidentiality, in which any information about the identities of biological and adoptive parents was withheld from each other ("closed" adoption procedures), to a system allowing for varying degrees of indirect and direct contact between all parties involved (varying degrees of "openness"). A common middle-ground ("semiopen" procedure) has involved mediation by a third party, who communicates nonidentifying information between the birthmother and adoptive parents.

The clinical literature suggests that the most positive outcomes for adopted children and adolescents result when their adoptive parents provided them with information about their birth parents (e.g., Melina & Rosnia, 1993). Such procedures at least provide young adoptees with a sense of continuity in their life histories—a feature Erikson (1968) stressed as vital to the adolescent identity-formation process. Such procedures may also give the child a greater understanding of the reasons for his or her adoption, which may help alleviate potential feelings of rejection.

Among adolescents who were adopted as children, both clinical and personal accounts point to a developmental sequence in how an individual comes to construct a sense of adoptive identity. Grotevant (1997a) has proposed that an initial state of unawareness or denial may be followed by disequilibrating experiences that can precipitate a crisis or exploration phase. Following this period of questioning, the realities of one's adoptive situation can be more fully integrated into one's sense of identity. This cycle may repeat itself several times over the life span. Similarly, Brodinsky (1987) has proposed an adaptation of Marcia's identity-formation model to suggest that adoptees may assume quite differential responses to identity questions. Some may struggle with, but ultimately resolve, issues of their adoptive identity (i.e., proceed through a moratorium to become identity achieved), whereas others may never seriously consider issues related to their adoptive position (i.e., remain identity diffuse). Or, one may accept their adoptive status but never seriously question one's origins (i.e., remain foreclosed). Both proposals have yet to be examined empirically, however. It may be that adolescents who lack information about their personal birth histories find the adolescent identity-formation process far lengthier and more complex than those nonadopted or adopted youths who have such knowledge of their personal birth histories.

It is when adopted children reach adolescence that most will develop more sophisticated cognitive capacities to think about the meaning of their adoption. Some research has directly investigated the relationship between adoption and identity among adolescents. Benson, Sharma, and Roehlkepartain (1994) found over one-quarter of adolescents who were adopted as infants said that adoption was a big part of how they thought about themselves. In addition, nearly half of adopted adolescents taking part in the survey reported thinking about their adoption at least two or three times per month or as frequently as daily. More recently, Kohler, Grotevant, and McRoy (2002) worked with a national sample of adolescent adoptees to address the question, "Which adopted adolescents are most preoccupied with their adoptive status?" Researchers found that those adolescents who experienced greater alienation from their adoptive fathers experienced high levels of preoccupation with their adoptive status. Those adolescents who were extremely preoccupied with their adoptive status reported significantly higher levels of alienation and lower levels of trust for both mother and father than adolescents with extremely low levels of preoccupation about their adoptive status. Thus, adoption status seems to play an important role in how a number of adopted teenagers view themselves as they work toward developing a sense of personal identity.

In terms of outcomes for identity development and mental health, a number of investigations have taken place. Hoopes (1990) summarized earlier adoption research to suggest that adoptive status, alone, is not associated with positive or negative identity resolutions among adolescents. Rather, many additional factors such as the ease and style of communication within the adoptive family and other personality and contextual variables seem to play key roles in the identity-formation process of adolescent adoptees. More recent research has supported this conclusion, even though a far greater variety of family configurations exist for adolescent adoptees today, including gay and lesbian households, stepfamilies, and extended families. Grotevant, Wrobel, van Dulmen, and McRoy (2001) examined the issue of social competence and engagement among adopted adolescents having differing levels of compatibility with their parents. Results showed that higher degrees of compatibility (as reported by parents) that were maintained over time from the primary school years through adolescence were associated with higher social competence and attachment, along with lower levels of problem behavior among the adopted adolescents. The results were similar for both male and female adolescents. Family functioning appears to be an extremely important variable in the identity-formation process of adopted adolescents.

A further issue for identity development among adolescent adoptees is whether the adoption is visible or invisible. Visible adoptions are those adoptions across ethnic groups, whereas invisible adoptions are those in which the ethnic origin of the child matches that of at least one of the adoptive parents. Although issues of biological origin most commonly mark the identity concerns of those young people in invisible adoptive situations, a concern with ethnic origin is the most common identity issue of those in visible adoptive situations (Irhammar, 1997). A survey of visible adoptees in Sweden found about one-third of young people take an active interest in their ethnic origins (Irhammar, 1997). Families of these youths were often uninterested in their child's ethnic origin, and the adoptee often felt a lower sense of self-esteem regarding his or her physical appearance. Conversely, an interest by the adoptive parents in their child's ethnic origin seemed to diminish the adoptee's interests in questions regarding his or her ethnicity.

International adoptions have become more commonplace in many countries over the past decades. In situations of visible difference between international adoptees and their new families, attitudes toward the child's ethnic group by the adoptive parents as well as by society more generally have been viewed as critical in the young person's ethnic identity development (Dalen & Sætersdal, 1992). In the United States, some research has found problematic mental health and low self-esteem to be common among children in visible adoptive situations (e.g., Gaber, 1994). However, children in visible adoptive situations studied in Sweden and Norway who have assumed a Swedish or Norwegian self-identity have been shown to have a better mental health status than counterparts who have not assumed a Swedish or Norwegian self-identity (Cederblad, Hook, Irhammar, & Mercke, 1999; Dalen & Sætersdal, 1992). It may be that international adoptions are more commonplace in many countries of Europe compared with the United States, and that social acceptance in the new context may be strongly linked with adoptee adjustment during adolescence.

Assumption of a new national identity by international adoptees appears linked with optimal adjustment during adolescence. However, this process does not imply that internationally adopted young people have denied their ethnic origins. Cederblad and colleagues' (1999) research in Sweden found that those international adoptees who were engaged in questions of identity during adolescence and who felt mostly non-Swedish had more behavior problems; however 90 percent of the sample of adoptees felt mostly Swedish, and 70 percent of the sample felt no connection to their country of origin.

In the Netherlands, similar longitudinal research has been undertaken with internationally adopted children. Higher levels of behavior problems did appear among adopted versus nonadopted children and youths; again, however, the majority of international adoptees functioned quite well during adolescence. Indeed, internationally adopted adolescents in Italy actually perceived better communication with both parents than did biological adolescents; also, it was the adolescents from separated families who had more difficulties in relationships with parents than adopted or biological children of intact families (Lanz, Iafrate, Rosnati, & Scabini, 1999). Both the Swedish and Dutch studies previously noted that preadoption conditions experienced by the adoptees were strongly linked to behavior problems during adolescence. Extreme deprivation during early childhood for many of the international adoptees was as or more important than status as an international adoptee for mental health functioning during adolescence.

Finally, comment must be made on the prevalence of the searching for biological origins phenomenon among some adolescent adoptees. Much controversy has surrounded the extent to which curiosity about one's genealogy characterizes the identity-formation process for all adolescent adoptees. Some have proposed that curiosity about one's genealogy is more associated with particular personality traits an adolescent may hold, whereas others have argued that a search for information about one's past may be primarily associated with poor experiences in one's family of adoption. Recent longitudinal research is helping to clarify this matter.

From the Minnesota-Texas Adoption Research Project, Wrobal, Grotevant, and McRoy (2004) focused on the question of which adolescent adoptees search for their biological parents and which adolescents do not as they begin to deal with issues of identity. Adopted adolescents most likely to search for biological parents were those who experienced some openness in their adoption, were least satisfied with that adoptive openness, and were most preoccupied with their adoptive status. Desire on the part of adolescent adoptees to search for biological parents was not related to family functioning or adolescent problem behavior. The issue of searching versus non-searching is likely to change dramatically in coming generations, for many adoptions in the United States now enable direct contact between members of the adoptive and birth families from the outset (Grotevant, personal communication, 1998).

Section Summary and Implications

Providing adopted children with information about their birth parents is not problematic for identity development, according to research by Wrobel and colleagues.

Adoptive status, alone, is not associated with positive or negative identity resolutions among adolescents. Many additional factors such as ease and style of family communication within the adoptive family and other personality variables play key roles in the identity-formation process of adolescent adoptees.

Adolescent adoptees who are preoccupied with searching for their biological parents tend to be those who are preoccupied with their adoptive status, experienced some openness about the adoption process but were least satisfied with it. Family functioning and problem behaviors have not differed between searchers and nonsearchers.

Identity and Unemployment

Erikson (1968) has noted that it is the inability to find a meaningful vocation that most disturbs young people, and research reviewed in Chapter 4 indicates this to be still the case. Increasing levels of unemployment have characterized life in most Organisation of Economic Co-operation and Development (OECD) countries since 1990, and often, the rate of youth unemployment in these countries is some two to three times the rate of unemployment found within adult populations (Winefield, 1997). From U.S. Census data (U.S. Bureau of the Census, 2003), some 12.7 percent of youth in the 16- to 19-year-old age range in 2002 were unemployed; however, rates were far higher among some ethnic minority groups. In this same age range and year, some 29 percent of African American and 17.7 percent of Hispanic youths were unable to find work in the United States. Between ages 16 and 24 years, about 2.6 million young Americans were out of work in 2002. Within Europe, a wide range of youth unemployment rates is present among OECD nations. Such unemployment rates for 15- to 24-year-olds have typically ranged from 6.6 percent in the Netherlands to 20–30 percent in France, Finland, Spain, and Italy, to more than 40 percent in Poland (OECD, 2004). In both Europe and the United States, rates of unemployment among youth in the 18- to 24-year-old age group are far higher than all other adult rates. And furthermore, all of these figures may underestimate the actual rate of unemployment among youths, for many stop looking for work after a period of time and are not registered as unemployed.

Many writers have pointed to the detrimental effects that unemployment or underemployment have on youth in particular. The identity-formation process is critically dependent upon matching one's own skills, talents, and interests with those required by the vocational context. Recognizing and being recognized as one "who counts" is an interactive process, dependent upon motivated youths and receptive contexts. Youth unemployment has been commonly linked with low self-esteem and negative feelings of psychological well-being and self-worth (Feather, 1990; Winefield, 1997)—a difficult base from which to enter the adult world.

Prause and Dooley (1997) point out that the job market does not just provide conditions of unemployment or employment. Rather, it also presents various intermediary positions of involuntary part-time employment and underemployment (defined as the underutilization of one's level of skills and/or educational background or inadequate monetary compensation for them). With many OECD countries undergoing economic restructuring, more workers are finding themselves underemployed as well as unemployed; the risk of underemployment for school leavers in the United States was rising faster than for adult workers (Prause & Dooley, 1997). Prause and Dooley noted that whereas unemployment is likely to be a transient state, underemployment is often of longer duration. Unemployment and underemployment are often both situations beyond an individual's control that nevertheless have important implications for the identity-formation process.

Youth unemployment is, to a large extent, associated with macrolevel factors within larger social systems as well as individual factors. Reasons for high levels of youth unemployment differ from one country to another, and unemployed youths themselves vary enormously in terms of their work ethics, social supports, and various personality factors (Gumbel, 2005; Meeus, Decovic, & Iedema, 1997). Among common causes of youth unemployment may be the fact that many unemployed youths will be high school dropouts, and many employers require minimal levels of training and skill among their workers. Among the total number of unemployed youths in the United States in 2001, some 20 percent were high school *dropouts;* however, rates for unemployment among African American youths who were high school dropouts were far higher at 41 percent. Certainly rates of unemployment among high school *graduates* dropped to about 12 percent in the United States in 2001 (U.S. Bureau of the Census, 2003). Additionally, when minimum wages go up relative to the lower productivity levels of younger workers, many employers prefer to hire older workers with more general life experience. Also for steady jobs, employers may prefer to hire older workers where turnover rates are considered to be lower. Within a number of European countries, social entitlements following World War II provided generous safety nets for those who do not work; while current economic circumstances have changed, many of the post–World War II safety provisions have not. Thus, motivation may not be high among some youthful segments of the population to seek employment. Furthermore, practices such as high minimum wages in many countries make it unattractive for businesses to hire younger workers (Gumbel, 2005).

Following a review of a number of studies of youth unemployment, Fryer (1997) drew the general conclusion that mental health indices of those adolescents who become employed after leaving school diverge from those who become unemployed. Negative self-esteem and psychological distress have commonly been associated with unemployment after leaving school (e.g., Feather & O'Brien, 1986; Patton & Noller, 1990). Some debate, however, has surrounded the question of causation regarding youth unemployment; researchers have questioned whether poor mental health is the result of unemployment due to social circumstances or, rather, whether poor mental health itself leads to youth unemployment. This debate has been referred to as the social causation versus individual drift discussion. Fryer points out that economic conditions in the labor market must be considered when trying to integrate findings from studies of adolescents who become unemployed. In times of relatively low unemployment, individual factors are more likely to be associated with unemployment, whereas in times of high unemployment, the proportion of those whose mental health has deteriorated because they have become unemployed is likely to increase. However, Fryer cautions against a simplistic attempt to dichotomize forces responsible for unemployment and notes social causation and individual drift are usually inextricably intertwined.

Whatever the reasons for unemployment, adolescents seeking work who are unable to find suitable jobs face a number of latent consequences that are likely to impact on identity development. These youths will often miss a clearly defined sense of purpose and structure in their daily lives; they will also miss participation in goals and purposes beyond themselves, and recognition by a significant reference group for personal status and accomplishments. Winefield, Tiggerman, Winefield, and Goldney (1993) pointed out that unemployment is a different experience for youths compared with adults. In a longitudinal study of youth unemployment, Winefield and colleagues found that unemployment may become a critical factor in determining a late adolescent's outlook on life; at this age, unemployment has an impact on so many aspects of one's social relationships. A youth's family support system, parental employment status, and geographical setting mediated such negative effects on relationships, however. One particular difficulty that long-term unemployed adolescents may face is the possible adoption of the identity of an "unemployed person." Such an identity resolution may seem all too tempting when one is struggling to find a sense of self within a particular social context that provides limited opportunities for vocational expression.

A number of factors may affect the way in which adolescents cope with unemployment. Understanding the reasons for their unemployment plays an important role in youth's identity development. Levine (1982) found that if youths see their unemployment as a result of external forces beyond their control, have confidence in themselves, and experience some academic or social success, identity will not be as threatened as it is for youths who attribute their unemployment to their own lack of ability. More recent research with unemployed late adolescents has found that youths' relational and work identities are affected differently by unemployment (Meeus et al., 1997). Their sense of relational identity did not seem related to employment status, but unemployment was strongly associated with their sense of vocational identity in this research. Furthermore, relational identity seemed to act as a buffer against psychological distress for those unemployed youths under study.

Many different avenues of approach have been taken to deal with youth unemployment in different countries. One common intervention effort in the United States, however, has been to target youths at risk for dropping out of school, because rates of unemployment for this group have been particularly high. Efforts to include vocational apprenticeship programs in the curriculum of many high schools to show youths the links between school and work have generally proven popular. Efforts have also been made with groups of potential school leavers to provide opportunities for community service, in principle helping better to integrate youths into the community and giving them opportunities to interact with adult role models. Studies on the impact of such community service programs have found increased self-esteem and feelings of efficacy, decreased problem behaviors, and improved mental health more generally (e.g., Hansen, Larson, & Dworkin, 2003; Scales, Blyth, Berkas, & Kielsmeier, 2000). A recent report on practices developing in some European countries, such as Denmark, requires unemployed youths to participate in job-training placement schemes in order to receive unemployment benefits; indeed, Germany now slashes unemployment benefits to youths who do not work or participate in such schemes (Gumbel, 2005).

Prause and Dooley (1997) have pointed out that youth employed in jobs in which they were dissatisfied and/or underemployed were as at risk in terms of various mental health factors as their unemployed counterparts. In a study involving three random samples of school leavers born in the United States between 1957 and 1964, these authors examined several groups of adolescents. These groups included the adequately employed, the unemployed, the involuntary part-time employed, the intermittently employed, and the inadequately employed (those in a poverty income group of recent school leavers). Several categories of underemployment seemed to retard development of self-esteem. When compared to the adequately employed, the unemployed *and* all underemployment groups showed lower levels of self-esteem, even when adjusted for earlier self-esteem measures taken at school and other variables such as aptitude, age, ethnicity, and parental years of education. Findings of this longitudinal study suggest that underemployment as well as unemployment are harmful to youthful workers' senses of self-esteem. The authors conclude that "thrusting young people into an unwelcoming economy may carry a social cost that we do not fully appreciate either in its magnitude or its duration" (Prause & Dooley, 1997, p. 258).

Section Summary and Implications

Mental health indices show lower self-esteem and higher psychological distress for those who become unemployed after leaving school compared with those finding work. Research suggests interventions that help youth attribute their unemployment to social rather than personal factors reduce the negative impact of unemployment.

Youths experiencing job dissatisfaction and/or underemployment are as at risk in terms of mental health factors as unemployed adolescents. Work training programs must stress preparing for employment that suits individual identity needs and interests rather than merely learning a random variety of useful skills.

Identity and Ethnicity

> *When my family first migrated here, our parents separated us from the majority culture largely because they knew so little about it. Physical appearance for us was always a barrier, too. Our mother strictly forbade us girls ever to date a "European boy," and with us living at home, she was easily able to do this. But last year I left home for university, and that was a year full of experimentation and exploration. I was curious to discover what I was doing here, and who I really was. I wanted my own set of morals and beliefs. Questions like "Where am I going?" and "Who will I become?" are still unanswered, but I feel certain that I will one day find some answers. I think feeling comfortable with my ethnic identity is a prerequisite to discovering my personal identity.*

—18-year-old female university student

Thinking about one's ethnic origin is not often a key identity quest among Caucasian North American adolescents; values in the home are generally similar to mainstream values for these adolescents, so concerns with one's ethnic identity often do not arise (Rotheram-Borus, 1993). However, for many adolescents of ethnic minority groups, ethnic identity concerns become central to the identity-formation process, as illustrated in the previous quotation. Phinney and Alipuria (1990), in fact, examined the ethnic identity search and commitment process for college students within three ethnic minority groups and one Caucasian comparison group. The researchers found that ethnic identity exploration was significantly higher among the three ethnic minority groups (Asian American, African American, and Mexican American) than the comparison Caucasian majority group. Furthermore, ethnicity was rated as significantly more important to overall identity by all minority groups compared with Caucasian college students. A number of more recent works also support this finding; ethnicity and, in turn, ethnic identity have appeared to be far more salient issues for ethnic minority adolescents than for those members of the ethnic majority (e.g., Branch, Tayal, & Triplett, 2000).

How does a sense of ethnic identity emerge? Erikson (1964) has noted that "true identity depends on the support that the young receive from the collective sense of identity characterizing the social groups significant to [them]: [their] class, [their] nation, [their] culture" (p. 93). Being a member of a particular ethnic group holds important identity implications. Young children are certainly aware of differences in ethnicity and culture. But it is during adolescence, with capacities for reflecting on the past and the future, that one may develop a greater interest in one's own ethnic background. And it is during adolescence that one may have wider experiences within multicultural groups and experience ethnic discrimination. (More than three-fourths of subjects in Chavira and Phinney's [1991] study of Hispanic adolescents reported experiencing discrimination, and nearly 90 percent believed society held negative stereotypes of Hispanics.) Experiences of discrimination complicate efforts by adolescents to develop a strong sense of cultural pride and belonging. Spencer and Dornbusch (1990) have noted how adolescent awareness of negative appraisals of their cultural group can negatively influence the adolescent's life choices and plans for the future.

Growing up as a member of an ethnic minority group within a larger, mainstream culture additionally complicates the identity-formation process by providing alternative role models for identification to adolescents (Phinney & Rosenthal, 1992). There may be conflicting values between the minority group and mainstream cultures, which require the minority group adolescent to choose in the identity-formation process. Such conflict of values has been particularly noted for Native American adolescents, faced with their minority culture's emphasis on tribal spirituality, freedom to experiment and operate semi-independently, and participation in ceremonies that may violate the school-attendance policies of the dominant culture (LaFromboise & Low, 1989). The statement from one of my New Zealand sophomore university students that follows describes the process she experienced in trying to find a sense of her own ethnic identity within the mainstream culture.

> *As a child, I was pretty insulated within the Chinese culture. But as I grew older, many of my Chinese peers went through an assimilation stage. They dressed and spoke as they perceived the majority to do—all because they wanted to be accepted. Physical appearance was a barrier; they felt like outcasts simply because they were not comfortable with themselves being Chinese. They tried to assimilate into the European culture, norms, and standards, but unsuccessfully, for their parents, like my own, were constant reminders of their ethnicity.*
>
> —19-year-old female university student

Phinney (1996) has defined ethnic identity as an enduring and basic sense of oneself that includes a sense of membership in an ethnic group, coupled with the attitudes and feelings of individuals in that ethnic group. For adolescents in any ethnic minority group, identity development is a more complicated task, involving decisions about the roles that two or more sources of identification will play in their own identity-formation process.

How does a sense of one's ethnic identity emerge? Several writers have posited stages in the ethnic identity-formation process for adolescents within various ethnic minority groups. In Cross's (1987) model, there is an initial *pre-encounter* stage in which individuals identify with the dominant culture. Although individuals here are aware of differences between themselves and the dominant culture, such differences are not considered to be important. In the next, *encounter* stage, adolescents come to experience discrimination, which leads to greater awareness of the cultural values present within their own ethnic group. At this time, they are likely to reject values of the dominant culture and strongly uphold those of their own ethnic group. Cross calls the next stage, *immersion,* in which young people strongly identify with values of their own ethnic group and may become politically active or even militant in rejecting the dominant society. However, through this stage, individuals may come to feel discontent with the rigidity of the initial immersion process and no longer find it necessary to reject everything from the dominant culture. In the final *internalization* stage, new recognitions emerge as people come to be appreciated more as individuals rather than as members of a particular ethnic group. Here, individuals experience a sense of fulfillment in integrating their personal and cultural identities. Although one still retains a sense of one's ethnic origins, a general attitude of tolerance and consideration of all people is present.

Phinney (1989, 1996) also suggests a stage model of ethnic identity development, based on Marcia's ego identity status framework. Although Marcia did not include the issue of ethnicity as a domain of study in his Identity Status Interview, Phinney has examined the variables of exploration and commitment with regard to the ethnic identity-formation process. In studies with adolescents from various ethnic backgrounds, Phinney has proposed a three-stage developmental process: unexamined ethnic identity, ethnic identity search, and achieved ethnic identity. These stages correspond to Marcia's diffuse/foreclosed, moratorium, and achieved identity statuses, respectively. These stages of ethnic identity development have correlated positively with measures of ego identity-status development. The stages are also found among adolescents of many cultural minority groups. Phinney (2003) considers that many contemporary adolescents of ethnic minority groups find resolution to questions of their ethnicity ultimately by adopting a *bicultural* identity.

How do adolescents of mixed minority and majority group parentage experience the identity-formation process? Research by Grove (1991) suggests the process may not be as difficult as one might imagine. In a study including small samples of Asian, Asian/Caucasian, and Caucasian college students, the Asian/Caucasian group rated race as significantly less important to their sense of identity than did the Asian group. Results from Marcia's Identity Status Interview did not indicate significant differences in identity status distributions across the three ethnic groups. From qualitative accounts, Grove suggests that being partially Caucasian allowed those in the Asian/Caucasian group to question their Asian identity from a "safe place." In fact, being of mixed racial origins was often regarded positively by these students. Because they were not easily stereotyped by physical appearance, Asian/Caucasian students often reported feeling freer to choose their own ethnic identity commitments. Although this preliminary work with adolescents of mixed parentage suggests such teens may be less at risk than one might expect, research with larger samples of adolescents from different mixed ethnic origins is needed.

Self-esteem is one variable that has been studied extensively in relation to ethnic identity development. Phinney and Chavira (1992), for example, examined the relationship of ethnic identity to self-esteem. They found that self-esteem, especially among minority group students, was related to the degree of exploration and commitment around issues regarding their ethnicity. Those who had undertaken more extensive levels of exploration, followed by commitment with regard to their sense of ethnic identity had higher levels of self-esteem. Similar findings have emerged across a diversity of adolescent ethnic groups. Among Hispanic, African American, and Caucasian early adolescents girls, for example, ethnic identity was a significant predictor of global self-esteem (Carlson, Uppal, & Prosser, 2000). Smith, Walker, Fields, Brookins, and Seay (1999) examined relationships between self-esteem and ethnic identity among early adolescents in a diversity of ethnic groups. The investigators found that self-esteem and ethnic identity were distinct constructs that contributed to young adolescents' perceptions of their abilities to achieve in school, find meaningful work, and relate well to others in this process. And within a large sample of Mexican-origin adolescents attending three schools of varied ethnic compositions, Umaña-Taylor (2004) also found significant positive relationships between self-esteem and ethnic identity emerging in all three contexts. Furthermore, when generation and maternal education level were controlled, those attending a predominately non-Latino school reported significantly higher levels of ethnic identity than those attending either predominately Latino or balanced Latino/non-Latino school contexts. All of these studies point to the centrality that ethnic identity holds in the global identity development of ethnic minority youths.

Spencer and Markstrom-Adams (1990) have provided suggestions for some specific interventions that may assist in promoting a sense of identity achievement, ethnic group pride, and observable competence among ethnic minority group youth. Among their suggestions is finding methods to keep minority youth in school and academically oriented, because lack of education ensures future socioeconomic disadvantages for these teens. Also important are affirming constructive social networks and support systems for minority families and promoting the teaching of native languages in schools in an atmosphere of biculturalism. Additional suggestions are offering special training for teachers of ethnic minority students and offering a media-focused cultural emphasis that affirms ethnic group identity and group pride for all youths.

Section Summary and Implications

Growing up as an ethnic minority group member within a larger culture complicates the identity-formation process for many adolescents by the availability of varied role models holding possibly conflicting cultural values.

Ethnic identity emerges as adolescents experience a sense of difference. As a result, youths often immerse themselves in their own ethnic group values and reject the mainstream culture. Optimally, however, adolescents learn to integrate their own personal and cultural identities, achieving a sense of tolerance for and consideration of all people.

Steps to enhance ethnic identity might include finding methods to keep ethnic minority group adolescents involved with school and having schools that, in turn, promote an atmosphere of biculturalism.

Identity and Residential Relocation

When I was sixteen, I moved to [names city]. It was a huge change for me. I had to leave my friends, my school, my home, and my community behind. All of a sudden I found myself lost, and although I was with my family, I felt very lonely—sort of like a pariah. I was very unsure of myself and basically didn't know who I was and how I should be or act. After a few years at school, then teacher's college, then being a full-time worker I started to get to know myself through courses, reading books, and meeting people. I started to set goals for myself, relating to my future career and actually began to enjoy being the person who I was.

—22-year-old female, returning to university study

Geographic migration, whether within a county or across continents, raises important identity issues during the years of adolescence. Adolescents may undergo residential relocation for a variety of reasons, ranging from having upwardly mobile parents who wish to purchase a larger home to being forced to emigrate from homelands undergoing political turmoil or other forms of upheaval. Moving may involve a change of residence within the same city to a move between cities to a complete change of culture and traditions across national boundaries. Across all of these situations, however, the importance of "an average, expectable environment" has been stressed by Erikson (1968) as central to the identity-formation process of adolescence. Through such experiences, one ideally acquires a sense of inner sameness and continuity with one's past, which must be integrated into the present and the sense of identity that is forming. The reasons for residential relocation, magnitude of the contextual change, frequency of residential changes, age at the time of transition, and family supports available through the process are all extremely important variables to consider in understanding the impact that residential relocation may have on adolescents. However, this section will explore some of the many identity-related issues that a change of residence—in some of its many forms—may bring.

Several investigations have explored the identity-related impact of residential relocation on adolescents within the United States. Simmons, Burgeson, Carlton-Ford, and Blyth (1987) asked the question of whether or not an environmental change is more difficult if it coincides with other changes (such as pubertal development, change of school systems, early dating behavior, family disruption) in the transition to early adolescence. Results indicated that there were negative consequences for those early adolescents who made multiple changes at once. A family's residential mobility experienced at the very time an adolescent was entering puberty and changing the type of school system was associated with lowered self-esteem for girls, whereas both boys and girls experienced lowered grade point averages and more restricted extracurricular participation as multiple transitions increased. The authors proposed the need for some "arena of comfort" in at least some life spheres for such early adolescents.

These findings have been supported by more recent investigations into identity issues associated with residential relocation. For example, the type of family structure and family cohesion experienced by children and young adolescents experiencing residential relocation is an important mediator for identity-related outcomes of the experience. Tucker, Marx, and Long (1998) found that children and young adolescents who had experienced an average or above average number of residential changes in their lives appeared to suffer no psychological ill-effects if they resided in families in which both biological parents were present; however, for children and early adolescents residing in single parent or reconstituted family structures, change of residence was associated with both behavioral and academic difficulties in school. Similarly, Crowder and Teachman (2004) found family residential mobility and neighborhood context to be important mediators through which one's family structure is associated with at risk behaviors among adolescents. Among adolescent women with premarital pregnancies, those living in solo, single-parent families at some time during adolescence had experienced almost twice as many residential relocations as those living in other family structures. (They also were exposed to neighborhoods with far higher levels of social and economic disadvantage than pregnant adolescents raised in other types of family structures.) Among school dropouts, the number of residential moves and level of neighborhood disadvantage increased sharply with increasing exposure to a solo, single-parent family structure during adolescence. Thus, family structure appears as a crucial mediator in the impact of residential relocation on adolescent social and academic behaviors. And work by Scanlon and Devine (2001) similarly found adverse associations between residential mobility and academic functioning and social well-being to be particularly high for poor children and adolescents living in single-parent families.

How has residential mobility been associated with feelings of well-being more generally during adolescence? Brown and Orthner (1990) researched the impact of recency of residential mobility and moving rate on early adolescents' feelings of well-being. Neither of these two mobility variables were associated with feelings of well-being among boys, but life satisfaction was negatively affected by the two mobility variables among girls. In addition, levels of depression were higher among those girls who had moved more frequently. The authors suggested that results may reflect the greater length of time taken by girls to develop a more intrinsic basis for their relationships with friends. Similarly, high rates of depression have been found among high-mobility adult women, but not high-mobility men, after controlling for social class, marital status, and employment (Magdol, 2003). In sum, residential relocation may be particularly disturbing to early adolescents, who are already adjusting to changes in physique, school setting, and friendship networks. Girls may be somewhat more vulnerable than boys in adjusting to residential relocation.

Among early adolescents, several researchers have also addressed the social implications for building a sense of identity that residential relocation involves. Vernberg (1990) found mobile adolescents of junior high age generally had fewer contacts with friends and reported less intimacy with a best friend. Furthermore, boys who had moved were more likely to experience rejection by friends than nonmobile counterparts; this pattern was not in evidence for girls, however. Vernberg, Ewell, Beery, and Abwender (1994) also examined the sophistication of various interpersonal relationship skills of mobile early adolescents and their abilities to develop new friendships. Results suggested that the ability to coordinate social perspectives exerts a strong influence on the ability to make new friends following a move.

Another group of adolescents experiencing residential relocation are those who cross national and cultural boundaries and face the many demands that adjusting to a new culture, new patterns of communication and expectations, and possibly a new language brings. Bledin (2003) likens the experience of emigration to one of a separation-individuation process; emigration involves leaving behind both the external and internalized "motherland" (and often one's own physical parents in the homeland). For adolescent emigrants, the adolescent separation-individuation process (see Chapter 4) may be particularly complex when it is compounded with this additional "home-leaving" process. The new emigrant needs to resolve not only his or her adolescent separation-individuation issues, but also undergo the process of separation from the mother(land) in order to attain autonomous functioning in the new context. Bledin also suggests that the process for an emigrant of "bridging and arriving" in the new context can be facilitated by finding reference "groups of belonging" that provide a sense of place in the new environment.

However, it is finding such a reference "group of belonging" that can be a difficult task for immigrant adolescents in their new cultural settings. Qualitative work examining cross-cultural adaptation styles of immigrant youths from former USSR in Israel found themes of powerlessness punctuating the interviews of both male and female immigrant adolescents. From this study, males found it particularly difficult to function in a subordinate position with respect to peers in the Israeli context. They coped by retreating to their own ethnic groups and keeping interactions with host-culture peers to a minimum. Females were, by contrast, able to acknowledge and discuss their feelings of powerlessness more readily. This feat enabled them to cross cultural borders with Israeli peers more freely.

Attaining a sense of belonging to a peer group, which often holds social and cultural values contrasting markedly to those of an adolescent's immigrant parents, is a complex task for the immigrant adolescent. However, if attained, such social support and feelings of belonging do appear to act as a buffer against the many difficulties faced by immigrant adolescents. Assimilated Mexican American adolescents, for example, evidenced significantly fewer symptoms of depression than their nonassimilated peers (Cuéllar & Roberts, 1997).

Does emigration threaten one's sense of identity continuity? Ward and Styles (2003) examined the impact of multiple losses through the emigration process on identities of emerging adults as well as older women. These researchers were interested to learn if the loss of home, community, and social and cultural networks could threaten one's sense of identity and invoke a grief reaction. They were also interested to learn of strategies that might be used to buffer the impact of migration on one's sense of self. They found, in general, that reinvention of the self following emigration occurred over differing lengths of time for different people. The development of the self does not occur in isolation, and those emigrant women who worked through the grieving process to feel a sense of belonging in the new country were able to "reinvent" themselves using social strategies. However, those less able to adapt to new conditions used solitary strategies in trying to adjust. While the majority of participants experienced growth within themselves through the experience of emigration, not all reported a sense of belonging in the new context. This study highlights the importance of social context to identity formation and affirmation during adolescence that Erikson described many years earlier.

Vercrysse and Chandler (1992) were interested in coping strategies of American adolescents during their first year of living in a European country. Both approach and avoidance coping strategies were commonly used by these adolescents. (Adolescents generally use more approach than avoidance strategies.) The authors point out that these adolescents were unable to avoid geographical relocation as many adults can and therefore perceived relocation as an uncontrollable event. In so doing, they were more likely to avoid than approach that which they cannot control—hence the relatively common use of avoiding difficult situations. Teens with a higher self-concept and better behavioral adjustment tended to use approach strategies when dealing with stressors in the new situation, while those with lower self-concepts and behavioral adjustment avoided stressors in the new situations.

In many European countries, large numbers of immigrants are seeking refuge from political unrest or upheaval in homelands and/or a better future in the new locale; a similar phenomenon has also occurred within the United States. Within the United States, Goodenow and Espin (1993) point out that developing a firm sense of identity among immigrant adolescents seems to involve steering a course somewhere between refusing to adapt to American life at all and acculturating too quickly. In their case studies of Latin American immigrant adolescent women, initial language difficulties posed an important impediment to adapting to the new context at first, and the resulting isolation from peers was particularly distressing to them. Negotiating different expectations in friendships and sex roles, in turn, brought new tensions in mother-daughter ties.

Within Europe, several empirical studies have addressed immigrant adolescent identity development in contexts undergoing rapid social change. Silbereisen and Schmitt-Rodermund (1995) examined the processes and outcomes of acculturation among ethnic German immigrant adolescents. Ancestors of these ethnic German immigrants had immigrated to countries within eastern and southeastern Europe some centuries earlier. With the change in political liberalization of Germany in the late 1980s, many such ethnic Germans returned to Germany, coming "home" as strangers. Silbereisen and Schmitt-Rodermund were especially interested in the timing of transitions to autonomy for ethnic German immigrant adolescents and the processes leading to their adaptation in a new land. They studied groups of settled immigrants, who had lived in Germany about one year longer than newcomers. Transition to assuming various aspects of autonomy by the newcomer adolescents was about three years later than the control group German counterparts; transition timetables for settled immigrants, however, were about one year closer to those of local German youths. Acculturation by immigrant German parents did not take place quickly, although settled immigrant parents allowed their adolescents more leeway from parental supervision than did newcomer parents. Peer involvement was an important factor in the acculturation timetables for transition to more autonomous functioning by both groups of immigrant adolescents.

Section Summary and Implications

Residential relocation may be particularly problematic for early adolescents, who are already adjusting to changes in physique, school structure, and friendship networks. However, being a member of an intact family acts as a buffer for many risk factors associated with residential relocation.

Receiving social support from significant others as well as having a reference "group of belonging" is associated with reduction in the negative impact on self-concept and identity that a move may bring.

Adolescent immigrants may best develop a firm sense of their own identity by steering a course between refusing to adapt to the new context at all and acculturating too quickly.

Back to the Beginning

This chapter began with three questions and a quotation from Sophia, a 19-year-old female university student who felt that the need to discover her ethnic identity to be a crucial prerequisite for discovering and developing her personal identity. For many adolescents facing special identity issues, it is sometimes the need to discover their own particular minority group roots or response to a situation of difference that may be a prerequisite to resolving other important identity issues of adolescence.

Answers to Chapter Questions

◈ **How does knowledge of one's adoption impact identity?**

Providing children and adolescents with information about their birth parents does not have negative consequences for their identity development. Other factors such as the ease and style of family communication and personality factors of parents who have adopted are more important to adolescent identity formation than knowledge of one's adoptive status alone.

◈ **Does immigration change one's sense of identity?**

Optimal identity formation among adolescents who have immigrated involves developing a sense of personal identity that integrates elements from ones identifications and experiences in different cultural settings. So yes, immigration does require changes in one's sense of identity.

◈ **Is a sense of ethnic identity critical to one's ego identity?**

For many adolescent members of an ethnic minority group who live within a larger, mainstream culture, integrating a sense of ethnic identity within one's sense of ego identity is a critical task. Ethnic identity has been positively linked with self-esteem.

PART III
Adulthood

To truly meet others with whom to share a "We," one must have a sense of "I."

—Erik Erikson, *The Life Cycle Completed*

Now, in my late 20s, I sometimes stop to wonder about my life.

—28-year-old female nurse

6

Identity in Early Adulthood

- Are there further major identity developments during early adulthood?
- How does the identity established during late adolescence affect expression of intimacy during young adulthood?
- How does one find the right balance between one's own identity needs and those of significant others?

I feel like I'm still hovering somewhere between adolescence and adulthood, and I'm in my 30s! In terms of feeling responsible and taking charge of the directions for things I want, I don't feel like an adult at all—and certainly my wife would agree with that. I guess maybe I'll feel like an adult proper when I've got my "act" together.

—Paul, 32-year-old theater worker

Can I be happy not being single anymore, with the loss of some independence? What will my future be like with my fiancée? What do I really want to do with my life? Can I really make it out there? Who will be with me to share my life? What matters most to me now? How am I going to make financial ends meet? Do I really just want to climb the career ladder? What are effective ways of maintaining my relationship with my partner? How can I meet my family's needs without totally sacrificing my own? Will I see my son live to adulthood? What kind of a world will he live in?

These identity-related questions were foremost in the minds of some young adults I interviewed who were undertaking an adult education course at a local continuing education center. Individuals were asked what kinds of questions were foremost in their minds as they thought about who they were as people and about their own identities. These young adults were preoccupied with questions of the future—particularly with getting established in vocational and family arenas and making things work. Putting an identity consolidated during late adolescence to the test of early adult social- and work-role demands best captures the identity concerns of these young adults.

Themes of biology, psychology, and societal response described by Erikson (1968) as the main ingredients of the ultimate identity outcome can be seen here in early adulthood in somewhat altered proportions to those that appeared during adolescence. Now moving into various work and social roles within their communities and establishing intimate partnerships and beginning families, these young adults showed far fewer concerns with matters of biology in considering who they were as people. Certainly gender played an enormous role in vocational and interpersonal identity commitments, but one's sense of identity as male or female and considerations of gender roles could now be taken for granted. In fact, biological themes appeared only in relation to concerns regarding childbearing and expressions of sexuality among the young adults interviewed in the previous paragraph. Some individuals were uncertain of their ability to develop vocational competencies or to manage the new demands of becoming half of a partnership. Others who had established vocational and familial or alternative interpersonal roles showed concerns of generativity—how they might best contribute to the healthy development of their children, their community, and the future world in which their children would live. I turn now to the world of early adulthood, to give an overview of the key biological, psychological, and societal influences that continue to shape and reshape that identity formed and consolidated throughout the adolescent years. I define early adulthood here again in terms of both chronological age and psychosocial tasks—as the time between about 23 and 39 years of age, when one normatively enters and becomes established in vocational and interpersonal roles and actualizes a meaningful philosophy of life.

Intersection of Biological, Psychological, and Societal Influences on Identity in Early Adulthood: An Overview

Erikson has asked some profound questions regarding adulthood (Hoare, 2002). What does it mean to be an adult? Are adults merely "grown up editions" of their prior selves? Why do so many adults seem to settle for a restricted version of what they might become? To Erikson, adults need both individual identities as well as group-based identities for survival. Erikson viewed a fully functioning adult as someone who is moral, ethical, and spiritual. Nearly all adults are moral, he believed, but only some are ethical (Hoare, 2002). Moral adults live by rules; ethical adults enable others to develop, building their own and other's strengths without control or judgment. A fully functioning, mature adult, additionally, is able to retain a childlike sense of wonder; identity, in its mature adult form, cannot coexist with cynicism and rejection. The mature adult is self-renewing, refusing to become a mere puppet of institutions or social convention. Erikson also pointed to insight, wisdom, and the ability to consider one's own life in a broader cultural and historical perspective as features of the mature adult—someone far different from a "grown up edition" of his or her adolescent self (Hoare, 2002).

Entry into early adulthood marks a major milestone in identity terms. For better or worse, one now faces the test of bringing into reality the sense of identity that was formed and consolidated through the years of adolescence. How does that sense of I, prepared, tested, shaped, and reshaped within the safe confines of the family, friendship networks, and educational institutions, meet, accommodate to, and become accommodated by larger psychosocial orders as well as interpersonal partners?

For some individuals, this transition will be smooth, as the conferred identity of childhood provides the framework through which young adulthood is entered. In some social and cultural contexts, this type of identity structure will even be adaptive. However, with the demands presented by many complex, Western nations for the development of a more differentiated sense of self through which to enter and meet the challenges of adult life, the process is more complex. For some young adults, this movement, both intrapsychically and externally, will be tumultuous. Yet, for most, the transition will be challenging although not overwhelming in its demands (Offer, 1991).

A wide range of lifestyle, identity-expressing options become available for young adults as they seek self-expression and satisfaction in the adult world. Decisions by young adults must be made not only regarding personally meaningful vocational, ideological, and sexual roles and values, but also concerning balances of energy that will be expended across these domains. Numerous studies have found women to be particularly concerned about such "metadecisions" (balances across identity-defining domains of commitment). Indeed, certain identity-defining interests for some women may be sent to the sidelines, as other identity dimensions demand more immediate priority (Archer, 1989; Kroger & Haslett, 1987, 1991).

An understanding of the interplay among individual biology, psychological variables, and societal and cultural demands is central to an appreciation of identity issues for young adults within many contemporary Western cultures. Within such contexts, for example, there has been a growing acceptance of a diversity of family structures, which, in turn, provides greater scope for an individual to find expression of psychological identity needs and interests. Furthermore, biological capacities for reproduction are optimal for women in early adulthood; thus, many couples wish to begin their families, a further expression of identity, as well as intimacy and generativity needs, during early adulthood before the biological clock limits procreational potential. Gradual biological aging processes also produce some noticeable changes in appearance for both men and women. Those individuals who have placed high value on physical appearance in constructing their sense of identity may need to reevaluate the basis for such a decision as they near the end of early adulthood.

Biological Processes

During the years of early adulthood, there are wide variations in rates of aging—from one person to another and even from one biological system to another within any given individual. These changes are controlled both by genetic and environmental factors. Furthermore, an individual's psychological response to the aging process may also accelerate or compensate for biological changes (Whitbourne, 1996b). Although the cause of aging is a complex question that is difficult to answer, the body copes with aging by integrating the changes in tissue structure to new levels of organization. In this way, life and functioning are preserved as long as possible.

What are some of the normative biological changes of early adulthood that may have identity-related implications? Typically, many biological changes of early adulthood affect appearance, which, in turn, affects identity. From age 20 throughout the years of early adulthood, an individual's weight generally increases. Furthermore, there is a redistribution of body fat; subcutaneous fat decreases in the extremities while increasing in the abdominal area for both men and women (Shock et al., 1984). Thus, limbs become thinner in appearance as the trunk thickens, with "middle-age spread" beginning to appear for many as they approach middle age. There is also a height loss for both men and women between ages 30 and 50; these losses result from loss of bone density, compression of cartilage in the spine, and postural changes (Hoyer & Roodin, 2003). For those whose identity and sense of self-esteem are strongly tied to a slim, lean, youthful appearance, such changes may prove problematic. Indeed, individuals such as professional athletes may feel older and more negative about their age and appearance than those who do not assess themselves primarily in terms of physical features.

Other biological changes of young adulthood that affect physical appearance include changes in skin, hair, and facial structure (Whitbourne, 1996b).

Skin may gradually become drier and less resilient by age 40, and there may be graying of hair pigmentation due to a decrease of melatonin production in the hair follicles. In addition, hair often begins to thin as one approaches 40 for both men and women; some men experience a genetic form of hair loss during early adulthood, whereby the hair begins receding at the temples and eventually proceeds to the top of the head as well. The face changes in appearance as there may come greater wrinkling, puffiness, and a deepening of pigmentation around the eyes (Whitbourne, 1996b). Such normative changes of aging will demand some readjustment and response by all young adults in relation to the individual identity issues raised.

In terms of physical functioning, young adults are generally healthy and at their time of peak performance. Nearly 95 percent of those living in the United States between ages 15 to 44 consider their health to be excellent, very good, or good (Federal Interagency Forum on Aging Related Statistics, 2000). Although all organs of the body change with age, major organ systems usually function smoothly and efficiently throughout early adulthood. Sensory systems operate at maximal efficiency, although there may be some decline in certain aspects of visual ability (nearsightedness generally increases dramatically from childhood through young adulthood). Muscle tone and strength, however, generally are at their peak from 25 to 30 years of age (Whitbourne, 1996b). Through the 30s, there is often a gradual decrease in muscle fibers (hence muscle mass) and a replacement by fat tissue; in fact, between ages 24 and 50, about 10 percent of muscle mass is lost (Booth, Weeden, & Tseng, 1994). A high-fat diet and inactivity may greatly accelerate this process.

Reproductive functioning for most young adults is also at its peak. Expressions of sexuality, both in terms of reproduction and sexual gratification, are important identity issues of early adulthood (Erikson, 1963). The large National Health and Social Life Survey (Michael, Gagnon, Laumann, & Kolata, 1994) surveyed Americans aged 18 to 59 years. The investigation found that couples in their 20s tended to have sex far more frequently than couples in their 30s and 40s. There are both biological and social factors that may help explain the reduction of sexual activity with age. Biologically, both the sex drive and the pressure to have children decrease with age. (However, levels of sex hormones are not much changed until the 50s or beyond.) Social factors such as increasing demands of work, commuting, and balancing other family demands in a complicated life may also reduce the available time for sexual activity (Michael et al., 1994).

Psychological Issues

Taking hold of "some kind of life" becomes a primary task as late adolescents move into young adulthood. Erikson (1968) has pointed out that the identity established during late adolescence serves as the basis for resolution to future psychosocial tasks during the years of early, middle, and late adulthood. At the same time, however, he points out that the identity consolidated at the end of late adolescence is not the final identity, but rather a structure or framework providing some direction for entering young adulthood. Optimally, one's identity established during late adolescence will remain flexible, open to change or modification from both external experiences and new internal awareness over the remainder of the life span.

As adolescent explorations give way to adult commitments, early adulthood sees the consolidation of initial identity decisions for most individuals. Erikson (1963) describes the tasks of Intimacy Versus Isolation as the primary preoccupation of those in their early adulthood years, although concerns with Generativity Versus Stagnation also emerge as middle adulthood approaches. As noted in Chapter 4, identity resolutions adopted at the end of late adolescence set limits on the kind of intimacy that one is able to experience in the early years of young adulthood. Those who have achieved a sense of their own identity are most likely to engage in an intimate relationship (a relationship characterized by mutual respect, depth, and sharing), whereas those foreclosed in identity are most likely engaged in more stereotypic forms of relatedness (Marcia, Waterman, Matteson, Archer, & Orlofsky, 1993). Intimacy may undergo further forms of development during late adolescence and early adulthood.

How do successes and difficulties with various life tasks of young adulthood relate to experiences of well-being and identity development during this time? Different trajectories of well-being have appeared for young people making the important life transition into young adulthood (Schulenberg, Bryant, & O'Malley, 2004). In their large survey of 18 to 26 year olds, there was much continuity in the experience of psychological well-being. At the same time, however, opportunities for amending existing developmental pathways did appear. Maintaining or gaining in feelings of well-being was associated with more success and less stalling, particularly in areas of work, romantic involvements, and citizenship domains. Compensatory effects, like succeeding in one domain but not another were also in evidence and associated with well-being (Schulenberg et al., 2004).

Erikson's seventh psychosocial task of Generativity Versus Stagnation emerges as middle adulthood approaches. One's way of coping with Generativity Versus Stagnation rests upon resolutions to identity and intimacy issues, as well as preceding psychosocial stages of development. Erikson (1963) defines generativity as the desire to establish and guide the next generation. Although many young, middle-age, and older adults will express generativity needs through parenting roles, parenting is not the only form through which generativity may be expressed. More broadly, generativity refers to the desire to foster one's creative productions, sharing one's knowledge, skills, and talents so that one's community is enhanced and one's offspring can survive. Where generativity fails, Erikson describes the dangers of stagnation or self-absorption. Certainly, the act of parenting is not necessarily an expression of generativity (Erikson, 1963).

Vaillant and Milofsky (1980) have been concerned with a psychosocial task accompanying intimacy and preceding generativity that they find omitted in Erikson's life cycle scheme. From the early 20s until the mid-30s, Vaillant has observed and described a psychosocial task of "career consolidation," which preoccupies many in their years of early adulthood. Many empirical studies do point to the identity-enhancing experience that accomplishments in one's chosen vocation can bring (e.g., Warr, 1992). It may be that fostering the development of one's creative products in the vocational arena and creating and guiding one's own offspring in the parental sphere are both tangible expressions of the single underlying desire for generativity.

Cognitive processes during the years of early adulthood also undergo further changes having identity implications as the cognitive operations developed during adolescence are applied in new contexts. Hoyer and Rybash (1994) point out that early adult cognitive development sees the emergence and increased differentiation of domain-ordered knowledge specializations. Thinking and reasoning during early adulthood may be less constrained by developmental processes than by the demands of the contexts to which individuals must adapt (Hoyer & Rybash, 1994). Thus, those in their early adulthood years may be effective functioning in some cognitive domains but not in others.

Several writers have pointed to the possibility of further stages in cognitive development in adulthood beyond Piaget's (1972) stage of formal operational logic (see Chapter 3 for a definition of formal operations). Arlin (1989) proposed and empirically defined a fifth "problem-finding" stage of reasoning beyond formal operations that involves the capacity to generate new questions based on existing information. One could argue that this ability is central to potential identity reformulations during the adulthood years. Labouvie-Vief (1990, 2005) has also proposed additional stages of cognitive development during adulthood years: *intrasystemic, intersystemic,* and *integrated* levels of thinking. The intrasystemic level corresponds to Piaget's stage of formal operations, in which people can reason within a single system of thought like Christianity or Buddhism, but they cannot reflect upon that system itself. In the intersystemic level of thinking, people become aware of multiple, often contradictory systems of thought that are seen as irreconcilable. At the next integrated level, people operate with responsible, autonomous reflection as they adopt their own views while viewing diversity as positive and conducive to further growth.

While people generally do not reach formal operational thought levels until late adolescence or early adulthood, midlife-aged adults are not necessarily using more mature forms of logic than those in their early adulthood years. Much research remains to be undertaken with regard to adult cognitive structures, although there is evidence that cognitive development during early and middle adulthood is less absolute and more tolerant of uncertainties than cognitive development during adolescence (Labouvie-Vief, 2005).

Societal Influences

The path of identity during the adulthood years is shaped to a large extent by the supports and sanctions provided within the host culture for choice of differing lifestyle options by its young adult members. Neugarten and Neugarten (1986) suggested that different societies have a particular social age clock, or series of age-related expectations about what an individual is supposed to accomplish by a particular time. They suggest that such timetables provide guidelines for our lives, and individuals who are "off-time" for a particular event such as getting married or having children are likely to experience much stress in their lives. However, they also maintain that now, in contrast to the first half of this century, there is much less agreement on particular life events that should be experienced at a particular time during adulthood. In identity terms, the lack of clear guidelines and timetables for adult development in most Western cultures presents a dilemma similar to that experienced by many adolescents in the absence of puberty rituals. One might again argue, as has Marcia (1983), that such conditions are optimal for facilitating individual identity development. However, much research remains to be done on conditions that best facilitate optimal identity formation both during adolescence and adulthood.

Societies also change over time and people change alongside or perhaps as a result of such social forces. The participation rate of women in the labor force within the United States, for example, has changed dramatically over the past few decades. Between 1980 and 2000, the percentage of men in the United States who held at least a college degree increased by about 8 percent, while the percentage of women holding at least a college degree have nearly doubled (from 13 percent to 24 percent) over this same time period (U.S. Bureau of the Census, 2003). From 2000 Census data, almost equal percentages of men and women are college graduates (28 percent for men, 24 percent for women), and about 76 percent of all young adult women participate in the civilian labor force. It is projected that by 2010, about 80 percent of all young adult women will be employed outside the home (U.S. Bureau of the Census, 2003). Greater possibilities for economic independence among women have removed pressures to marry purely for economic reasons. Thus, the last half-century has seen enormous change in the type, pattern, and reasons behind work for many young and middle adulthood women. Although many problems remain, such as inequality of pay and opportunity structures within many work contexts for women compared with men, many Western contexts have sanctioned a greater number of vocational possibilities and lifestyle options for women compared with those available to them even 25 years ago.

This greater range of choice, in turn, has presented new issues for identity consideration among many contemporary young adults. Decisions by couples must now be made in terms of various options for full- or part-time work in combination with family responsibilities for each partner. For those couples with children, consideration must also be given to when and how much time to work by each member of the partnership. Options chosen by many women now include remaining in full-time or part-time employment throughout the years of raising young children, returning to full- or part-time work after the children are older, or becoming a full-time homemaker throughout the years of child rearing. Although possible, a similar diversity of lifestyle options has not been adopted among men (Kroger & Haslett, 1987, 1991). Indeed, even the decision of whether or not to commit oneself to a partnership is a greater option for many women with sufficient earning power now to ensure the standard of living they desire. This greater diversity of possible lifestyle options for at least some young adults has been associated with different patterns of identity development, particularly among young adult women, even when level of education and family responsibilities have been controlled (Kroger & Haslett, 1987, 1991). Further differences in identity development have been found across groups of young adult men and women who have followed different lifestyle arrangements (Pulkkinen, 1994). For example, women who chose full-time homemaking responsibilities throughout adulthood were likely to be foreclosed in a number of identity-defining domains, even when education level was controlled (Kroger & Haslett, 1987).

In addition to considering a range of identity-defining lifestyle options, young adults who become parents will also be helping to transmit important cultural values regarding optimal identity development through their child-rearing practices. Cultures vary in their emphasis on what constitutes an optimal sense of identity among individuals. Socialization practices reflect differing understandings of what constitutes a healthy sense of identity across cultures.

One important cultural dimension affecting the later identity development of children is the extent to which collective versus individual values are stressed. Parents raising children within collectivist cultures stress placing the needs of the group above needs of the self, teaching their children obedience to authority and conformity to group values, while those in individualist cultures stress personal over group goals in addition to self-reliance and independence. As a result, definitions of what constitutes well-being and an optimal sense of identity differ dramatically across cultural contexts (Ryff, Lee, & Na, 1996).

Section Summary and Implications

Young adults generally experience good health and are at their time of peak physical performance. There are wide variations in both intra- and interindividual rates of aging, however. An individual's psychological response to aging may accelerate or compensate for biological changes of aging.

Concerns with Intimacy Versus Isolation dominate the years of early adulthood, according to Erikson. However, most young adult couples are also beginning to establish families, and the task of Generativity Versus Stagnation also enters their lives. Vaillant also believes a task of "Career Consolidation" preoccupies many from their late 20s through mid-30s.

Greater vocational and lifestyle options now exist for young adult men and women than in previous generations. Such choices have presented new implications for identity development, often requiring more extended phases of exploration and decision making than previous generations experienced.

The Course of Identity in Early Adulthood

Erikson (1968) suggests that issues of identity and role confusion fade into the background for most young adults who have achieved a sense of identity, as issues of intimacy followed by generativity come to the fore. However, Erikson (1968) also proposed that an adolescent's resolutions to identity-defining issues do not remain fixed but rather retain flexibility for modification through various life experiences and new awarenesses during the adulthood years. Questions thus arise regarding the course of normative identity development during adulthood. Sufficient research within an Eriksonian framework has now been conducted at least among young adults to give some indication of normative movements and impetuses for change in identity during early adulthood. This section will overview theoretical ideas as well as key longitudinal and retrospective studies to shed light on the evolution of identity in the initial years beyond late adolescence.

Marcia (2002) has proposed some interesting notions about how identity itself may be reformulated throughout the psychosocial stages of adult development that Erikson (1968) has described. During young adulthood, any identity commitments formed during adolescence are likely subject to disequilibrating events through the circumstances of everyday life. Normal, expected disequilibrating events of young adulthood might involve issues with partnerships, friendships, intimacy, and getting started in work and leisure commitments. In addition, there may be nonnormative, critical life events that occur, such as loss of loved ones or loss of employment, that an individual must deal with. Marcia (2002) suggests that during such times, the individual may temporarily regress to earlier identity modes in meeting disequilibrating life events. Thus, one who has constructed a sense of his or her own identity during late adolescence (attained identity achievement) may experience a phase of diffusion as an old identity structure must be revised during young adulthood, following a disequilibrating event. He or she may behave erratically, impulsively, or otherwise inappropriately. Following this period of disorganization, an individual may attempt to return to old identity commitments, cycling briefly through a foreclosure phase. Eventual searching for better identity options would precipitate a moratorium phase and, optimally, new identity commitments eventuating in an identity-achieved structure. Thus, each reconstructed identity structure following the disequilibrating life event accommodates to a wider range of life experiences than previous resolutions. However, no longitudinal work has been conducted on Marcia's (2002) proposal to date.

Earlier, Stephen, Fraser, and Marcia (1992) described such identity reformulations in terms of "MAMA" (moratorium-achievement-moratorium-achievement) cycles. These authors proposed that progressive (optimal) identity development throughout the adult years is likely to be characterized by repeated phases of commitment and later reassessment. Some empirical support for this suggestion has come through the longitudinal studies of Anthis (2002) and Josselson (1996) and retrospective work of Kroger and Haslett (1987, 1991). Anthis (2002), for example, found an increase in identity exploration and a decrease in identity commitment over a five-month interval among women who had experienced a stressful life event related to death and dying, health care issues, crime, financial/economic issues, and family-related events.

Through qualitative analyses, Kunnen and Wassink (2003) have also turned their attention to the process of identity development during young adulthood. They explore ways in which individuals may react to particular disequilibrating life events as well as steps that may be involved for those who do accommodate, or change their identity structures, to meet the new life circumstances. An understanding of such processes involved in ongoing identity development during adult life remains a rich and important area for future longitudinal research.

Perhaps one of the most interesting issues to appear in studies of identity-status change through the years of late adolescence is the fact that the majority of youths about to leave college and enter young adulthood have not attained a sense of their own identity. All published longitudinal investigations of late adolescents and young adults have produced samples with fewer than half of subjects attaining the status of identity achievement (forming meaningful commitments following exploration) by young adulthood (e.g., Cramer, 1998; Kroger, 1988, 1995; Marcia, 1976; Pulkkinen & Kokko, 2000; Waterman, Geary, & Waterman, 1974; Waterman & Goldman, 1976). Cross-sectional studies have shown (similarly) low percentages of individuals rated as identity-achieved across global identity or individual identity domains in late adolescence and early adulthood. That such a large proportion of those entering young adulthood do not appear to have achieved a sense of ego identity suggests considerable scope for development during the years of young adulthood.

How likely is it that one's identity status will change during early adulthood? And when identity status does change, what are the most common patterns of movement? Here, further interesting findings appear within the existing longitudinal and retrospective studies from the late adolescent through early adult years (e.g., Josselson, 1987; Kroger & Haslett, 1987, 1991; Marcia, 1976; Pulkkinen & Kokko, 2000). In these investigations, movement from a low (diffusion or foreclosure) to higher (moratorium to achievement) identity status occurred, but this trajectory was not as frequent during young adulthood as during late adolescence. Openness to the exploration of further identity-defining commitments appears more limited during the years of early adulthood compared with late adolescence. There may also be fewer institutional supports for young adults to undergo or continue identity explorations compared with adolescents, and there may be less willingness or possibility on the part of individuals to remain open to different identity alternatives once assuming the many family and work responsibilities of early adult life. Where identity status change has occurred in the previously mentioned studies, the most common movement has been from a lower (diffusion or foreclosure) to higher (moratorium to achievement) identity status, as both internal awareness and external events have been associated with change. However, some additional identity status movements occurred during young adulthood sufficiently often to warrant comment.

Attaining identity achievement in late adolescence does not yield a style of continuing identity achievement for many. The theoretically anomalous movement from identity achievement or moratorium to foreclosure occurred in all of these studies at a rate greater than might be explained by measurement error alone. (Indeed, in Marcia's 1976 investigation, over half of the subjects rated moratorium or identity-achieved in terms of overall identity status in late adolescence were rated foreclosed or foreclosed/diffuse in their mid-20s.) Such individuals seemed to have "reclosed," or retreated to an earlier foreclosed identity position by withdrawing into a constricted and rigidified life plan. Such anomalies led Valde (1996) to differentiate and offer some empirical support for an "open-achieved" versus a "closed-achieved" identity status to describe potentials for modification to one's late adolescent identity-achieved position. However, a more common pattern of movement for those identity-achieved individuals during late adolescence was to shift to a moratorium (and often a further identity-achieved) position during young adult life.

The Contents of Identity in Early Adulthood

Now, in my late 20s, I sometimes stop to wonder about my life. Many of my friends are moving up the corporate ladder and have married and started families. This, at times, can be a little disconcerting and prompts me to question where I'm going and where I'll be in 10 years' time. I really don't know if I want to go either of those routes. And if I do, what will matter most?

—28-year-old female nurse

The identity-defining domains of meaningful vocational directions, political, religious, interpersonal, sexual, and life philosophy values remain key foundations of identity for most young adults, regardless of culture. In addition, most early adults are making decisions regarding possible partnership and parental commitments as well. Vaillant and Milofsky (1980) have suggested young adulthood is a time of developing and consolidating goals, particularly in areas of vocational commitment and family life. In looking at vocational hopes, much research attention has been directed to the area of career choice and implementation. And although women have been entering the paid work force in increasing numbers, one must not lose sight of the fact that for many young adult women, "the goal" will still involve full-time homemaking. This vocation receives no salary and often little recognition or status but reflects an important identity choice.

Super (1980, 1994) has offered a theory of vocational development that suggests that the self-concept plays an important role in career choice. His model describes various changes in self-concept that occur during late adolescence and adulthood years. Following the *crystallization* phase during mid-adolescence (approximately 14–18 years) in which young people consider possibilities for a vocational direction that meshes with their existing self-concept, late adolescents (approximately 18–22 years) narrow their range of career choices in the *specification* phase and begin to follow a particular vocational path. During the initial years of early adulthood (22–24 years), individuals complete their education or training and begin work during the *implementation* phase. Between about 25 and 35 years of age, a specific career choice is made during the *stabilization* phase. *Career consolidation* follows after the age of 35, leading to *deceleration* in the late 50s, and *retirement* usually in the mid-60s.

These stages have been criticized as not reflecting women's career development, for many women tend to move in and out of employment roles in response to various life events (e.g., Ornstein & Isabella, 1990). Furthermore, vocational choice for both men and women frequently does not follow such an orderly path, for many people select work on the basis of chance factors or contextual constraints, and many also change vocational directions during adult life (Ornstein & Isabella, 1990).

In response to such criticisms, Super has broadened his model to examine the interplay of major life roles with his career development model (Kulenovic & Super, 1995). Super notes that some roles assume great importance (e.g., as a family member or as an employee) at certain points in time and must be resolved, while others do not demand urgent attention. The ascendancy of certain life roles at particular points in time may impact stages in one's career development. For example, one may put one's career establishment "on hold" while critical family issues are addressed. Or one may retrain, rather than maintain a particular line of work as the work is phased out. With such modifications, Super's model has provided a useful description of how a sizable percentage of young adults select, implement, and consolidate vocational decisions.

Entering the labor force marks a central transition in the lives of many young adults, and failure in this transition often has both negative financial and psychosocial outcomes (Wiesner, Vondracek, Capaldi, & Porfeli, 2003). In an effort to predict career development pathways among young adults, Wiesner and colleagues conducted a prospective longitudinal study to look at childhood and adolescent precursors. Four career pathways were identified among a sample of several hundred at risk men, aged 23 to 24 years:

long-term unemployment, short-term unemployment, full employment, and college education. The most important predictors of the differing career pathways were educational attainments, arrest record, and mental health problems. The long-term unemployed men, as a group, had the poorest levels of educational attainments, family and peer relations, and personal adjustments during childhood and adolescence. The short-term unemployed and employed groups had intermediate levels of educational attainments and intermediate levels of difficulties in personal and social adjustments.

For many during the early adult years, some time may be spent fine-tuning personal interests and talents with those of potential vocational settings, and turnover rates in one's work experience are high. And values associated with work motivation have shown some dramatic changes over the past three decades. A recent longitudinal study of some 3,290 African American and Caucasian young adults found young people consistently place greater emphasis on intrinsic rather than extrinsic work values (Cotton, Bynum, & Madhere, 1997). Finding a vocational context that can express identity-related needs and interests rather than just bringing in a paycheck appears crucial to the lives of many contemporary young adults.

In addition to implementing a vocational pathway, the demands of partnering and parenting raise new issues for many young adults trying to live according to their selected values and implement meaningful philosophies of life. Dual-career partnerships raise many considerations among those couples wishing to pursue their individual vocational interests. Decisions must be made as to whether or not to delay marriage until careers have been established, or indeed whether or not to marry at all. For those couples wishing to have children, decisions must also be made as to when to begin a family and how large it will be. Certainly, becoming a parent profoundly affects one's self-concept and identity, and balancing that role with the demands of establishing a new marriage as well as vocational direction are difficult ventures for most young adults to undertake concurrently (Levinson, 1978, 1996).

Recent research has suggested that in moving from early to mature adulthood, men and women frequently change in their goals and values, in what they find important in their lives, and what they are striving toward more generally (Harker & Solomon, 1996). Both men and women of this retrospective investigation declined in gender-traditional goals and values and increased in individual goals and values. Although such findings may reflect the contextual effects of the rise of the women's movement and greater support for women assuming traditionally masculine roles over the young and middle adulthood years of the study's participants, such cohort effects do not explain the shift in values for men.

Identity and Intimacy in Early Adulthood

I suppose I now feel solid enough in my relationship to my part-
ner to be able to disagree or argue, for example, and know that's
not a dangerous thing. In fact, quite the reverse—it's actually
healthy, and the dangerous thing is if disagreements go undis-
cussed and that becomes the predominant way of relating.

—31-year-old male administrator

Achieving a sense of identity opens the possibility to more mature forms of intimacy according to Erikson (1963). Intimacy, as defined by Erikson, refers to the mutual trust and sharing in a relationship with a loved partner of the opposite sex in which there is a mutuality of orgasm and the regulation of work, procreation, and recreation (Erikson, 1963). Others, such as Orlofsky (Orlofsky, Marcia, & Lesser, 1973), have broadened notions of intimacy to include relationships involving mutuality and trust in friendships as well as in heterosexual relationships; in addition, one might question now whether or not all intimate relationships must involve heterosexual or even sexual forms of self-expression. In Chapter 4, we have illustrated some of the attempts to operationalize intimacy and its relationship to identity during late adolescence (e.g., Levitz-Jones & Orlofsky, 1985; Orlofsky et al., 1973). Various styles of intimacy have been described by Orlofsky and his colleagues, and these intimacy styles have shown strong relationships to different identity statuses adopted by late adolescents. But what styles of intimacy are most frequently used by young adults, and are these styles related to Marcia's identity statuses in young adulthood? How does intimacy commonly develop over the course of young adulthood? And how does identity contribute to the furthering of intimacy and intimacy to the furthering of identity during young adulthood? It is interesting that much research has been conducted on various forms of intimacy (intimacy statuses) and their relationship to different forms of identity (identity statuses) during late adolescence, but even now, little research has been conducted on the forms and development of intimacy during young adulthood. Research has similarly not focused on how various forms of intimacy may enhance or impede identity development during the young adult years.

Whitbourne and her colleagues (Tesch & Whitbourne, 1982; Whitbourne and Tesch, 1985), Marcia (1976), Raskin (1986), and Kahn, Zimmerman, Csikszentmihalyi, and Getzels (1985) have all attempted to address the relationship between identity status and intimacy during the years of young adulthood through longitudinal or cross-sectional research. In their investigations, a greater proportion of young adults were involved in relationships of mutuality and long-term commitment (intimate) than late adolescents or those just out of college. Furthermore, a greater proportion of late adolescents were in relationships that involved little commitment or mutuality (i.e., stereotyped and isolated). Thus, young adults may develop increasingly intimate forms of relationship beyond late adolescence. Significant links between mature forms of intimacy and high identity status have also appeared across these studies, as they did in adolescence, with somewhat different patterns appearing for some women, again as in adolescence.

Like some of the men, some women from Whitbourne and Tesch (1985) showed mature intimacy development, but were low in identity. It may be that sex-role orientation mediates the relationship between identity and intimacy for young adults, as it seems to do among late adolescents. In a longitudinal study spanning 18 years from late adolescence to the late 30s, Kahn and colleagues (1985) found that those who had established a strong sense of identity during college had more enduring marital relationships some 18 years later. Men who lacked a well-developed sense of identity in late adolescence were likely to remain single until midlife; however, women lacking a strong sense of identity did marry but had problems in maintaining stable marriages.

And from work assessing identity in somewhat different ways, a 20-year longitudinal study of some 477 participants first assessed during early adolescence found that healthy identity formation in early adolescence facilitated the development of greater intimacy in young adulthood (Stein & Newcomb, 1999). Findings from the ego development literature present a similar picture. Indeed, those having higher levels of ego development during mid-adolescence reported more collaborative strategies for conflict resolution, greater interpersonal understanding, and more intimate sharing of experiences by age 25 years (Henninghausen, Hauser, Billings, Schultz, & Allen, 2004). Thus, the style of identity or ego development adopted during adolescence appears strongly related to one's style of intimacy both during adolescence as well as early adulthood.

How do social relationships change as people evolve from late adolescence through young adulthood? Reis, Lin, Bennett, and Nezlek (2004) provide some answers. These researchers undertook a longitudinal investigation of 113 young adults upon entry into college or as college seniors and again as young adults, aged 27 to 31 years. Detailed diaries from participants showed that through the college years, opposite-sex socializing grew at the same time that group interactions and same- and mixed-sex interactions decreased. This drop in same-sex socializing is noteworthy, for it is through such relationships that world views are often shared and identity and intimacy develop. By contrast, adults had roughly equal levels of same- and opposite-sex socializing. It may be that as participants became more comfortable with the opposite sex through college years, there was no longer the need to limit social contacts through heterosexual relationships alone. The data also suggested that increases in intimacy were experienced with age across all kinds of social relationships. It may thus be most useful to conceptualize the development of intimacy as a global style of interaction, rather than as a feature of specific relationships.

Identity and Generativity in Early Adulthood

Generativity Versus Stagnation, the seventh psychosocial task described by Erikson (1963), refers to the desire to guide and care for the next generation. "Generativity . . . is primarily the concern in establishing and guiding the next generation, although there are individuals who, through misfortune or because of special and genuine gifts in other directions, do not apply this drive to their own offspring" (p. 267). Parenting thus appears as an important focus of generativity for Erikson, although one's expressions of generativity can also appear in other forms, including productivity and the creation of works that contribute to the ongoing life of the community and society.

However, several writers have pointed out an anomaly in discussions of Erikson's writings on generativity (e.g., Peterson & Stewart, 1993). Although Erikson (1963) considers Generativity Versus Stagnation to be a psychosocial focus of mid-adult life (around age 40–50 years), the majority of adults will be beginning families and raising children long before this time. If generativity is an activity primarily associated with parenting, then Generativity Versus Stagnation must be an important issue in the lives of young adults as well as those at midlife. Although primary discussions of generativity and its varied forms and contexts will be overviewed in the next chapter, research on identity and generativity during young adulthood is briefly highlighted here.

Slater (2003) has proposed additional dimensions to Erikson's concept of generativity that emerge from a recent research review on the topic. From Slater's synthesis, there are a number of conflicts that provide further breadth to Erikson's writings on generativity: inclusivity versus exclusivity, pride versus embarrassment, responsibility versus ambivalence, career productivity versus inadequacy, parenthood versus self-absorption, being needed versus alienation, and honesty versus denial. Each of these generative conflicts captures themes from one of Erikson's earlier or later developmental tasks. In Slater's view, these themes could provide a stimulus for longitudinal studies that focus on antecedents and consequences of optimal resolution to the Eriksonian task of Generativity Versus Stagnation.

An important question one might pose is whether or not generativity in relation to parenting is an important feature for young adults as well as midlife adults. Several investigations have been undertaken to examine this question. Bailey (1992, 1994) found that for both men and women in their mid- to late 30s who were parents of young children and living in intact families, generativity was indeed an important feature of their lives and an integrated aspect of personality development. However, caregiving for one's own children was most frequently provided by the mother, with the father and mother equally involved in caregiving for their child's playmates. And generativity did not appear related to child rearing, but rather to social involvement more generally and to other personality traits such as self-esteem, locus of control, and instrumentality for both genders.

In more extensive research with young adults (mean age 28 years), Peterson and Stewart (1993) examined specific themes related to generativity and parenting in the lives of men and women. Some interesting gender differences appeared. Among women, an affiliation-intimacy motive was associated with many features of their generativity, whereas for men, it was rather the presence of children and needs for assertion that seemed to direct generative impulses. Generative activity in relation to societal concerns was minimal for both genders, reflecting the fact that these young adults were not generally engaged with broader social issues but rather with personal pro-ductivity. This research points to the fact that generativity is at least relevant to the arena of parenting among a sample of early adults. Generativity in relation to other arenas (i.e., societal concern or social roles), however, is likely to emerge as individuals grow older.

There is a great need for longitudinal research to understand the develop-ments of identity, intimacy, and generativity over the course of early adult-hood. A recent collection of works by de St. Aubin, McAdams, and Kim (2004) provides an excellent resource for considering a number of issues related to Erikson's concept of generativity. In a synthesis from a variety of researches over the past 15 years, McAdams and Logan (2004) conclude that generativity concerns and behaviors most likely peak during the years of midlife, but the developmental course of generativity is strongly shaped by social and cultural forces. Indeed, different dimensions of generativity may ebb and flow at different times over the adulthood years. Indeed, the *motivation* to be generative may be high in young adulthood, though it may not be possible to actualize one's concerns until midlife (Stewart & Vandewater, 1998).

Contexts Affecting Early Adult Identity Development

The research on the impact of different contextual features or events on young adult identity development has been limited. Indeed, whereas identity researchers have just begun to examine the impact of context on different facets of the identity-formation process during adolescence, similar work has hardly begun during the years of early adulthood. One issue facing researchers of adult identity development is trying to understand the impact of certain cohort effects on developmental phenomena. When an entire cohort of individuals experiences the impact of a particular social or historical circumstance, such as the rise of the women's movement, the Great Depression, or the terrorist attacks of September 11, 2001, one's sense of identity is invariably shaped by such experiences. Schaie and colleagues (Schaie, Labouvie, & Buech, 1973) recognized early the role that such historical events may have on many dimensions of personality. Thus, when conducting cross-sectional research over the years of early, middle, or later adulthood, one is faced with the problem of disentangling the normative effects of aging from those features that may characterize an entire cohort of individuals due to particular events and experiences a particular era brought. Those experiencing the rise of the women's movement during early adulthood, at the exact time they were making various vocational and lifestyle decisions, would undoubtedly hold different views on appropriate sex-role values compared with those in their later years of adulthood who were experiencing the rise of the women's movement. Thus, one must bear in mind the potential problems in comparing studies done on different cohorts of individuals over the years of both adolescence and adulthood. More sophisticated, cohort-sequential research designs now exist to try to untangle the impact of age, cohort, and time of measurement factors in the development of identity (Whitbourne, 2005).

The Family/Social Network

People that know me think of me as a highly capable person. That embarrasses me, for I get a lot of support and help from my family, so one has to look at the whole picture. I'm not just the liberated women doing my thing and having everything else running smoothly as well; my family gives me a lot of help.

—35-year-old female city administrator

Family and friendship networks of young adults can play important roles in the furthering of identity development. Long-standing friendships and family networks have been identified by young adults as becoming increasingly more important to them (Reis et al., 2004), and strong associations have been found between intimacy in social relationships and a strong sense of individual identity (Winefield & Harvey, 1996). At the same time, these social networks may also actually impede optimal identity development for some young adults. How do friendship networks among young adults contribute to identity development?

The role of friendships in young adulthood may also serve important functions for furthering identity development. From late adolescence to early adulthood, opposite-sex socializing grows, whereas same-sex, mixed-sex, and peer-group interactions decrease; young adult interactions are also significantly longer than those of late adolescents (Reis, Lin, Bennett, & Nezlek, 1993; Reis et al., 2004). It seems that compared to late adolescents, young adults desire to focus their time for socializing with a smaller number of close friends. Furthermore, intimacy seems to increase not just with one's primary partner, but with a range of individuals across different contexts (Reis et al., 1993). However, important gender differences have appeared. Men's interactions with other men were less intimate than either their interactions with women or than women's socializing with either sex (Reis et al., 1993).

The World of Work

I took a Sanity Day on Monday. I just didn't go to work, and I went back the next day and the children said they wanted me back so much. I'm really looking for a different purpose in life now. I'm looking to reduce stress in interpersonal and job relationships. There's just no way to meet all the demands, as things stand now.

—35-year-old female teacher

The work context not only plays a key role in structuring the lives of many young as well as middle adulthood adults, but also provides important feedback regarding one's capacities, skills, and interests. And increasingly today, continuing education contexts, particularly for many young and middle adulthood women, play a vital role in fostering or impeding optimal identity development.

How is identity development related to transition to the working environment during young adulthood? Recent longitudinal research suggests a reciprocal link between personality characteristics and one's work experiences from late adolescence through young adulthood. From a major New Zealand study, late adolescent personality traits at age 18 predicted the nature of young adult work experiences over the following eight years; additionally, young adult work experiences also predicted changes in personality between late adolescence and young adulthood (Roberts, Caspi, & Moffitt, 2003). Those late adolescents who scored high on personality measures of aggression, alienation, and stress at age 18 had a difficult and unsuccessful transition into the working world. By contrast, those late adolescents who scored high on measures of achievement and social potency at age 18 experienced much work satisfaction and success and had far fewer financial difficulties by age 26. Additionally, those young adults who held higher status jobs that were satisfying and provided financial security also showed important personality changes between ages 18 and 26 years. These individuals showed increases in social closeness and feelings of well-being, as well as a reduction of aggression, alienation, and stress. This longitudinal investigation by Roberts and colleagues (Roberts et al., 2003) is important because it shows that work environments have the possibility to modify key personality features in the transition to young adulthood.

At present, a new type of worker and work context is emerging. From the National Study of the Changing Workforce (Galinsky, Bond, & Friedman, 1993), young adult workers today are less committed to their actual employers, career advancement, and places of work than they are to the quality of what they themselves produce. Commitment to and involvement in work remain high, but only insofar as work enables an individual to realize intrinsic goals. Working hard so that the company might succeed was a value endorsed by only about one-quarter of all workers in this survey. What factors may be responsible for this change? Through the 1980s and 1990s, there has been much corporate downsizing affecting workers at all levels. Many corporate mergers and sell-offs resulted in job losses for many. Galinsky and colleagues speculate that the impact of such uncontrollable external forces caused individuals to turn inward to the quality of their own work, something that they could control. In addition, such times of rapid restructuring in the economic sphere have caused many workers to redefine their lifestyle values and seek alternatives to traditional work regimens (Johnson, 1996). Certainly for many, such conditions in the workplace have raised issues regarding personal identity and how one can more meaningfully earn an income.

The Broader Community

> *Most important to me now are my faith, my continuing relationship with my wife, the love and affection of my children, and living in a national environment, which enables those conditions to continue. I want most to help retain an economic and political climate so that I as well as others, can continue to enjoy the quality of life that is possible in this nation. Here there is the freedom to shape one's own destiny, and there are many countries where you just cannot do that.*

> —38-year-old male engineer

The national and community context of the New Zealander quoted above vividly reflects the important role that the larger community and cultural ethos play in his identity-defining values. Unfortunately, the role of the larger social and cultural context on adult identity development is unsure. However, one direction that research on broader contextual issues for young adults has taken is the attempt to understand the impact that events which coincide with a particular life stage may have on individuals. Stewart and Healy (1989) have proposed a model linking the influences of social events with individual personality development. Generally, their model posits that at any particular point in time, events impact on individuals in a particular age cohort. These individuals are involved in different psychosocial tasks than those of other age cohorts. Thus, the same social event is likely to affect individuals of different age cohorts in different ways. For example, Stewart and Healy suggest that events experienced during late adolescence and young adulthood will affect perceptions of opportunities for commitment (fidelity) and identity formation. Events experienced during middle adulthood (after vocational and family commitments had been made) are most likely to affect behavior but not more fundamental features of personality, such as identity.

Duncan and Agronick (1995) were interested in testing this model with early adults. First they found support for the hypothesis that certain social events coinciding with early adulthood (when identity and intimacy commitments were being established) would be more salient at midlife than events occurring during childhood, early middle adulthood, or midlife. In four of five samples studied, broad social events that individuals identified as most influential in their lives occurred during early adulthood. Furthermore, the researchers found that social events coinciding with the time identity commitments were being made in early adulthood were most salient at midlife, even when major historical events were experienced at other life stages. The authors speculate that even if no major social events occur during one's early adulthood years, the prevailing social attitudes present during one's early adulthood years will still affect future decisions about family and career that carry well into midlife. Secondly, Duncan and Agronick focused on one particular historical event (the women's movement) to understand its impact on two cohorts of women: one group of early adults who witnessed the movement gaining strength at this stage of their lives and one group in middle adulthood at the time this movement gained momentum. The researchers again found that those who experienced this social event as young adults regarded it as personally meaningful in their lives in contrast to those who experienced the movement as midlife adults. The implications of these researches suggest that the phase of early adulthood is crucial for future family and vocational commitments during middle adulthood.

Section Summary and Implications

Young adults socialize with a smaller number of close friends compared with late adolescents. Intimacy increases not just with one's partner, but with individuals across a range of contexts during young adulthood.

A different type of worker and work context is currently emerging in which people place more emphasis on realizing intrinsic identity goals than on commitment to an actual employer, career, or place of work. More corporate mergers and downsizings may have caused workers to turn inward in order to gain satisfaction from the quality of their own work as well as to redefine fulfilling lifestyles in which traditional work regimes are seen as less important.

Certain social events coinciding with early adulthood have been found to be more salient at midlife than events occurring during childhood, early middle adulthood, or midlife. Prevailing social events or attitudes experienced during early adulthood may have a crucial impact on midlife family and vocational commitments.

Back to the Beginning

Three questions relevant to identity in early adulthood and Paul's statement opened this chapter. Paul, at age 32, still feels like he is hovering somewhere between adolescence and adulthood. He still feels unable to take charge of moving his life in desired directions for the things he wants. Paul feels his wife would agree with his statements. Certainly many identity issues seem to remain unresolved for Paul. Although it is during adolescence that identity issues come to the fore for many, Paul's statements indicate considerable scope for identity development also during the adulthood years of life. This theme has been reechoed through various sections of this chapter.

Answers to Chapter Questions

◈ **Are there further major identity developments during early adulthood?**

Yes. Research has indicated sizable proportions of adolescents have not achieved a sense of identity in many areas of their lives. Among young adults who have achieved a sense of their own identity, a continuation of moratorium-achievement-moratorium-achievement (MAMA) cycles may characterize the years of early adulthood. Marcia (2003) has also proposed that with disequili-brating life circumstances, there may be a recycling through diffusion, foreclosure, moratorium, and achievement statuses for each psychosocial stage of adult development.

◈ **How does the identity established during late adolescence affect expression of intimacy during young adulthood?**

The style of identity resolution adopted during late adolescence appears strongly linked to style of intimacy adopted during young adulthood. Where identity has remained foreclosed or diffuse during late adolescence, style of intimacy is more stereotypic or isolated in relating to others.

◈ **How does one find the right balance between one's own identity needs and those of significant others?**

There is no easy answer to this question. Different personal and situational circumstances may require different priorities to be adopted at different points in time. However, it does appear from research that those with more mature styles of identity resolutions are best able to care both for the needs of the self as well as those of others.

I really value the personal growth of my relationship with my wife. We've got it more together now than we've ever had. We've beaten the bad patches. And I also really value our growing relationship with our kids as friends, as distinct from being our children.

—57-year-old male educational administrator

7

Identity in Middle Adulthood

- Is a midlife identity crisis a common experience?
- How do biological changes affect midlife identity?
- Does having adult children alter one's sense of identity at midlife?

I'm now middle-aged, with all the connotations that has. Things are more limited now, in the sense that life might just stay more similar to the way it is at present, instead of presenting many possibilities for change, like it did earlier. I'm not as young as I used to be—I can't keep dancing all night now, and I don't even try to run for buses anymore. But I have a sense of personal power, a humble kind of personal power in my relationships with people and with the world. I feel more in control of my life now, and I believe I can make a difference to my family and community in ways that I never could before.

—Ian, 45-year-old freelance writer

W hat will I do in the years ahead, now that the children have all left home? What will I feel when I can no longer conceive? What do I truly want to do before my time runs out? Is this all there is? Could I die young? What do I really hope for the future, both for my children and grandchildren? What can I do to make a real difference to the people and work I care about? How can I give both my elderly mother as well as my children the time and attention they need and deserve? Is there a way out of the trap I feel in carrying on with the same work I've been doing for 25 years? Do relationships just naturally go stale over time? I feel such a strong sense of personal power now—how can I best use that energy in the time ahead?

The previously mentioned questions are some of the complex identity-related concerns raised by a group of midlife adults I interviewed as part of a large retrospective study of identity development from adolescence through middle adulthood. The participants were age 40 to 65 years, and their responses came in relation to queries regarding issues that were most on their minds as they thought about their identities and their relationships in and to the world at the present time. These individuals were again concerned with questions about the future, but not just their own futures, which typified concerns of younger adults. Rather, these midlife men and women were occupied with thoughts about their children and grandchildren, and the kind of world in which these new generations would live. They also expressed an increasing awareness of the finiteness of their lives and what they still wanted to do in the remaining years ahead. Sometimes, the future seemed ominous, as certain responsibilities (particularly for younger children) ended and the way ahead seemed uncertain. Sometimes, the future seemed infinite, with fears of boredom looming large. But sometimes, too, the future seemed exciting with opportunities to exercise a new sense of personal power and freedom to affect the world.

Themes of biology, psychology, and societal response, critical to the identity-formation process described by Erikson (1963), also occurred among the identity-related questions posed by these midlife adults. Although issues directly related to biological changes were not frequently mentioned, change in procreational and sexual capacities were clearly on the minds of some participants. However, of greater interest for most seemed to be a new psychological awareness of their own mortality and how to meaningfully fill whatever time there was that remained for them. In addition, the wish to contribute to the welfare of the general community surfaced in ways not described by previous age groups covered in this volume. And, in turn, community recognition of individual contributions was highly valued by many in the process of midlife self-definition. And so I proceed, now, to the time of middle adulthood to overview some of the key biological, psychological, and social factors that will shape identity during this time. I define middle adulthood again both in terms of chronological age and psychosocial tasks—the time between about 40 and 65 years of age, bounded for many at the beginning by decreasing time spent overseeing children and the assumption of senior roles in the workplace and/or wider community and at the end by diminishing involvement in the paid workforce.

Intersection of Biological, Psychological, and Societal Influences on Identity in Middle Adulthood: An Overview

Middle adulthood has no clear beginnings marked by biological events such as pubertal change, by societal demands such as finding a vocational direction and implementing life values, or by psychological issues such as readjustment to a rapidly changed body or new sense of gender identity. Nor does middle adulthood have a clearly defined end, although retirement from the paid workforce has been a socially determined marker event for many until recently. Thus, entry into and exit from middle adulthood have been described by a number of writers as times of transition, as new insights and awarenesses accompany changing biological abilities as well as family and community expectations (e.g., Kotre & Hall, 1990).

At midlife, however, one currently finds greater diversity of identity-defining roles and values among people than at any other stage of the life span. For example, a midlife adult woman today may experience the role of being not only a mother and grandmother, but also a daughter and granddaughter to living relations. During these same midlife years, one may find a 60-year-old father of a young infant, a 40-year-old-mother embarking for the first time in tertiary education, a 50-year-old retiree, and a 45-year-old great-grandmother (Kotre & Hall, 1990). With wide social acceptance for a variety of lifestyle choices among contemporary midlife adults, Neugarten and Neugarten (1996) claim that we are currently an "age irrelevant" society, without an "age clock" or socially approved guidelines for acceptable ways of behaving. Societal allowance for such diversity among contemporary midlife adults again raises a number of interesting identity issues for consideration.

Key biological, psychological, and societal identity-related issues of midlife are reviewed individually next, but their interaction must be appreciated to more fully understand identity development during midlife. Clearly, noticeable changes in body shape and physical stamina are difficult to ignore in life's middle years. Whereas this slow, ongoing process of biological change might easily be ignored throughout the years of early adulthood, midlife permits few illusions regarding one's youthfulness and energy. Changes appear in the skin tone and physical appearance more generally, along with the cessation of child-bearing capacities among menopausal women, and inevitably evoke changes in one's sense of physical identity (Whitbourne, 2005). In addition, the present generation of those entering midlife are products of the post–World War II baby boom. Numerous special identity issues face this particular generation of individuals, who must compete among vast numbers of counterparts for an ever-dwindling number of senior roles in business and management and find a place in which to complete their years in paid employment (Clair, Karp, & Yoels, 1993). Biological, psychological, and societal forces at midlife raise many psychosocial issues of identity, intimacy, and generativity for resolution by contemporary adults.

Biological Processes

As we have seen in the last chapter, biological systems begin the aging process during the 20s, though the process is slow, and significant declines in functioning are not generally apparent until the later years of young adulthood and midlife. Changes for both genders in physical appearance and in reproductive capacities for women are perhaps the most significant biological processes impacting on identity for many individuals at midlife. Health-related issues also become of increasing concern at midlife for some, precipitating important revisions to one's sense of psychosocial identity. In the overview of some of the common normative changes of aging that follows, it is again important to remember that people age at different rates, and much inter- as well as intra-individual variation in the aging process is common. For example, many, but not all, will experience thinning or graying of the hair during midlife, and many, but not all, physiological systems within any given individual will age at the same rate of change.

Perhaps the most noticeable and common transitions in physical appearance during midlife include changes in the skin, hair color, and facial features (Whitbourne, 2005). Wrinkling and sagging of the skin gradually increase through middle adulthood, as the skin gradually begins to lose its firmness and elasticity. Brown pigmentation may also develop on exposed areas of the skin for fair-skinned people. Middle adulthood brings a greater likelihood that hair will become grayer (eventually turning white) due to loss of pigmentation. It is also likely to become thinner, especially for men, and male pattern baldness is likely to increase. In addition, the structure of the face changes, with a lengthening of the nose and ears and broadening of the jaw; puffiness and/or a deepening of pigmentation around the eyes for some may give the eyes a sunken appearance (Hoyer & Roodin, 2003). For many in their 40s, reading glasses also become necessary as lenses of the eyes thicken and harden, making it more difficult to focus on objects nearby.

Body build, for many, continues to undergo significant change during midlife. In terms of stature, a fairly consistent pattern of decrease in standing height has been found; furthermore, an Italian study found changes occur at a faster rate during the 50s compared with earlier adulthood age spans and are more pronounced among women than men (Pini et al., 2001). Such changes seem to result from loss of bone mineral content in the vertebrae, causing the spine to compress in length. In addition, weight gain through the years of middle adulthood is common, followed by a reduction of weight during later adulthood. This weight gain often observed among midlife adults results from an accumulation of body fats particularly around the waist and hips; middle-aged women are particularly prone to experiencing this accumulation of body fat around the torso. Many factors that will impact on body health and functioning during middle and later adulthood lie within our control; such factors include diet, exercise, personality patterns, and various lifestyle choices.

The functioning of many of the body's systems brings about more marked performance changes during the years of midlife. The heart, for example, may function well under everyday requirements, but use less oxygen, beat more slowly, and pump less oxygen when under stress; changes also result in the lungs' capacity to take in oxygen (Kotre & Hall, 1990). Thus, those at midlife may find themselves more breathless during intense physical exertion than they were when younger. There is also often a decline in muscle strength after age 50, with nearly 50 percent of individuals affected by late adulthood (Roubenoff & Hughes, 2000).

While the relationship between many of the previously mentioned biological changes during midlife and one's sense of ego identity have not been extensively researched, recent work has suggested high body dissatisfaction at least among midlife women in the United States. A study of 54-year-old women participants in the National Survey of Health and Development Study indicated that women were most dissatisfied with their bodies at midlife relative to all earlier life periods; some 80 percent of the sample were dissatisfied with their weight, including 50 percent of all normal weight women (McLaren & Kuh, 2004). Additionally, an increasing sense of control over one's own life course has been demonstrated to have a buffering effect on genetic variance in physical health (Johnson & Krueger, 2004). These studies suggest that biological status at midlife may hold important implications for identity readjustments. The high rates of body dissatisfaction among midlife women warrant further research attention.

Perhaps one of the most well-researched areas of biological change having identity implications at midlife has been that of sexual functioning and reproductive capacity. For men, changes in sexual functioning will take place slowly and gradually over the course of middle and later adulthood, but for women, the change in reproductive capacity will be more dramatic with the cessation of the menstrual cycle at the time of menopause. Kotre and Hall (1990) point out that during their 40s, men may notice little change in their sexual responsiveness. However, during the 50s, there is a change in the basic biological pattern of the way in which the pituitary releases the sex hormones so that a difference in sexual performance becomes noticeable to many men. The concentration of testosterone in the blood remains more constant throughout the day among midlife males, resulting in a slower sexual response rate through nearly all phases of sexual activity. However, most middle-aged men have better control over ejaculation than they did during early adulthood. Furthermore, most men will remain fertile throughout middle adulthood. Although these biological changes may lead to performance anxieties and questioning of sexual capabilities and masculine identity for some men, an active sex life is still possible to enjoy for many years to come.

Among women, Kotre and Hall (1990) report that through the 40s, the ovaries begin missing signals from the pituitary to release an egg. In response, the pituitary sends increased hormonal messages to the ovaries to get to work; in this way, the hormonal balance shifts and the climacteric begins. By around 50 to 55 years of age, the ovaries stop releasing eggs and producing estrogen altogether, resulting in menopause or cessation of the ability to reproduce. Although menopause used to be considered a time of psychological upheaval and distress for many women, current research finds no rise in the rate of depression for women in menopausal years compared with other phases of the life span. Nor does menopause mean serious physical discomfort for most; around 85 percent of women seem only mildly affected by the physical signs of menopause, such as hot flashes, headaches, or feeling tired (Whitbourne, 1996a). Loss of reproductive capacity does not end a woman's capacity to enjoy sexual relations, though some alterations in behavior may need to be made (Whitbourne, 2005). For both genders, an individual's interpretation of his or her changing biology plays a major role in the impact such biological change will have on one's sense of self-esteem and psychosocial identity.

Finally, it must be noted that although many continue to maintain healthy, active lives during middle adulthood, there are definite changes in health status between young and midlife adults. The rates for both chronic conditions and serious physical illness requiring hospitalization begin to increase during middle adulthood. Most common among these conditions are hypertension and heart conditions, chronic sinusitis, diabetes, arthritis, and hearing problems (Lemme, 1995). Some of these conditions may be fatal. Thus, significant identity reassessment may be experienced by those who undergo a marked change in the state of their health.

Psychological Issues

Theorists and researchers have pointed to middle adulthood as an important time of identity reevaluation and transition for many, as they are called on to assume new roles in their relationships both with important others and with the broader community. At the same time, many important internal psychological changes are often taking place, including a change in time perspective, a growing awareness of one's own mortality, and a recalibration of one's dreams in the light of current realities. During middle adulthood, those who are parents are often involved in launching their adolescent children toward greater financial, physical, and psychological independence as well as negotiating new forms of connection with them. Those who have not become parents must face crucial final decisions on this issue before the biological clock brings procreational capacities for women to a close. In this same middle adulthood age span, many will become grandparents and develop new roles in assisting with the upbringing of their grandchildren. At the same time, many at midlife will assume greater responsibility for their own parents. And, it is also during midlife that most will come to experience the death of one or both of their own parents.

In paid employment, midlife adults are often senior members in their working environment or owners or partners of their business firms. They are now called upon to make crucial decisions in the running of their respective organizations. At the same time, a number of women who have had primary responsibility for raising children will return to further their education and/or to establish themselves in varied employment settings. The community, too, will often seek assistance from midlife adults to assume leadership roles in various religious and service organizations. Thus, the years of middle adulthood have been dubbed by a number of writers as the "age of responsibility" (Kotre & Hall, 1990).

Middle adulthood has been characterized by Erikson (1963) as a time when people offset fears of stagnation with expressions of generativity— with leaving some kind of legacy for the generations that will follow. Generativity refers not only to the care and nurturance of one's own children but also of one's own life values, work, and other creative projects, which will eventually outlive the self. Detailed expansions to Erikson's views on generativity and new developments in the study of its relationship to identity at midlife are described in a later section of this chapter. However, at this point, it should be noted that Vaillant (1977) again suggests some modification to the span of Erikson's Generativity Versus Stagnation task. Vaillant proposes that the task of Keeping the Meaning Versus Rigidity best captures energy during the era of middle adulthood between about 45 and 55 years. At this time, attention often focuses on themes of coming to terms with met or unmet life goals and finding some meaning in current life circumstances rather than adopting a rigid orientation to life.

Jung (1969) has described midlife as a time of great transition resulting in an increased sense of individuation and integration. By this time, careers have been secured and established, and children have been raised and launched. Thus, middle adulthood enables individuals to have more time and freedom to explore their own needs and reintegrate important identity elements that may have been left behind as life structures were set up. Jung has also described midlife as a time of increased introspection. There may be a growing desire to express feelings of masculinity that may have been denied by women and feelings of femininity that may have been denied by men during early adulthood. Furthermore, the death of a parent often enables people to experience a greater sense of freedom toward fulfilling their own wishes rather than those of parents. All of these factors contribute to an increased sense of individuation during midlife, according to Jung. The following statement by an individual I interviewed for a research project on identity development during middle adulthood vividly illustrates the impact that the death of a parent may have, once initial feelings of loss subside:

> I'm more certain of myself than I've ever been. I suppose it sounds like a crazy thing, but since the death of my parents about three or four years ago, I feel that for the first time I really am an adult in my own right, and I'm sort of spreading my wings in a way.
>
> —50-year-old female teacher

Is there a midlife identity crisis? Certainly the media suggests that after age 40, life presents itself as a time of stress and difficulties until one reaches the shores of late adulthood. Not only does one hold responsibilities for one's (often teenaged) offspring, but also one is often called upon to take more responsibility for one's aging parents. However, a review of the research literature suggests that only about 10 percent of men in the United States may undergo a midlife identity crisis (Brim, 1992).

More recent literature based on participant reports rather than investigator evaluations, presents a somewhat different picture. A large-scale, semistructured telephone survey investigation by Wethington (2000) suggests that about 25 percent of both men and women experience midlife as a time of stress and confusion. Furthermore, about 20 percent of respondents who reported a midlife identity crisis indicated that awareness of aging and time passing were the source of the crisis. A further 13 percent of both men and women reporting a midlife crisis described the experience as a major life review or time of reevaluation. Thus, the experience of a major midlife identity crisis does not appear to take place for the majority of midlife adults.

Cognitively, little or no decline in speed, reasoning, and short-term memory measures of midlife adults have been found relative to young adults; additionally, vocabulary measures show midlife adults outperforming those at younger ages (Soederberg Miller & Lachman, 2000). And relative to later life adults, those at midlife have scored higher on all these cognitive tasks except vocabulary, where no differences occurred. Expansions beyond Piaget's (1972) formal operational reasoning stage have remained largely unexamined during middle adulthood. However, Labouvie-Vief and Hakim-Larson (1989) describe a new mode of thought that may evolve during middle adulthood, which is characterized by considering more pragmatic and subjective aspects of reality. This mode contrasts with the first mode of thought, a characteristic of youth, which involves thinking about reality in abstract and objective ways. The new mode of middle adulthood thought also brings the capacity for integrating both cognitive and emotional dimensions of one's life experiences as well as increasing flexibility and openness to new experiences. Such reasoning may, in fact, underpin many of the identity-related transformations commonly seen during midlife. However, Labouvie-Vief and Hakim-Larson (1989) note that the emergence of this second mode of midlife thought is profoundly influenced by cultural and historical circumstances; thus, the possibility of any midlife identity transformation will vary greatly across cultural and historical settings.

Societal Influences

Middle adulthood is a relatively recent phenomenon. At the turn of this century in the United States, only about half of all children born in 1900 could expect to live to age 50. Less than 5 percent of individuals born in the United States at that time could expect to live until age 65 (U.S. Bureau of the Census, 2003). However, with better medical knowledge and care available and improved nutrition, the life expectancies of men and women have greatly increased. For those men and women born in 2000, life expectancies are 74.1 and 79.5 years, respectively (U.S. Bureau of the Census, 2003). Thus, many individuals in the United States (as well as other Western nations) are now living to experience middle as well as late adulthood. The emergence of midlife as a distinct phase in the adult life span has resulted from both the increase in longevity as well as the decrease in time spent raising children. These two demographic changes have particular significance for women, who are likely to live longer than men as well have greater involvement in family responsibilities (Moen & Wethington, 1999). And until recently, midlife has been relatively neglected by researchers, as merely a "staging area on the way to old age" (Baruch & Brooks-Gunn, 1984, p. 1).

However, with the baby boom generation has come the demand for new social norms and expectations, social attitudes and behaviors during midlife (Moen & Wethington, 1999), coupled with more research attention. The work of Mary Catherine Bateson (1989, 1994) suggests how the increasing length of life expectancy impacts middle age. She points out that midlife adults are now faced with the task of composing a satisfying life beyond the time of childrearing. Since individuals now can anticipate spending about one-third of their lives beyond age 50, this task must be taken quite seriously. Bateson (1994) uses the analogy of adding a new room to one's existing home. By having such a new addition, traffic patterns throughout the whole house will change to take advantage of this new space. Furthermore, one usually does not go to the effort of creating such a new space just to store old baggage and household effects; one wants to make optimal use of this new extension to one's daily life space. Similarly, one's increased years of life expectancy in later adulthood should have the effect of changing the traffic patterns through the middle adulthood years. In identity terms, one can begin to prepare the financial and psychological bases for extending one's interests and talents and other psychosocial expressions of identity well into the many years of later adulthood.

A further demographic issue holds enormous identity implications for today's midlife adults—the impact of the postwar baby boom. Following World War II, between 1946 and 1964, a baby boom, or great increase in the number births, occurred within the United States (as well as many other nations) as servicemen returned home. Today, about one-third of the total U.S. population belongs to this baby boom generation (U.S. Bureau of the Census, 2003). The sheer size of the baby boom population bulge has meant increased competition among its members for vocational positions and community services; relative wages, rates of employment, and opportunities for upward mobility have all been affected by the large numbers of those born after the war. Furthermore, current baby boomers in the United States are better educated than any previous generation of Americans and are thus more likely to be aware of a vast range of possibilities for the expression of vocational and other identity-defining values. However, for those with certain vocational interests (for example, in managerial roles), there may simply not be sufficient opportunities available to express such identity preferences. In addition, the sheer numbers of postwar baby boomers have driven up demand for housing and many other services. It may thus become more difficult for the present generation of midlife postwar baby boomer adults financially to set up life structures that are most expressive of their identity interests and values. Indeed, a number of writers have suggested that the present generation of midlife adults may be the first generation of individuals who are less well-off financially at the time of their retirement than their parents. Certainly, the home ownership rate of baby boomers is much smaller than that of their parents (Easterlin, Schaeffer, & Macunovich, 1993).

Additional trends among the current generation of midlife adults have helped to transform more traditional "social age clock" to "age irrelevant notions of what are appropriate psychosocial roles for those traversing middle adulthood" (Neugarten & Neugarten, 1996). More baby boomers have remained single, and more of those in partnerships have remained childless, compared with previous generations. Furthermore, those baby boomers that have had children have had a smaller number and have more frequently combined childrearing with employment responsibilities to supplement the family income, compared with previous generations of midlife adults. And a greater number of separations and divorces also characterize the lives of those currently at midlife compared with previous generations (Easterlin et al., 1993).

Section Summary and Implications

Normative biological changes of aging markedly affect physical appearance and endurance at midlife. There are negative changes in health status between young and middle adulthood. These issues may spark significant identity reassessments during middle adulthood for many.

Psychologically, midlife often is a time of increased introspection, a time in which new potential identity elements may be explored and expressed. The death of one's own parents, often experienced by those at midlife, may contribute to a greater sense of one's own autonomy.

Middle adulthood involves significant role changes for many, as parenting demands diminish and the need to care for one's own parents increases. Those at midlife also adopt senior roles in the workplace and community. In addition, midlife adults currently experience greater role flexibility than in previous generations. Living in an "age irrelevant" society may bring identity issues to the fore for many during middle adulthood.

The Course of Identity in Middle Adulthood

These days I'm in kind of a holding period, a hiatus stage, and I know something will come out of it in the end. I know I can't hurry it, so I'm taking things slowly. Healthwise, this is a resting or recuperating period; I know that, so I don't fight it as I would have in the past. I'm taking time away from work now. Out of this I think I will find something that will then be the next stage for a new beginning, perhaps not just in terms of my career but in other things as well.

—55-year-old male former school administrator

This poignant statement reflects the time of identity reevaluation by many at midlife, as they attempt to lay the groundwork for pathways into the future. Whereas Erikson (1963) focused primarily on the ways in which one's identity is expressed through acts of generativity and struggles with stagnation, several major longitudinal and retrospective researches have now examined the course of identity development during the years of young adulthood and midlife in various cultural settings.

Long-term longitudinal studies using various Eriksonian measures of identity have all found continued growth in identity development during both young adulthood and midlife. For example, in the Rochester Study, Whitbourne & van Mannen (1996) followed two cohorts of individuals from ages 20 to 31; one of these cohorts was also followed up again at age 42. Both cohorts showed increases in positive scores of Identity Versus Identity Diffusion (as well as Intimacy Versus Isolation) on Constantinople's (1969) measure of Eriksonian psychosocial stages over the time spans covered. In Finland, Pulkkinen and Kokko (2000) and Fadjukoff, Pulkkinen, and Kokko (2005) used Marcia's (1966, 1967) identity status interview to assess patterns of identity formation among participants in the Jyväsklyä Longitudinal Study of Personality and Social Development through early and middle adulthood. Participants in the Pulkkinen and Kokko (2000) study were followed from ages 27 to 36 years, while those of Fadjukoff and colleagues (2005) were 27 to 36 to 42. Development from diffusion to foreclosure to moratorium to achievement was the most common identity trajectory in all identity domains except political identity, where diffusion predominated. An increase in the salience of identity domains could be attributed to an increase in the commitment process.

Josselson (1996) also examined the evolution of identity status from late adolescence through middle adulthood among a sample of women. Josselson conducted extensive interviews with 10 women in each of Marcia's four identity statuses during their college years. At ages 33 and 42, some 30 of these women were reinterviewed about the courses that their lives had taken during the intervening years. By midlife, many of the initial foreclosures (or guardians of the culture) had broken free from the earlier charted life courses, whereas many of the initial diffusions (drifters) had made commitments, often in quite traditional ways. Relationships remained an important identity element for these women throughout the course of their lives.

Using Mallory's (1989) personality profiles for men and women in each of Marcia's four identity statuses, later researchers have studied identity status movements in longitudinal investigations of personality development over time. All of these studies have indicated considerable identity-status movements over the course of early and middle adulthood and patterns of identity development that are strongly related to social context (e.g., Hart, 1989; Helson, 1992; Stewart & Vanderwater, 1993). Hart (1989), for example, reanalyzed personality data in terms of identity status for women at Mills College when the women were ages 21 and 43 years. Women who had achieved an identity at age 21 showed the greatest likelihood of positive life outcomes at age 43 years. Women who were foreclosed at age 21 lived fairly traditional female lifestyles, with only modest personality growth at age 43. Women classed as moratorium at age 21 entered the labor force earliest, led fairly untraditional lives compared with those of other identity statuses, and were the most discontent at age 43. Only about half of the sample was assigned the same identity status at age 43 that they had been assigned at age 21.

Cramer (2004) has also used Mallory's (1989) measure to examine identity status changes over a period of 24 years of adulthood: from early adulthood (ages 30–37), through middle adulthood (ages 40–47), to late-middle age (ages 54–61). Drawing on 155 participants from the Intergenerational Study, from the Institute of Human Development in Berkeley, Cramer found increases in identity achievement, moratorium, and foreclosure statuses, with a decrease in diffusion from early to middle adulthood; late-middle age also evidenced an increase in the foreclosure identity status. Additionally, Cramer found identity status change to be predicted by use of certain defense mechanisms (similar findings have also emerged during adolescence). In early adulthood, use of the defense mechanism of identification was associated with both achieved and foreclosed identity statuses.

Change in identity status during early and middle adulthood was predicted by both personality characteristics and life experiences from Cramer (2004). Among the many interesting results were the following: An increase in identity achievement during middle adulthood was predicted by intelligence, success in work, family and marital situations, and being involved in community and political activities. Increases in the foreclosure status during middle adulthood were predicted by intelligence, quality of marital relationship, and its duration. At higher levels of intelligence, activity in social lodges also predicted increases in the foreclosure status, as did becoming more conservative in political attitudes. An increase in the moratorium status by middle adulthood was predicted by use of identification and positive family relationships, as well as absence of lodge activity. At higher levels of intelligence, less visiting with relatives, greater community activity, and increased liberal attitudes predicted an increase in the moratorium status by midlife. Taken together, these findings show that the defense of identification is the primary predictor of identity status and identity status change at midlife; the defenses of denial and projection were unrelated to adult identity status change.

Longitudinal work has also assessed identity development during adulthood more indirectly. From Helson and Sanjay's (2001) study of Mills College women, the style of identity obtained at age 43 mediated the influence of a number of personality variables obtained at age 21 to predict mental health at age 60. This study found that young adult personality characteristics exhibit much of their influence on positive mental health patterns by facilitating or inhibiting the formation of different identity structures. Conservers, seekers, achievers, and depleted styles were patterns of identity that were defined in this study, based on measures of personal growth and environmental mastery. (These styles showed marked similarities to Marcia's foreclosure, moratorium, achieved, and diffuse identity statuses, respectively.) Conservers, seekers, and achievers at age 60 moved toward different goals in life that were all associated with positive patterns of mental health.

All of the long-term longitudinal studies cited in this section point to a common finding: that considerable identity development occurs over the course of early and middle adulthood for many.

The Contents of Identity in Middle Adulthood

Kotre and Hall (1990) point to identity issues of middle adulthood in terms of one's shifting time perspective, greater sense of personal power, and the reclaiming of opposite-sex qualities in their discussions of changing personal identity issues at midlife. Erikson (1963) and Vaillant (1977) have all described middle adulthood according to the development and consolidation of generativity drives and the beginnings of the search for an ultimate meaning to one's life and life experiences. Psychosocial cornerstones of identity in midlife once again seem to involve issues of vocation, meaningful personal values, and important relationships with others for most individuals.

> *I suppose I'm in a bit of a rut, really. In the same job 13 years, getting on the same train at the same time every morning, press the elevator button at the same point. How do you think it feels for a man on the verge of retirement to have to have his work still checked by someone else—how's that for job satisfaction? . . . In a nutshell, I'm not totally dissatisfied, but I'm in a rut. I would like to be doing something different, but it's hard.*

> —60-year-old male city administrator

In the area of vocation, a number of individuals at midlife will reevaluate their level of vocational satisfaction, and some will make new commitments to carry them through their remaining middle adulthood years. Those nearing retirement will often be making evaluations of the vocational paths they have chosen and considering different roles in the years that will lie ahead postretirement. Levels of vocational satisfaction have been examined in relation to various personality and demographic variables. By midlife, established workers seem to find greatest satisfaction from such issues as autonomy in the work setting, freedom for creativity, feelings of mastery and personal achievement, and seeing one's work as contributing to some greater whole (Galinsky, 1993). Quality of the work environment, recognition of influence, and opportunities for balancing family with work responsibilities were also of great importance to those expressing work satisfaction at midlife (Galinsky, 1993). All of these issues are related to the expression of personal identity. Where such opportunities are lacking, many will experience job dissatisfaction and remain bored, burned out, unfulfilled, or willing to seek a new line of work.

In addition, many women will be entering or reentering the workforce or continuing education after childcare responsibilities have diminished during this age span. Recent work has examined diverse patterns of vocational identity development for women at midlife. Roberts and Friend (1998) examined some 83 women from the Mills Longitudinal Study in their early 50s at the time of interview to determine whether they reported a subjective sense of increasing, maintaining, or decreasing momentum in their careers. Researchers then divided the women into three groups based on reported career momentum to examine the importance of work to personal identity, personality characteristics, and psychological well-being. Those in the high career momentum group were in higher-status employment and viewed their work as more central to their identities than women in the other two groups. These high career momentum women also scored higher on measures of self-acceptance, independence, effective functioning, and physical health than women in the other two groups. Surprisingly, they also had more children than women of the other groups. Furthermore, from this prospective, longitudinal study, personality and life context patterns differed for the three work momentum groups some 30 years previously (Roberts & Friend, 1998).

High career momentum women were the most confident and independent 30 years before career momentum was evaluated; they were also highest in well-being and effective functioning from age 43, compared with the other two groups. The career-maintaining women began the study at age 21, scoring high on measures of effective functioning and well-being, but then showed large drops on these two scales between ages 21 and 43. This group also felt they were closer to retirement and in the last stages of their careers, compared with other groups. The low career momentum women scored continuously low on self-acceptance and well-being across the 30 years of the study. Results indicate that vocational identity (as gauged by career momentum) seems to result from a combination of one's work situation, personality characteristics, and one's life stage or developmental age.

Retirement from paid employment will bring a number of identity-related adjustments for many. Although the act of leaving paid employment is a single marker event, identity-related decisions regarding retirement have generally occurred over many years preceding this time. In the years before retirement, talking to others about retirement and reading material related to the topic does increase, whether or not one has been satisfied with one's employment (Evans, Ekerdt, & Bossé, 1985). In studies of both male and female retired workers, relationships between self-investment in the roles of worker and spouse and postretirement self-esteem have been explored (Reitzes, Mutran, & Fernandez, 1996b). Interestingly, commitment to the role of worker and having a worker identity before retirement seems to have a positive influence on self-esteem in postretirement years. Furthermore, pre-retirement self-esteem is positively related to postretirement self-esteem. In a further longitudinal study of workers ages 58 to 64, these authors found no change in self-esteem scores for those who continued to work; however, depression scores declined for those who retired during the two-year interval of this investigation (Reitzes, Mutran, & Fernandez, 1996a). Such studies indicate considerable continuity between pre- and postretirement self-esteem.

The study of moral reasoning among midlife adults has been limited. Skoe, Pratt, Matthews, and Curror (1996) found that the way in which people reasoned about moral dilemmas involving situations of caring for another was relatively stable from mid- to late adulthood (see Chapter 4 for a description of Skoe's measure). People scoring higher on the ethic of care interview (ECI) also felt more positively about their physical health and their experience of aging. In addition, Pratt, Diessner, Hunsberger, Pancer, and Savoy (1991) examined how midlife and older adults reason about personal dilemmas. He and his colleagues again found no significant age differences from middle to later adulthood in reasoning about personal dilemmas, once level of education was controlled. However, those who were more sensitive to aging changes were apt to use more complex modes of reasoning about moral dilemmas in later adulthood. Thus, there is some evidence for consistency in the way in which one reasons about moral issues involving care and personal dilemmas across the years of middle adulthood.

Identity and Generativity in Middle Adulthood

Erikson, Erikson, and Kivnick (1986) have described midlife as a time of expressing generative concerns for those who have found optimal resolutions to earlier psychosocial stages. Generativity involves the expression of care, both for the present as well as future generations. Difficulties in attaining generativity can lead to a sense of stagnation, according to Erikson (1963). Stagnation means self-absorption and self-indulgence in this context. Erikson (1982) elaborated elements of stagnation in his later discussions of rejectivity and authoritism. *Rejectivity* involves the exclusion of individuals or groups of people from one's caring attention, and *authoritism* involves the use of power alone for regimenting economic and family life. Erikson suggests that finding some optimal balance favoring generativity over these elements of stagnation during midlife is necessary in order for one's caring attentions to have maximal impact on the generations to come.

Generativity among midlife adults can be expressed in many ways. Kotre (1984) has elaborated on some of Erikson's ideas about generativity by describing four specific arenas in which generativity is often expressed: biological, parental, work, and cultural. Biological generativity refers to conceiving and giving birth to a child, who will in turn contribute to future generations. Parental generativity refers to providing care and guidance for children as they mature and assume greater roles in the community. Work generativity denotes guiding, providing assistance, and/or mentoring younger workers as they acquire the skills and knowledge necessary in one's given line of work. And cultural generativity describes the care that adults give to their cultures, through acts of creation, conservation, material acquisitions, and/or community participation to ensure that the culture itself will survive and flourish. In sum, leaving some kind of legacy for future generations is an important focus for many at midlife (Kotre & Hall, 1990).

A number of recent researchers have attempted to operationalize and further examine aspects of generativity during midlife. One innovative effort based directly on Erikson's proposals has been that of Bradley (1997) and Bradley and Marcia (1998a, 1998b), who have developed a status approach to qualitatively understand different styles of generativity. Whereas most other researchers have conceptualized generativity along a continuum ranging from high to low, Bradley's status approach identifies different styles of generative expression in which both generativity and stagnation are captured in varied ways. Bradley (1997) proposes five styles of generativity, defined on the basis of two variables as they relate to self and others: involvement and inclusivity. *Involvement* is primarily a behavioral indicator of generativity; low involvement suggests little generative action. *Inclusivity* addresses the scope of one's generative concerns; one can show generative actions that are inclusive or exclusive of both the self and of others. On the basis of these two criterion variables, the following generativity statuses have been defined:

- *Generative*—Involvement in both self and others is high, and inclusivity of both self and others is high.
- *Agentic*—Involvement in self is high, while involvement with others is low; inclusivity of others is low, whereas inclusivity of the self is high.
- *Communal*—Involvement with the self is low, whereas involvement with others is high; inclusivity of self is low, while inclusivity of others is high.
- *Conventional*—Involvement with self is high, whereas involvement with others is low; inclusivity of both self and others is low.
- *Stagnant*—Involvement with both self and others is low; inclusivity of both self and others is also low or laissez-faire.

Construct validity for these generativity statuses has been supported by investigations of predicted relationships between these statuses and other measures of generativity as well as confirmation of predicted personality variables associated with each status (Bradley & Marcia, 1998a, 1998b). Further research needs to examine the ways in which resolutions to earlier identity and intimacy tasks impact on the style of generativity one is able to adopt at midlife.

Additional investigations have been conducted into the expression of generativity at midlife. Two of the more extensive research programs include those of McAdams, Ruetzel, and Foley (1986) and Snarey (1993). McAdams and colleagues investigated power and intimacy motives in Thematic Apperception Test (TAT) stories and found that both agency and communal needs were related to the achievement of generativity at midlife. McAdams and de St. Aubin (1992) have also developed a self-report Loyola Generativity Scale, which assesses generative concerns on a high to low continuum.

Snarey (1993) conducted a study of men over four decades to learn more about the role of fathering in the development of mature generativity. He found a successful marriage to be a crucial predictor to the father's socio-emotional involvement with his first-born child; this involvement, in turn, predicted the child's educational and occupational attainments beyond those of the father himself.

More recent work has also pointed to generativity as an important midlife issue. Stewart, Ostrove, and Helson (2001) used three samples of women to examine themes of identity certainty, generativity, confident power, and concern about aging during young and middle adulthood. All themes were more prominent in the decade of the 40s, compared with the 30s, and these themes were rated even more highly in the 50s, compared to the 40s. In a sample of educated women at midlife, Peterson (2002) found that generative women at age 43 reported greater involvement in intergenerational care and less of a subjective sense of burden in caring for aging parents a decade later than less generative women. In a longitudinal study of men spanning 32 years, Westermeyer (2004) has shown an important young adult predictor of midlife generativity to be young adult social relationships; those raised in warm family environments with an absence of troubled parental discipline, coupled with good peer relationships and a strong mentor relationship were likely to be generative adults in midlife. About 56 percent of the men in Westermeyer's study had achieved generativity by age 53.

What is the relationship between identity and generativity? Links between identity and generativity have been examined directly by several investigations. Christiansen and Palkovitz (1998) explored the relationships among fathers and their involvement in childcare, paternal identity, psychosocial identity, intimacy, and generativity to learn which variables best predicted these men's level of generativity. The father's paternal identity was the best predictor of level of generativity. However, psychosocial identity and intimacy also predicted the father's level of generativity. Gillespie and MacDermid (1993) compared groups of both older and younger women on measures of global generativity, role-specific generativity, and ego identity, as well as additional personality variables. Their findings showed role-specific generativity scores (i.e., work generativity, parenting generativity, spouse generativity, civic generativity, religious generativity) to be significantly related to role-specific identity assessments; only occupational identity and work generativity did not show a significant relationship. In addition, identity achievement scores were positive predictors of well-being among these women at midlife. However, the relationship between identity and generativity in young adult and midlife development is an area in need of further research investigation.

Other investigations have examined the relationship between feelings of well-being and generativity at midlife. Engagement in multiple roles during early adulthood has been found to facilitate the development of identity; identity, in turn, has predicted generativity and role quality, which, in turn, have predicted well-being at midlife (Vandewater, Ostrove, & Stewart, 1997). Ryff and colleagues (Ryff & Keyes, 1995) have found dimensions of well-being at midlife strongly related to feelings of autonomy, environmental mastery, personal growth, and purpose in life (all elements of identity), as well as positive relations with others and self-acceptance (elements of generativity). And in a nationwide study of well-being at midlife in the United States, Ryff, Keyes, and Hughes (2004) found that midlife adults from a variety of ethnic backgrounds reported fewer frustrating stressors during which they felt little or no control. Results, in general, indicated that although midlife is a time of increased responsibilities, often involving caring for others, it is also a peak time for feelings of competence and a sense of mastery. Optimal identity development does seem to show a strong positive relationship to generativity and feelings of well-being at midlife.

Contexts Affecting Identity Development During Middle Adulthood

Many contexts affect the lives of midlife adults as they assume greater responsibility for others—as parents of growing children; as children of aging parents; as owners, managers, and/or executives of businesses; as administrators of government and community agencies; and as leaders of various community organizations. Certainly, these varied contexts both affect and are affected by those who function within their parameters. Research is greatly needed into ways in which midlife adult identity both shapes and is shaped by surrounding social contexts and historical circumstances. Rice (1992) looks particularly at how identity issues for adolescents strongly parallel those of their midlife parents and at how the timing of these parallel concerns may only exacerbate a number of identity issues for midlife parents. Somewhat similar situations may be occurring among those in mentoring roles for younger adults within other social contexts as well.

The Family/Social Network

I think I have recently had the feeling that I'm on the downward side of life, which comes as a bit of a surprise because you think of yourself as young and full of opportunity and things like that. It's partly by seeing the children growing up with their whole lives ahead of them. It's hard not to feel a little bit envious at times.

—47-year-old female teacher

Rice (1992) considers the family situation of many midlife adults and how the identity issues of one's own adolescents reverberate with those of their parents. As adolescents adjust to new feelings of sexual identity, midlife parents are also facing issues of readjustment to their sexuality. As menopause brings to a close a woman's childbearing years and physical signs of aging become more apparent for both midlife men and women, concerns may arise regarding their own continued sexual desirability. The youthful physique and athletic prowess of one's own adolescents may precipitate a variety of reactions by midlife parents. Similarly, Rice notes that both midlife parents and their teenagers face decisions regarding future roles. As parents evaluate accomplishments and failures in their vocational hopes and consider possible pathways into the future, adolescents, too, are considering how best they may find expressions of their own identities in future social and vocational roles. And midlife parents alongside their adolescents are undergoing many emotional readjustments, including renegotiating what the roles of parents and adolescents will involve. Desires on the part of teenagers for greater autonomy has been associated with midlife identity reassessment by many parents (Silverberg & Sternberg, 1987); furthermore, intense midlife identity concerns among women seem to be associated with diminished satisfaction with parenting (Koski & Steinberg, 1990).

Many older midlife adults will have both adult children and grandchildren. The impact of one's adult children's accomplishments has been investigated in relation to midlife self-esteem (Ryff, Lee, Essex, & Schmutte, 1994). Ryff and her colleagues hypothesized that midlife parents who think that their children have turned out well would have more positive views about themselves in terms of self-acceptance and would have a greater sense of purpose in life than would parents who believed their children had not done so well. "Turning out well" was defined particularly in terms of educational and occupational achievements as well as personal and social adjustments. Indeed, parental self-esteem was strongly linked to children's personal and social adjustments, whereas only weaker links were found between parental well-being and educational and occupational achievements of adult children. The effects did not differ for mothers or fathers in any of the analyses undertaken. The authors present arguments suggesting that for parents, adult children present a kind of validation of parental efforts and actions; in addition, results suggest some of the complex ways in which parental identity may be influenced by the lives of their adult children.

The departure of children from the family home has also been frequently linked to one's sense of marital satisfaction and relationship identity. It seems that satisfaction with one's marriage generally reaches a low point while the children are in elementary and high school and rises after the children have left home (e.g., Harris, Ellicott, & Holmes, 1986). The following statement clearly reflects one individual's experience of the changing nature of relationships with his spouse and children over his years of middle adulthood.

> *I really value the personal growth of my relationship with my wife. We've got it more together than we've ever had. We've beaten the bad patches. And I also really value our growing relationship with our kids as friends, as distinct from being our children.*

—57-year-old male educational administrator

And becoming a grandparent is a new role that many midlife adults will come to experience. With increased longevity, adults now may spend a number of decades as a grandparent during middle and later adulthood. Reitzes and Mutran (2002) found that in the United States the role of grandparent was regarded as the most important social role in one's life by both men and women; grandparenting was also regarded as more important than the role of worker. From the Reitzes and Mutran's (2004a) investigation of both African American and Caucasian grandmothers and grandfathers, having an identity as a grandparent that was central to one's sense of identity was positively related to amount of social contact with grandchildren for men. Among women, however, frequency of contact with grandchildren was not related to a grandparent identity and grandparent centrality variables. It may be that traditional gender norms require women to embrace the grandparenting role regardless of its role in their own identity development at midlife, while for men involvement with grandchildren is a more voluntary behavior. Self-investment in the role of grandparenting was positively related to role satisfaction.

The World of Work

Recent research attention has been devoted to understanding more about the working environment and its impact on midlife identity for men and women. There have been a number of demographic changes in the workforce over the past 20 years, as baby boomers move toward their retirement years. With increasing trends toward downsizing of many companies, greatly decreased attitudes of loyalty, both on the part of companies toward workers and on the part of workers toward companies, have been reported by many employees compared with their circumstances 10 years earlier (Kleinfield, 1996). This situation has generated a new system of values for many employees that are no longer able to rely on their companies for financial security or provision of a continued work role. For those whose identities have been tied to a job rather than a more general career role, this situation may precipitate a reconstruction of one's worker identity itself.

In addition, the length of the retirement period has been growing, due both to increased life expectancies as well as a trend toward earlier retirement. The median age of retirement in the United States is age 64.6 years for men and 63.4 years for women; furthermore, about a quarter of both men and women in the United States leave the workforce by age 59 years (U.S. Bureau of the Census, 2003). The tendency for many to leave the workforce before age 65 is due in part to early retirement incentives offered by many organizations as well as changing social views toward retirement (Schulz, 1992). At the same time, the 1987 Age Discrimination in Employment Act makes mandatory retirement based on age illegal, assuming workers remain capable of acceptable performance (U.S. Senate Special Committee on Aging, 1991). Coberly (1991) has noted that in 1965 the rate of participation in the labor force for men between the ages of 55 and 64 years was 84.6 percent; by 1990, it had fallen to 67.7 percent. (During the same period, however, rates of employment for women in the same age group rose from 41.1 percent to 45.3 percent.) Thus, socially sanctioned and supported opportunities for older midlife adults to consider various possibilities for continuing to work full time, part time, or not at all in their later years holds important identity implications.

What are some of the identity implications of preparing to exit the work force? Reitzes and Mutran (2004b) have addressed this question through a longitudinal sample of older workers who were followed through their retirements to 24 months postretirement. The researchers were interested to explore any stages in psychological and practical adjustment leading up to retirement as well as the impact of various demographic variables on retirement adjustment. They found that preretirement self-esteem, as well as relationships with friends and pension eligibility, were positively associated with attitudes toward retirement at 6, 12, and 24 months after retirement. Furthermore, planning for one's retirement while working and retiring voluntarily increased one's positive adjustment to retirement in the early phases of postretirement. By contrast, poor health decreased positive attitudes toward retirement two-years postretirement.

The Broader Community

Broader community values again play an important role in identity evaluations and reevaluations by those at midlife as do resolutions to previous Eriksonian stages. In research directly examining the impact of various historical epochs on Eriksonian stage resolutions, Whitbourne, Zuschlag, Elliot, and Waterman (1992) examined three cohorts of men and women who were college students in the United States in 1966, 1977, and 1988, respectively. Two of the cohorts were in their early 40s at the time of the final follow-up. Using Constantinople's (1969) Inventory of Psychosocial Development, which assesses resolutions to all of Erikson's stages, Whitbourne and her colleagues found evidence of increasingly favorable resolutions to early Eriksonian stages up through the oldest age group studied within all cohorts. However, scores for Ego Integrity Versus Despair declined markedly in the first two cohorts through the 1980s and were generally low for the third cohort, who were college students at this time. The authors interpret the rise of materialism in the 1980s (which led to reduced social welfare programs and an emphasis on the acquisition of wealth and possessions rather than a meaningful philosophy of life) to be associated with this pattern of scoring. Broader social values present during a particular historical epoch within a community may be reflected in the quality of later psychosocial stage resolutions.

From the large Midlife in the United States (MIDUS) investigation, Markus, Plaut, and Lachman (2004) found strong links between how one comes to represent and experience feelings of well-being in areas of health, autonomy, self-acceptance, emotion, focus on others, and social responsibility according to geographic, and hence social-cultural regions of the country. For example, New England was noteworthy for the high levels of positive relations with others and social well-being, along with meaningfulness of society reported by midlife participants. The West-South-Central region was noteworthy for its levels of self-satisfaction and self-acceptance well-being. The authors indicate that the presence of strong regional variations in how midlife adults come to represent and experience feelings of well-being suggests again the complex interplay between broader community ethos and individual development during adulthood.

Section Summary and Implications

Parallel identity issues affect both parents and their adolescents; the intensity of midlife identity concerns with physical aging, sexuality, and readjustments to many familiar roles may be heightened.

For those whose sense of identity may have been strongly tied to the work context, recent trends for company mergers and downsizing may precipitate a reconstruction of one's identity. Many employees may also now be generating a new system of work values, no longer advocating loyalty to a particular employer.

Age of retirement is now a much more open-ended matter. Legally, individuals cannot be forced to retire on the basis of age alone. There are also social supports for different work patterns so that older midlife adults may continue to work full-time, part-time, or not at all in their later adult years. These possibilities raise a number of identity issues for employed, midlife adults nearing retirement.

Back to the Beginning

This chapter opened with three questions and a statement from Ian, a 45-year-old freelance writer. Ian describes what his identity at midlife feels like. He finds that life is more limited, for there are unlikely to be wide-open possibilities for change as there were when he was younger. Physically, he notices a decline in his energy level. But at the same time, Ian comes to experience a greater sense of personal power than he has known in earlier decades. This power enables him to feel more in charge of his own destiny and in his relationships with others and the world. Ian's newfound power also finds expression in generative concerns with his family and wider community. Ian's comments suggest optimal identity development at midlife.

Answers to Chapter Questions

⬦ **Is a midlife identity crisis a common experience?**

Midlife brings considerable identity readjustments and transitions in roles for most. A shift in perspective often occurs and life may be viewed in terms of time left to live. However, the experience of a major midlife identity crisis does not appear to occur for the majority of midlife adults from studies conducted in many Western contexts.

⬦ **How do biological changes affect midlife identity?**

The body undergoes significant changes during midlife, including hair becoming grayer and thinner and the accumulation of body fat around the waist and hips. For those who have tied their identities to a sense of youthfulness, biological changes at midlife may bring considerable consternation.

⬦ **Does having adult children alter one's sense of identity at midlife?**

Yes. Parental self-esteem (both mother's and father's) has been strongly linked to the personal and social accomplishments of one's adult children. Adult children who "turn out well" may provide a kind of validation of one's identity as a parent.

If I knew tomorrow that I had only six months to live, what would I do? I would complete writing the history of my tribal origins. I would work to strengthen the economic base of my people. I would have time with my family. I would do a little sailing. And while I was physically capable, I would give as much loving as I possibly could.

—70-year-old male community elder

8

Identity in Late Adulthood

- How does an aging body affect one's sense of identity in later adulthood years?
- Are cognitive declines inevitable in old age?
- How is identity related to one's resolution of Integrity Versus Despair issues in old age?

I feel that the death of my mother in the year I turned 65 really put me up a generation so that I became superannuated, as it were, officially. I was pleased that I felt ready to move out of paid employment. But I'm also very conscious of the feeling of transition now—this sense of a very large challenge looming ahead, and a sense of preparing for that. The older I get, the more I worry about the constraints of aging and the physical problems that might come up.

—Alison, 67-year-old retired community worker

What will I do to structure my time in the years ahead? There's just never been time to think about it before now. What do I still want to do? How can I make these later years the best of my life? If I hadn't retired when I did, I wonder if I would have been happier these days? Will my children be all right? Will I be remembered at all? How will I be remembered? Getting back, once you've lost your footing, is so very, very hard. I don't feel old inside, but the mirror tells me otherwise—how did I get to be so old? Memories are surely one's most precious possessions, aren't they? I've been through it all—3 wars, 2 marriages, 15 grandchildren; I'm doing pretty well, don't you think?

The previous questions and statements reflect identity issues important to some old and very old individuals I spoke with in a community facility for various levels of nonassisted and assisted living. Residents, ranging from 67 to 98 years of age, shared these and other thoughts when asked about the kinds of questions that came to mind when they thought about their identities and their relationships in and to the world at the present time. For those younger old adults, many of whom had recently retired themselves or had spouses who had done so, adjusting to new psychosocial roles occupied their current life energies. A changed vocational status seemed not only to generate new questions about how to structure time but also about how to respond to changed social expectations both within the family and community.

Foremost in the minds of many of the very old adults were concerns for their children and grandchildren and hopes for their futures in a world that they themselves would soon be leaving behind. Leaving some impression in the world and finishing unfinished business, in relationships as well as creative projects, were forces giving very old age important meaning for many interviewees. Adjusting to a changing biology and increasing physical limitations was experienced by all during their older years of later adulthood, while reminiscing, bringing memories of past events into present reality was a stabilizing identity task for many.

These concerns of younger old and very old adults still reflect well the intermingling of biological, psychological, and societal considerations described by Erikson as key elements of ego identity. I turn now to the world of later adulthood and some of these key biological, psychological, and social factors that will interact to shape the course of identity over the final stages of the life span. In viewing the years of later adulthood and the increased years of life experienced by many, I will refer to the younger old adult (66–79 years) and the very old adult (80 years and beyond) age groups, for identity issues are often quite different during these two spans of time.

Intersection of Biological, Psychological, and Societal Influences on Identity in Late Adulthood: An Overview

There is growing consensus among gerontologists that with the increasing longevity of many older adults, the later adulthood years are best considered in at least two separate phases. At present, one might, indeed, find oneself in the time of late adulthood for some 30 to 40 years—longer than any other time of the life span. Although much individual variation remains in both physical and mental ability among both the younger old and the very old, the latter often appear to be coping with newfound identity issues more related to a changed biology than changed psychosocial roles, as was the case with younger old adults.

Again, the interrelationships among biology, psychology, social networks and culture more generally are essential to understanding identity concerns for those in the years of late adulthood. The trend for increasing longevity continues, and the percentage of individuals reaching very old age is greater than in any previous era in the United States (U.S. Bureau of the Census, 2003). Those 65 years and over comprised 12.6 percent of the total population from the 2000 census data. The highest rate of increase in those aged 65 and over is among the oldest old—those aged 85 years and over. Currently those 65 and older comprise at least 15 percent of the total population in many European and Asian countries (U.S. Bureau of the Census, 2003).

At this time of growing numbers of older adults in the general population in many Western nations, however, socially constructed meanings of old age often serve to curb identity expression and potential for many. Stereotypic attitudes toward older adults, the perception that they are feeble-minded at best, senile at worst, may give rise to painful forms of social discrimination having negative identity repercussions for a number of later life individuals. Eisenhandler (1990) has demonstrated the intrinsic value for many older adults of merely holding a valid driver's license, which serves as a social disidentifier of late adulthood and the accompanying stigma of an old age identity. At the same time, the interaction of biological and social factors—of having good physical health, financial security, and supportive family and friendship networks—has been associated with psychological well-being and a satisfying sense of identity during late adulthood years across four continents (Fry et al., 1997).

Biological Processes

By late adulthood, virtually no one can remain oblivious to the physical signs of aging and the identity-related readjustments that such changes demand. As Erikson and colleagues (1986) have noted,

> As the overall tonus of the body begins to sag and innumerable inner parts call attention to themselves through their malfunction, the aging body is forced into a new sense of invalidness. . . . The elder is obliged to turn attention from more interesting aspects of life to the demanding requirements of the body. (p. 309)

Whereas some of these biological changes may be merely annoying, others may be painful, difficult, and sometimes even shame inducing.

Although Erikson has presented a somewhat sobering view regarding the psychological impact of the aging process, it is important to note that in the United States, a substantial proportion of adults over the age of 80 years do function reasonably effectively. Indeed, the majority continue to live in the community, and of these individuals, more than one-third report that their health is good or excellent (Suzman, Harris, Hadley, Kovar, & Weindruch, 1992). Nevertheless, the rates of disease do increase dramatically for those over age 65 years, and the majority of those over age 80 do have some type of physical impairment.

In turning to the course of biological changes in late adulthood, it is important to distinguish normal physical changes of aging from physical changes caused by disease. Reviewed in the following paragraph are some of the normative biological changes of aging holding potential identity implications; discussion of severe illnesses and their threats to identity and physical integrity will be presented in the next chapter.

Changes in body build and composition continue during the years of late adulthood, although much individual variation exists in the rate of such changes. Some bodily systems also decline more rapidly than others. Longitudinal studies have demonstrated a continuing decrease in standing height during late adulthood and some loss of bone tissue in the skeleton (Whitbourne, 1996a). Where loss of bone tissue is severe, osteoporosis (the extensive loss of bone tissue) results and causes individuals to walk with a marked stoop and become particularly vulnerable to bone fractures. In the United States, osteoporosis affects some two-thirds of all women over the age of 60. During late adulthood, weight loss is a frequent experience due to loss of lean body mass in muscle and bone tissue rather than fat reduction in the torso. Thus, very old adults may have very slender arms and legs while retaining fat deposits acquired during middle age in the torso (Whitbourne, 1996a).

Aging changes to the skin can result in dramatic alterations to one's appearance. Common during late adulthood are the continuing development of wrinkles, furrows, sagging skin, and loss of resiliency of the skin. The face, always exposed to the elements, may particularly suffer the harmful consequences of sun exposure. The skin loses its firmness and elasticity, leading to areas of sagging such as the double chin (Whitbourne, 2005). In addition, the nose and ears lengthen and broaden, and there is frequently a reduction in the amount of bone in the jaw (Whitbourne, 1996a). Thinning and graying of the hair continue, although there are great individual differences in the degree of hair grayness, largely due to genetic factors.

Declines in the acuity of all five senses are experienced over the life span, with vision and auditory loss often reported to be the most problematic ones by late life adults. Reduced vision may severely restrict an individual's independence as well as pleasure in a number of activities (Rubert, Eisdorfer, & Loewenstein, 1996). About 92 percent of older adults wear glasses to help them cope with problems of decreased lens accommodation, acuity, and depth perception. Hearing loss is experienced by about 50 percent of individuals over 75 years of age. Such loss may greatly impair an older adult's sense of safety and pleasure as well as increase one's sense of social isolation (Rubert et al., 1996).

Motor ability and cardiovascular and respiratory systems also commonly undergo marked changes during the years of late adulthood. There is generally a gradual reduction of speed of walking from midlife (Whitbourne, 2005). Reduction of bone strength as well as strength and flexibility of joints, muscles, ligaments, and tendons may also place an individual in considerable pain; the muscle aches and stiffness of arthritis are frequently ascribed to getting old (Leventhal, 1996). The cardiovascular and respiratory systems also undergo changes that decrease one's capacity for exercise tolerance (Leventhal, 1996).

Reproductive capacities for women have ended in middle adulthood at menopause, when women stop ovulating and the menstrual cycle ceases. After this time, estrogen levels decline, and women become more vulnerable to strokes, coronary artery disease, and osteoporosis. Men do not experience the abrupt change in fertility that women do. In fact, they will be able to produce mature sperm throughout most of their lives, with declines coming only in their seventh and eighth decades (Leventhal, 1996). Indeed, an older person's sense of self-worth and the partner's health status were the best predictors of sexual activity among older adults (Marsiglio & Donnelly, 1991).

Psychological Issues

The majority of younger old adults (66–79 years) in many contemporary Western nations are now enjoying many years of relatively good health, burdened by only minor physical impairments. No longer viewed as responsible for the "maintenance of the world," many of these individuals will find new roles as providers of experience and wisdom in family, friendship, and community networks without the level of responsibility that came during the years of middle adulthood (Erikson, Erikson, & Kivnick, 1986). The role of grandparent is one that many younger old adults report enjoying, as well as coming into a new relationship with their own children. The loss, for many, of paid employment gives rise to a new search for vocational satisfaction. Some individuals will find ways to reintegrate previous identity elements that may have been long neglected, where as others may find this task too daunting and retain a sense of unfulfilled potential throughout their remaining years of adulthood (Erikson et al., 1986).

Among very old adults (aged 80 and above), physical decline is generally much more evident and progresses much more rapidly than for those in the younger years of late adulthood (Suzman et al., 1992). As a result, many of the very old must rely on assistance from family members and institutions, and their sense of a previously defined autonomous identity may be required to undergo significant revision. In the United States, financial concerns are likely to increase for those who have outlived their planned retirement incomes, and fear of financial dependency may also threaten their sense of autonomous functioning and competent identity. And certainly the losses of friends, associates, loved ones, and even important contexts (for example, one's family home or community of residence) through death or relocation bring continual readjustments. Such changes cannot help but challenge that sense of continuity that is so vital to optimal identity functioning.

Erikson (1963) has described the psychosocial task of Integrity Versus Despair as the final challenge to be resolved during these last decades of life. He choose integrity and despair to represent opposite poles producing a key tension in the psyche—the tension felt as older individuals struggle for a sense of wholeness and purpose despite deteriorating physical capacities. Important in this task is one's ability to remember early life events and internal states and to reweave what may have been more disparate identity elements back into some form of coherent whole. Erikson chose *wisdom* to symbolize the key strength that emerges from an optimal resolution to the older individual's struggle for integrity and integration.

The importance of the life review in optimal identity integration has been the subject of much empirical study during the later years of adulthood. The task of Integrity Versus Despair requires considerable time in review of one's life and is the grounding for Kierkegaard's well-known observation that although life must be lived forward, it can only be understood by looking back. Robert Butler (1968) initially proposed that a life review is crucial in old age for optimal psychological functioning, and his proposal has spawned several decades of research efforts into this phenomenon. Some of the findings from these studies are reviewed in a later section of this chapter. Cognitive functioning is critical to the psychological process involved in the life review and in finding some resolution to the tension between ego integrity and ultimate despair.

There has been much debate about the issue of cognitive decline during the years of late adulthood. Earlier studies showing cognitive declines in inductive reasoning during late adulthood were commonly based on cross-sectional data, but more recent longitudinal work has found only slight declines beginning in the early part of late adulthood (Schaie, 1994). However, enormous variation in cognitive functioning among the very old has also been observed (e.g., Bäckman, Wahlin, Small, Herlitz, Winblad, & Fratiglioni, 2004). From the Heidelberg Centenarian Study (Kliegel, Moor, & Rott, 2004), about half of centenarians (people 100 years of age and older) showed moderate to severe cognitive impairment, but about one-fourth of the same sample suffered little, if any, cognitive impairment. Furthermore, the strong performance of this latter group of individuals was rather stable over one and a half years. Thus, enormous variation in cognitive functioning among the very old has been found, and significant numbers of individuals may reach very old age with few signs of cognitive impairments.

Researchers have often found it necessary to examine specific types of cognitive capacities, and the ability for older adults to recall information on long-term memory tasks has shown significant declines (Rybash, Roodin, & Hoyer, 1995). This difficulty may, indeed, present some obstacles to the life review process. Also difficult for many late life adults have been declines in free recall; however, the ability to use cognitive supports such as retrieval cues and increased time for task completion have facilitated these memory skills among those in the Swedish Kungsholmen study of cognitive abilities in old age (Bäckman et al., 2004). Other studies conducted with late-life adults have confirmed the slowing of cognitive processing speed, a major mediator of working memory (Baudouin, Vanneste, & Isingrini, 2004). Many individual factors such as education level, social supports, activity levels, and genetic and health-related factors contribute to the variation in cognitive performance in late adulthood, but recent studies have portrayed a somewhat more optimistic picture of cognitive abilities among late-life adults.

Results from the Berlin Aging Study, however, have shown that old age holds more promise than is generally expected (Baltes & Kunzmann, 2004; Baltes & Staudinger, 1993; Lindenberger & Baltes, 1997). Paul Baltes and his colleagues have been asking questions such as "How can one measure wisdom-related knowledge and skills?" and "Which groups of people are likely to show high levels of wisdom-related knowledge and skills?" in studies of the gains and losses of the aging mind. When one looks at more biologically controlled issues of cognitive mechanics (visual and sensory memory, processes of discrimination, categorization, and coordination), aging does indeed seem to take its toll. However, when one examines intellectual problems in which culture-based knowledge and skills are in the foreground, the situation is much different. Certain groups of older individuals perform far better than younger adults with respect to reading and writing skills, language comprehension, and even strategies to manage life's highs and lows—in short, in the skill of wisdom, conceived as expert knowledge. Chronological age alone is not a sufficient condition for wisdom. But age, in conjunction with lack of disease affecting cognitive functioning, openness to new experiences, good mentoring of younger adults, extensive training in certain life contexts, and broad experiences with the human condition are all elements that contribute strongly to the superior performance of older adults on tasks requiring wisdom. Research on wisdom continues in the Berlin Aging Study, and early indicators suggest that many in their last season of life obtain wisdom-related knowledge.

Societal Influences

Americans are growing older and doing so at an accelerating rate. A child born in 1900 could expect to live to about 47.3 years; a child born in 1960 could expect to live to 69.6 years (U.S. Bureau of the Census, 2003). Current total life expectancy statistics in the United States indicate that men and women who were born in 1970 could expect to live to ages 67.1 and 74.7 years, respectively; for those men and women born in 2000, life expectancies are 74.1 and 79.5 years, respectively (U.S. Bureau of the Census, 2003). For those who are 50 in 2000, the average life expectancy was 77.9 years for men, and 81.8 years for women. The rate of acceleration for those entering late adulthood slowed during the 1990s and will do so in the first decade of the new century due to low fertility rates during the Depression. However, the number of those older than 65 years will more than double when the baby boomers enter late adulthood. From population estimates, in the year 2030 there will be as many individuals older than 65 as younger than 18 (about 20 percent of the U.S. population in each age group; U.S. Bureau of the Census, 2003).

This increase in longevity and its accelerating rate will hold enormous implications for social service requirements of older adults in the years ahead. A society must allocate its social resources according to the age structure of its citizens. Such resources come through the tax base provided by industries and individuals employed in public and private sectors. Birth rates and fertility rates have been declining since 1965 at the same time that longevity has been increasing. This situation means that fewer working individuals will be available to support those in late adulthood years, and competition for social services among the elderly will be great. In identity terms, anxiety must exist among those midlife and younger old adults anticipating an increased life expectancy with fewer available community supports and services in the years ahead.

Recent investigations in the United States have also begun to consider how social policy differentially impacts identity issues in all age groups.

Public policy frequently dictates roles, relationships, and access to opportunity. With reference to late life adults, public policies such as Social Security or Medicaid access deeply impact not only the quality of life possible through economic supports, but also the nature of the relationship of late life adults to other members of their families (Hendricks, 2004). Further research into the ways in which entitlements and public policies influence key aspects of one's sense of self and one's worldview are badly needed. Many European countries have public policies and provisions offering strong economic and health supports to those in their years of late adulthood. Comparative research across nations offering varying types of support systems available to older adults is an important area for future research focus in understanding links between identity and context in later life.

The fact that larger percentages of individuals are now living into very old age means that few role models exist for current cohorts of very old adults of how one can cope successfully with the demands of very old age. In their extensive interviews with late life adults, Erikson and colleagues (1986) noted how frequently study participants discussed the important role model for aging that an older relative or friend had provided. However, the study's subjects, aged 75 to 95 years at the time of the last interview, had now outlived many of their previous guides and were having to face problems of physical disability, illness, or just general physical limitations that many of their predecessors had never lived long enough to experience. Finding ways to cope with diminishing capacities without role models has proved a great challenge to those living into very old age today.

Late adulthood women may also expect to outlive their male contemporaries. In 1990, men slightly outnumbered women in all age groups under 35 years, but women greatly outnumbered men by age 65 and above at a ratio of 3:2 (Longino & Mittelmark, 1996). This trend continues today (U.S. Bureau of the Census, 2003). Thus, married women or those in long-term stable relationships may expect to outlive their partners. Adjusting to a single lifestyle in late adulthood is likely to pose difficult identity adjustments, particularly for those coping with the new psychosocial roles of retiree or pensioner in addition to dealing with loss and increased physical limitations.

Social attitudes toward those in late adulthood differ greatly across cultures, and such social attitudes carry important identity implications regarding one's value as a later life adult. In some societies, it is only in later life that positions of full power and authority are attained (Achenbaum, 1993). Such societies are called *gerontocracies,* and in agricultural gerontocracies, for example, control of property most frequently occurs through inheritance. Thus the elders of a village become more powerful in community affairs than junior residents through their ownership of property. In the United States, however, the elderly are often unjustly stereotyped as nonproductive at best or incompetent at worst. *Ageism* is a term coined to describe the unjust stereotyping or prejudiced behavior of a society toward its older members. Negative labels such as "feeble," "old buzzard," and "old crow" are frequently applied to older men and women, communicating their lack of value. Such negative, repeated messages communicated to many older adults cannot help but erode their sense of identity and self-esteem during the late adulthood years.

Indeed, Tougas, Lagacé, Sablonnière, and Kocum (2004) in Canada have found that negative views regarding older workers in the workforce have increased. These researchers investigated how negative attitudes (ageism) that 149 older workers had experienced in the workplace impacted their senses of self-esteem and life satisfaction during retirement. Results from their study showed that end-of-career experiences had a strong impact on the identities of new retirees. Feelings of personal discrimination were damaging to one's personal sense of identity. However, internalizing the negative feelings of one's work group did not impact self-esteem directly; it was when one internalized the negative feelings of one's coworkers and also felt a sense of deprivation in comparing one's own circumstances with younger workers that the self-esteem of older workers was negatively affected. Furthermore, one's self-esteem upon leaving the workforce was strongly correlated with one's sense of self-esteem in retirement. Comments offered by participants at the end of the study conveyed a sense of struggle in finding their place in society.

Erikson (1997) noted that our culture lacks a viable ideal of old age and thus, the whole of life. As a result, our society does not know how to integrate its elders into its vital functioning. And so, adults in later life are often overlooked and regarded negatively rather than as bearers of wisdom, according to Erikson.

Section Summary and Implications

Rates of disease do increase for those over age 65, and the majority of those over age 80 do have some type of physical impairment.

Among younger old adults (66–79 years), the majority will experience relatively good health and find new roles as providers of experience and wisdom in family and community roles without the level of responsibility held by those in their middle adult years.

Americans are growing older and at an accelerating rate. Living into very old age (80 years and older) now means that many will have few if any role models for how to cope with the identity adjustments and other demands of aging.

The Course of Identity in Late Adulthood

I know who I've been, but who am I now?

—70-year-old female retired teacher

By contrast to the volume of research on identity development during adolescence and young and middle adulthood, far less work has been undertaken on the process of identity development during the late adulthood years. Within an Eriksonian framework, Vaillant (2002) has reinterviewed participants from three major longitudinal studies conducted in the United States. Participants were primarily in their eighth and ninth decades of life at the time of follow-up. Among the many surprising findings from this large body of interviews was the fact that individual lifestyle choices played a far greater role than genetics, wealth, and ethnicity in predicting life satisfaction during very old age. Furthermore, objective good health was less important to life satisfaction among the very old than was subjective good health; in other words, how one felt about one's health was more important to life satisfaction than what objective evidence from medical reports indicated. More important than one's level of retirement income to life satisfaction (and one's subsequent feelings of integrity) were learning to play and create as well as gaining and maintaining friendships with younger adults as older friends were lost. Alcohol abuse consistently predicted unsuccessful aging, in large measure because it destroyed real and potential social supports.

Indeed Vaillant's (2002) findings for graceful aging reflect many of the concepts Erikson used to define ego integrity. Vaillant found that graceful aging involves the ability to remain open to new ideas, care about others, and accept the past and take sustenance from past accomplishments. Additionally, successful aging involved the ability to enjoy life and retain a sense of humor, to cheerfully accept the indignities of old age, to be graceful about dependency issues, to take care of the self, to cultivate relationships with both old and new friends, and to maintain positive resolutions to earlier Eriksonian psychosocial tasks.

Recently, I have undertaken a small, exploratory study to identify several identity revision as well as maintenance processes for both the younger old and the very old during late adulthood (Kroger, 2002). Among the younger old (defined in this study as age 65–75 years), important identity revision processes included reintegrating important identity elements from younger years before time ran out, rebalancing relationships and other roles, and re-adjusting to loss and diminished physical capacities. Among the older old, narrowing boundaries of physical and social worlds, finding life meanings, and readjusting following physical or social loss were often important identity processes. Important identity maintenance processes among the younger old included establishing visible forms of identity continuity, "tying up the package" (producing a single creative product that brings together important themes and events of their entire life cycles), and retaining important identity elements through loss. Among the older old, identity-maintenance processes included living in the present, maintaining visible forms of continuity (via important possessions), retaining important identity elements through loss, and maintaining a predictable, daily life structure.

Whitbourne (2005) suggests that both past and present life experiences are linked to one's identity through processes of *assimilation* and *accommodation* (concepts she draws from Piaget but links to Erikson's psychosocial identity construct). She defines adult identity as one's representations of oneself with regard to physical appearance and functioning, cognitive capacities, personality features, relationships with others, and in undertaking various social roles. Identity assimilation refers to the interpretation of life events relevant to one's current sense of identity—those cognitive and affective schemata that are presently held about the self. The forms that identity assimilation can take all involve, to some extent, distortion of facts that are inconsistent with one's current sense of identity. Identity accommodation, on the other hand, refers to some change in those cognitive and affective schemata so that one's sense of identity actually changes. A realistic appraisal of one's identity and life experiences is involved in the process of identity accommodation. The individual seeks a kind of identity homeostasis, in which experiences and identity are consistent or in balance. However, adjustments become necessary when one's identity does not match an experience. Hence identity assimilation and accommodation processes come into play.

Both identity assimilation and accommodation can take a variety of forms. Forms of identity assimilation give the individual positive information about the self, even if this information is inaccurate. Identity assimilation often involves twisting (distorting) one's perceptions of experiences so as not to have to change one's views of the self. Self-justification, identity projection (seeing one's own unacceptable feelings in others), defensive rigidity, and lack of insight are all forms of identity assimilation that protect positive self-attributions. For example, by using self-justification, an elderly person may refuse to acknowledge physical limitations and undertake highly stressful physical activity. From studies of aging and well-being reported by Whitbourne (2002), it seems that self-justification may be a common assimilation process for those who live into their late adulthood years.

The process of identity accommodation involves trying to arrive at a realistic appraisal of the self in relation to experiences; this process may ultimately result in changes to one's sense of identity. Identity accommodation often involves acknowledging areas of personal weakness and responding to them. Changes in identity commitments, self-doubts, looking at alternatives, and being responsive to external influences are all mechanisms of identity accommodation. For example, those who are highly susceptible to external influence are most affected by aging stereotypes of society. Whitbourne's model may assist in analyzing the ways in which the younger old and the very old adapt to new circumstances and life experiences.

The Contents of Identity in Late Adulthood

I actually think I value my sense of self more importantly than my family or relationships or health or wealth or wisdom. I do see myself as being on my own, ultimately, you know, and that means you have to be comfortable with that person. Statistics certainly show that older women are likely to end up being alone, so I really do value my own self when it comes right down to things in the end.

—69-year-old female retiree

Erikson (1997) has identified a number of identity components that require a readjustment in psychosocial roles during the younger and older years of late adulthood. These identity adjustments include developing a new lifestyle following retirement, continuing to evolve a meaningful set of ideological values, assuming new roles within the family and other social networks, adjusting to many forms of loss, and coming to terms with one's own death. Certainly, one great adjustment that many will make during their younger years of late adulthood is establishing new interests following retirement.

Current patterns of employment indicate that alongside the trend toward earlier retirement has also come the trend for increasing numbers of younger old adults to retain some level of part-time employment. In addition, there are some distinctive patterns of employment (e.g., alternating periods of unemployment and employment that may characterize some specific populations; U.S. Bureau of the Census, 2003). Certainly, changes in federal law (e.g., the Age Discrimination in Employment Act) enable older individuals to continue working beyond age 65 where age has no impact on job performance; indeed, older workers, considered as a percentage of the total workforce, have been steadily increasing since 1980 and currently constitute about 3 percent of the labor force (U.S. Bureau of the Census, 2003). Mandatory retirement has been banned for all but a few professions where safety or work performance is an issue, and firing older workers with seniority in cost-cutting efforts on the part of an employer is prohibited now in the United States. The meaning of work for both older men and women has been strongly linked to social contact, personal satisfaction, financial needs, and the need for generativity; some ethnic differences have been found, however, in areas regarded as most important to one's identity (Mor-Barak, 1995). Among those who do fully retire, a considerable realignment of role relationships is involved, as an important piece of one's identity is altered.

> *This is a very traumatic time for me in retirement. When I finished school, I went to sea and drifted for awhile. But then I joined the fire department and that was a 24-hour-a-day job. The job mattered a lot to me—I really committed myself to it. In fact, it was the job that was more important than money. Then all of a sudden that's gone. People keep telling you that you're retired and keep saying "Now you can enjoy your new life." But as far as I'm concerned, you're on the last train. Your career is finished, your kids are brought up, and you're in the doldrums. You just don't know what you're going to do.*
>
> —66-year-old retired male fire department administrator

Identity-crisis and identity-continuity orientations to retirement have been proposed in the gerontology literature as a means of understanding the impact of retirement on one's sense of ego identity. There are, however, many factors that may influence both one's adjustment to retirement as well as one's sense of identity in the period of time following this change. Issues such as the reasons for retirement, the conditions of one's health, personality factors, and one's financial circumstances upon leaving the workforce will all impact one's sense of self following this transition. Indeed, those who believe they will undertake this transition smoothly (holding a high degree of retirement self-efficacy) actually experience lower levels of anxiety following the transition than those with lower levels of retirement self-efficacy (Carter & Cook, 1995).

One of the most extensive studies of the retirement experiences of men and women is the Cornell Retirement and Well-Being Study (Quick & Moen, 1998). This study was based on the retirement experiences of men and women aged 50 to 72 years. Women's work lives were less continuous than those of men in this study. Generally, the longer that men worked, the lower their retirement satisfaction. However, the higher the level of advanced planning for retirement among men, the higher was their life satisfaction following retirement. By contrast, among women, higher retirement satisfaction was found among those with more continuous work histories. These gender differences were found even when factors such as income, one's health status, reason for retiring, and type of employment were controlled.

The single largest impact of retirement is generally a reduction of income, which may bring about additional role readjustments. Furthermore, the best predictor of life satisfaction and self-esteem after retirement is life satisfaction and self-esteem before leaving the workforce (Reitzes, Mutran, & Fernandez, 1996b). Such results suggest continuity, in identity terms, and that our life satisfaction may be less a function of ties to specific roles than it is to the attitudes and values we bring to various life circumstances.

The development of moral reasoning during the late years of adulthood has been a further identity domain receiving some research attention. Michael Pratt and his colleagues (Hunter & Pratt, 1988; Pratt, Diessner, Pratt, Hunsberger, & Pancer, 1996) have been extending Kohlberg's (1984) stage approach to moral reasoning to study the years of late adulthood.

Pratt and colleagues' (1996) longitudinal work involving older (64–80 years) and middle-aged (35–54 years) adults has examined relationships between the development of moral reasoning, integrative complexity of social reasoning, and perspective-taking levels over a four-year time period. Older adults, but not the middle-aged, showed significant declines in their levels of moral reasoning about issues of justice. Older adults also showed lower complexity of social reasoning scores than the middle-aged group. Furthermore, a lower reported level of social support was a predictor of decline in all three areas of reasoning for these older adults; greater opportunities for social interaction might be expected to stimulate older adults into thinking about moral and social issues in more sophisticated ways. Hunter and Pratt (1988) suggest that whereas older adults appear to be no longer evolving toward a higher stage of moral reasoning regarding issues of justice, they may, however, be better than younger adults at articulating the highest stage of moral reasoning that they are capable of understanding.

Relationships mark a further important element of one's sense of identity and well-being as an older adult. How do important relationships contribute to the process of self-definition among late life individuals? Numerous studies of actual and perceived social support have been conducted with older adults in relation to such factors as continuity in the sense of self (e.g., Troll & Skaff, 1997), life history perceptions (e.g., Rennemark & Hagberg, 1997), physical functioning (e.g., McIntosh, Kaplan, Kubena, & Landman, 1993), quality of life (e.g., Newsom & Schulz, 1996), and feelings of well-being (e.g., Gupta & Korte, 1994). Having at least one confidante as well as a peer group is positively related to one's sense of well-being and a stable sense of self in late adulthood; having a confidante alone has not been associated with the highest levels of well-being (Gupta & Korte, 1994).

The value of diverse relationships, each having a specialized provision, appears to be important to subjective experiences of well-being and one's sense of identity in old age. Different relationships fill different needs, particularly for those in late adulthood. Some of these relationships will be primarily for practical assistance; others may be for providing a sense of continuity via shared past experiences; others may fill specific emotional needs and provide intimacy, whereas still others will provide companionship in shared activities. Relationships with younger generations may exist to provide outlets for generativity, whereas relations with those of even older cohorts may provide models for aging or give new insights and experiences for the aging individual. The absence of any of these types of relationships may affect the subjective well-being and sense of self in later life (Gupta & Korte, 1994).

Identity and Integrity in Late Adulthood

> *I've seen many things in my life, both joyous and tragic, and I've been stretched in directions that I never would have imagined possible when I started out in my 20s. But what I think I value most in life now is a sense of integrity. "To thine own self, be true."*

> —80-year-old retired female teacher

Integrity Versus Despair is Erikson's eighth and final psychosocial stage in the human life cycle. Erikson (1997) has detailed some of the issues involved in this task by pointing to the struggle for finding a sense of integration in one's identity through the various situations and events that have helped to shape one's life. This integration occurs through such means as reviewing one's life to find threads of continuity and discontinuity and attempting to reintegrate or reconcile those elements that may have long been denied or abandoned. It also involves finding some kind of existential meaning in one's life cycle and coming to terms with the many changes and losses that any life is likely to encounter. Integrity's ultimate demand is facing death, ideally with some level of acceptance, peace, and sense of completion. In addition, Joan Erikson has recently described a ninth life cycle stage, to mark an extension of Integrity Versus Despair issues into very old age. In very old age, issues of despair arise in full force, as independence, control, and self-esteem are threatened by the physical declines of this ninth stage. However, as in all preceding stages, conflict is the source of growth, challenge, and potency even for the very old.

*As we passed through the years of generativity, it had never felt
as though the end of the road were here and now. We had still
taken years ahead for granted. At 90 the vistas changed; the
view ahead became limited and unclear. Death's door, which
we always knew was expectable but had taken in stride, now
seemed just down the block.*

—Joan Erikson, cited in Erikson, 1997, p. 4

It is only in recent years that social science researchers have begun to
explore and refine some of the constructs elucidated by Erikson in the final
stage of Integrity Versus Despair. Indeed, this stage is perhaps the least
researched of all stages in Erikson's life cycle scheme. Researches have now
attempted to test Erikson's assumptions about Integrity Versus Despair as a
primary focus of late adulthood. Sheldon and Kasser (2001) indeed found that
among their cross-sectional sample of Midwestern participants (ranging from
a university age group to late life adults) that generativity and integrity strivings did increase with age, while identity strivings generally decreased; however, only the integrity strivings evidenced a pronounced positive skew across
the four age groups studied. Thus strivings for integrity as well as psychosocial maturity occurred with increasing frequency across the adult life span;
however, strivings for intimacy remained equally salient across this time span.

Among other phenomena that have been attracting research attention are
ways of assessing Integrity Versus Despair, existential concerns in the stage
of Integrity Versus Despair, the role and function of the life review, the phenomenon of wisdom, issues of identity continuity and discontinuity in very
old age, general life satisfaction and well-being, dealing with losses and physical decline, and coming to terms with death. Examples of some of the directions research has taken in these areas are presented in the next paragraph,
although a more thorough discussion of identity readjustments following
serious illness and in the face of death will be addressed as special topics in
Chapter 9.

Several measures of Integrity Versus Despair have been developed. These
include the Inventory of Psychosocial Balance (which assesses degree of
resolution to all of Erikson's psychosocial stages; Domino & Affonso,
1990), the Integrity subscale of the Modified Eriksonian Psychosocial
Inventory (Darling-Fisher & Leidy, 1988), the Ego Integrity Status Interview
(Walaskay, Whitbourne, & Nehrke, 1983–84), and the Self Examination
Interview (Hearn, Glenham, Strayer, Koopman, & Marcia, 2006). The latter
two instruments adopt a status approach, again reconceptualizing Erikson's
bipolar task as one involving alternative styles of resolution.

One promising instrument developed by Hearn and colleagues (2006) has operationalized two dimensions of ego integrity inferred from Erikson's writings: *Perspective* (detachment, or the capacity to put aside personal views and self-interest in the service of a broader outlook) and *Connectedness* (vital involvement, deep and meaningful engagement with family, friends, and community). On the basis of these two dimensions, four integrity statuses have been postulated:

- *Integrated*—People who are knowledgeably committed to actions, values, and ideals, with a sense of continuity in their lives, present, past and future; they are deeply connected with significant others.
- *Nonexploratory*—People who are partially integrated, committed to a narrow scope of activities but not particularly knowledgeable regarding alternatives; there is little self-examination or deviation from the values by which they were raised, though they are generally content.
- *Pseudointegrated*—People who are also partially integrated but lack a depth of commitment to actions, ideals, and values as well as to others; there is an underlying sense of discontent with a life lived according to platitudes rather than according to genuine, deeply felt personal beliefs and values.
- *Despairing*—People who are not committed to current viable courses of action, ideals, or values and have little life satisfaction; they convey a sense of bitterness or regret about opportunities lost with little affirmation of their own or others' lives.

Initial steps have been undertaken to assess reliability of interview ratings and to validate these integrity statuses with measures of openness to experience, competence, geriatric depression, and the Integrity scale from the Modified Eriksonian Psychosocial Inventory.

Integrated people were found to be competent, open, likable, curious, and very much involved with the world, displaying qualities Erikson has associated with integrity. *Nonexploratory* individuals were generally extroverted and contented, although not open to new experiences, with concerns primarily centered on the family and immediate social group. They were resistant to introspection. *Pseudointegrated* individuals were often angry, preoccupied with interpersonal problems, and/or isolated in social relationships. They were less satisfied with life than individuals in the preceding two groups, and at the same time, more neurotic and less socially responsible. The *despairing* in this study, though too small in number for adequate analysis, were low on openness and high on depression measures, indicating little general life satisfaction.

What is the relationship between identity and integrity in late adulthood? When a subgroup of individuals assessed according to the previously mentioned integrity statuses were given Marcia and colleagues' (1993) Identity Status Interview by interviewers unaware of participants' integrity status assessments, some interesting links were found. Predictably, those who had achieved a sense of identity were also rated integrated, whereas those who were foreclosed in identity were typically rated as only partially integrated. Small numbers precluded any conclusions regarding the identity diffuse and their integrity status (Glenham & Strayer, 1994). Thus, preliminary evidence suggests that achieving a sense of ego identity is associated with attaining ego integrity in late adulthood. Several studies have also attempted to predict ego integrity from resolutions to earlier Eriksonian stages. Hannah, Domino, Figueredo, and Hendrickson (1996) have also found, for example, that adequate resolution of psychosocial tasks in earlier life phases to be a prerequisite for optimal resolution of ego integrity in old age.

General, existential questions of older adults has also been a focus of recent research attention, as individuals begin to understand the place of their own lives in broader contexts. Late adulthood holds a number of existential challenges, such as coming to terms with the transitory nature of life and its approaching end, dealing with questions of the meanings of one's life and ultimate religious or spiritual questions, and enduring possible illness, suffering, loss of significant relationships, and loneliness. Researchers in Graz, Austria, conducted several surveys with older and younger adults to show that the previous issues were important preoccupations among both younger and older adults as they considered their lives in old age (Längle, 2004). However, from these same surveys, late adulthood was also a time for greater tranquility, wisdom, maturity, independence, and special relationships, for example with grandchildren.

How is reminiscing related to ego integrity in old age? In recent years there has been a good deal of research focused on the role of reminiscence and the life review to identity consolidation and integrity in late adulthood. Research involving the life review and continuity of the self through time has been undertaken with older adults in relation to Erikson's concept of ego integrity. Boylin, Gordon, and Nehrke (1976) found high reminiscing frequency and affect to be positively correlated with a measure of ego integrity. Taft and Nehrke (1990) found reminiscence for the purpose of life review to be positively correlated with high ego integrity scores in a sample of elderly nursing home residents. While no relationship was found between reminiscing and life satisfaction in a sample of nursing home residents (Cook, 1991), group reminiscence did facilitate social interaction. Reminiscence may be an important process involved in the attainment of ego integrity.

Ego integrity has also been studied directly in relation to many other life adjustment issues, such as one's fear of death and continuity of identity over time. Older adults appear better able to face issues of mortality than younger or middle-aged adults, particularly those older individuals who have attained some resolution to Integrity Versus Despair (Goebel & Boeck, 1986). This finding may result from the greater likelihood that older people will have confronted the death of significant others more frequently than younger individuals; those finding greater acceptance of their own mortality were more likely to have achieved a sense of ego integrity. Fishman (1992) also found, when controlling for age and sex, that the higher the level of ego integrity, the lower the level of death anxiety among older adults.

What kinds of factors are associated with general life satisfaction and quality of life experienced among older adults? Life satisfaction and quality of life experiences are important indicators of resolution to Erikson's task of Integrity Versus Despair in late adulthood and a growing area of research focus. One's subjective experience of one's age has appeared as a more important predictor of physical and psychological well-being than actual chronological age. In general, people feel relatively younger as they get older, and age identity is closely linked to well-being (Kaufman & Elder, 2002); from this same work, old age was perceived to begin around age 74. Negative affect generally decreases as people age (Charles, Reynolds, & Gatz, 2001). In Great Britain, research has shown that quality of life, at least in the early years of late adulthood, seems very much influenced by current contextual factors and serious health problems; disadvantage from earlier childhood and adulthood years does not preclude a good quality of life at least in the early years of old age (Blane, Higgs, Hyde, & Wiggins, 2004). From the Berlin Aging Study, which assessed more than 200 people between 70 and 103 years, some three-quarters of all participants added new domains of hope (primarily self-improvement) to their future self images; indeed, far from disengagement in the future, these older adults demonstrated active involvement in both the present and future, even as length of time left to live became increasingly reduced. In sum, it appears that if current contextual circumstances are satisfying and one has relatively good health, then one is likely to experience high life satisfaction; furthermore, even very old adults have expressed interest in self-improvement as they think about possible future selves.

Contexts Affecting Identity in Late Adulthood

It is only in very recent decades that the oldest old have been available for study, so much remains to be learned about the impact of social context on late life adults. The study of aging has generated little of its own theory, apart from ideas regarding *disengagement* in which Cumming and Henry

(1961) argued that there was an inherent process of mutual withdrawal between the elderly and their societies. This framework for viewing the aging process was set up at a time in the United States when successful aging was viewed as remaining as much like a middle-aged person as possible (Coleman, 1995). Unfortunately, this perspective on aging was used as the basis for social policy that advocated no more than custodial practices in residential care facilities; furthermore, such facilities were usually placed on the outskirts of towns and cities.

In response to this theory of disengagement, a number of gerontologists through the 1970s advocated that there should be no social or cultural expectations of how older adults should live and behave; rather, they should create their own norms and values for living in later years themselves (e.g., Rosow, 1974). This view, however, proved equally detrimental, for it seemed that both society and the elderly needed some kind of framework as a basis for both social policy and individual adjustment during the later years of adulthood (Coleman, 1995). Thus, Erikson's contributions (Erikson, 1963; Erikson, Erikson, & Kivnick, 1986) have provided a valuable resource for practitioners as well as researchers and policy makers by illustrating how old age must be understood as an integral part of the life span. As a result, practitioners have been encouraged to consider an individual's strengths, which may have emerged over the course of a life span, rather than exaggerating disability (Coleman, 1995). Each of the general social contexts that follow plays an important role in helping to shape individual identity during the years of later life.

The Family/Social Network

Family structure and functioning, social network activity, and formal and informal supports all play an important role in successful identity adaptation to changes in physical and intellectual capacities resulting from the aging process. Some gender differences have appeared in the structures and functions of social networks and their associations with life history evaluations among the elderly (Rennemark & Hagberg, 1997). For women, social anchorage has been an important function of social networks, while among men, social influence was more important. However, social participation and social support are important issues for both men and women. Additionally, one's sense of personal coherence in later years is partly influencing the relationship between social network patterns and life history evaluations for both genders.

One important family-related issue that many in their late adulthood years will experience is becoming a widow or widower. Nearly half of all women over age 65 in the United States are widows, while only about

14 percent of men are widowers (U.S. Bureau of the Census, 2003). Women in the late adult years are far less likely to remarry than are men. The majority of widows live alone. In fact, the percentage of older women over age 75 living alone in the United States has been increasing to the extent that they are now the norm among elderly women (U.S. Bureau of the Census, 2003). Adjusting to widowhood and a new (often single) life is a key identity task of late adulthood for many older women.

How does widowhood affect identity in late adult life? As will be described in the next chapter, loss of a partner through death is one of the most stressful life events one may experience. Among other things, widowhood involves the loss of a shared reality that may have provided an important identity anchor. Widowhood may, however, bring new levels of identity integration, at least for some. Identity adjustments to widowhood have been examined by Thomas, DiGiulio, and Sheehan (1988). Using Marcia's (1966) Identity Status Interview, the researchers found the majority of older individuals in the sample to be identity achieved some five years following loss of a partner. Little support was found for the pathological cast often given to widowhood. Rather, the data best fit a developmental model of crisis resolution. However, the oldest age group (55–74 years) did report the highest percentage of negative as well as positive self-perceived changes following widowhood compared with midlife and young adult age groups.

How do one's connections with others relate to life satisfaction in late adulthood? Research on well-being and elders' social networks have generally focused on two important functions: social support and social comparison. Social support has been a demonstrated mediator in reported quality of life; lower reported social support is an important reason for decreases in life satisfaction and increases in depressive symptoms found among older populations (Newsom & Schulz, 1996). Social comparison processes have been shown to be important means by which the elderly maintain or enhance their feelings of well-being in the face of impairment, illness, and loss. More frequent social comparisons have been associated with lower physical health status, but more positive social comparisons have been linked to better mental health outcomes (Heidrich & Ryff, 1993).

Carstensen (1995) and Lang and Carstensen (2002) have provided an overview of some ways by which later life adults actively structure their social environments to maximize opportunities for positive emotional experiences and minimize negative ones. Whereas gerontology researchers have long noted that peoples' social contacts decrease with age, Carstensen (1995) has demonstrated that the frequency of emotionally meaningful contacts actually increases during the years of late adulthood. Relative to younger people, older adults are less motivated to engage in emotionally meaningless social contact. At the same time, late life adults are less likely to seek social interaction for purposes of gaining new information by contrast to those in early adulthood. In Germany, for example, Lang and Carstensen (2002) found that older individuals perceived their time as more limited than younger adults and thus prioritized emotionally meaningful goals such as being with close friends and family, rather than meeting new people.

The Broader Community

> *If I knew tomorrow that I had only six months to live, what would I do? I would complete writing the history of my tribal origins. I would work to strengthen the economic base of my people. I would have time with my family. I would do a little sailing. And while I was physically capable, I would give as much loving as I possibly could.*

—70-year-old male community tribal elder

Erikson and colleagues (1986) have argued that late-life adults are generally concerned with what will happen to their society after they die. The community, for some, has offered confirmation of one's ethnic identity and a chance to shape the future of one's ethnic group, as illustrated by the previous quote. For others, the community has offered recognition of other elements of ego identity as well as a focus for some forms of generativity. At the same time, however, one's society may have changed in the values once deemed important by an elder so that acceptance may be extremely difficult, and optimally balancing integrity with despair may be a formidable task. It is likely to be harder to die in a society holding values at some distance from those by which one was raised (Coleman, 1995).

What are the effects of living arrangements and of residential location and relocation on ego identity during the late adulthood years? From the 2000 census in the United States, nearly 22 percent of all householders were aged 65 and older (U.S. Bureau of the Census, 2003). Living arrangements for most people change markedly after age 75, however, with the younger old living predominantly in family households with a partner whereas nearly 60 percent of the very old live either alone or with people other than a spouse (U.S. Bureau of the Census, 2003). Of those living alone, women outnumber men by nearly two to one in the years of late adulthood (U.S. Bureau of the Census, 2003). Surveys have shown that the majority of older individuals in our society wish to live in their own homes and never move as they grow older (Rybash et al., 1995). Such desires to "age in place" may indicate the importance to one's identity in late adulthood of having a physical sense of continuity with the past while facing an unknown future. Through stability in living arrangements, older adults may also feel a greater sense of security in familiar places and life routines that they have created through identity-related interests.

Johnson and Barer (1993) have shown how boundaries around physical and social environments are often narrowed by those older than 85 as one of several adaptive strategies to cope with increasing physical impairments. However, not all are able to "age in place" as they grow older, and residential relocation has been shown to present a real challenge to personal identity for some (Elias & Iniu, 1993; Ryff & Essex, 1992). It seems that home may hold far greater meaning and identity-related links for older, compared with younger adults. For those who do have to cope with relocation, feelings of well-being are strongly linked to the congruence between personal needs and what the new setting provides (Ryff & Essex, 1992).

Section Summary and Implications

One important identity-related issue of late adulthood is the increased likelihood of becoming a widow or widower. Women are far less likely to remarry than men. Learning new skills to cope with a single lifestyle is a key identity task for many women in their late adult years. Involvement with family, a significant other, and the community have been linked with higher levels of life satisfaction for both men and women in late adulthood.

Many in their late adult years desire to "age in place." Stability of living arrangements for the very old is often not possible, and residential relocation may present very real identity challenges for some.

Back to the Beginning

Three questions and Alison's words introduced this chapter on identity in the late adulthood years. At age 67, Alison feels she is in another identity transition, as she reflects back over the past two years and the many changes that have come to her life. The death of her remaining parent at age 65 made her aware that she was now in the oldest generation of her family. Although Alison felt ready to leave paid employment, she now feels very much in transition, with another challenge yet ahead. Alison does not indicate what this challenge is, but she does express fears of physical decline in the years to come. It may be that the challenge Alison feels is that of finding an optimal balance between Integrity Versus Despair. Finding continued sources of identity expression despite the constraints that aging may bring and being at peace with the life lived while preparing for its end are some of the many tasks that this chapter has overviewed in its discussion of identity during the years of late adulthood.

Answers to Chapter Questions

◈ **How does an aging body affect one's sense of identity in late adulthood years?**

Among the younger old, many will lead active lives, although rates of disease increase dramatically. The majority of those over age 80 do have some physical impairment, however, such as hearing or visual loss. One's ability to enjoy previous roles and activities in modified form has been associated with a sense of well-being in late adulthood.

◈ **Are cognitive declines inevitable in old age?**

Some abilities, like visual and sensory memory, do decline in old age. However, Baltes found that wisdom is superior among some groups of older adults compared to those in early and middle adulthood. A breadth of life experiences may contribute to the greater likelihood of wisdom in old age.

◈ **How is identity related to one's resolution of Integrity Versus Despair issues in old age?**

Preliminary research suggests that attaining ego integrity is associated with achieving a sense of ego identity. Those foreclosed in identity in late adulthood have been found to be only partly integrated.

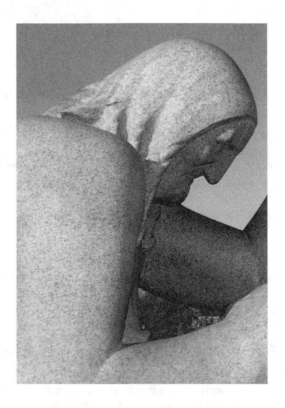

As we had passed through the years of generativity, it had never felt as though the end of the road were here and now. We had still taken years ahead for granted. At ninety the vistas changed; the view ahead became limited and unclear. Death's door, which we always knew was expectable but had taken in stride, now seemed just down the block.

—Joan Erikson, cited in Erikson, 1997, p. 4

9

Selected Identity
Issues of Adulthood

- How does loss of an intimate relationship impact one's identity in early adulthood?
- How does infertility affect identity and generativity at midlife?
- Are personality factors linked with a greater likelihood of mortality?

No theory of medicine can explain what is happening to me. Every few months I sense that another piece of me is missing. My life ... my self ... are falling apart. I can only think half-thoughts now. Someday I may wake up and not think at all ... not know who I am. Most people expect to die someday, but who ever expected to lose their self first.

—Elderly male Alzheimer's sufferer,
cited in Choen & Eisdorfer, 1986, p. 22

Four specific identity issues of adulthood have been selected for discussion in this chapter on the basis of the challenges each poses to resolving, optimally, one of Erikson's (1963) psychosocial tasks of adult life. As has been shown in the preceding chapters, resolutions to the tasks of Intimacy Versus Isolation, Generativity Versus Stagnation, and Integrity Versus Despair all rest on the foundations of an identity formed during adolescence, as well as preceding psychosocial stages of development. The loss of an intimate relationship, the inability to bear children, threats to physical integrity through serious illness or disability, and knowledge of one's own impending death will certainly provoke challenges to one's sense of ego identity at any time throughout adulthood. However, these selected issues have been chosen for discussion here specifically in relation to the particular psychosocial tasks of adult development that each phenomenon most challenges.

The loss of an intimate relationship through death, divorce, or relationship termination are discussed particularly in relation to young adulthood identity and the challenges posed to optimally resolving Intimacy Versus Isolation. The inability to bear children (infertility) is addressed in relation to identity issues of young and midlife adults, seeking resolution to Generativity Versus Stagnation. And the identity challenges posed by threats to one's physical integrity and knowledge of one's own impending death will be discussed in relation to those in their later adulthood years, struggling for an optimal balance between Integrity Versus Despair. These selected issues have affected the lives of significant numbers of young, middle, and older adults, respectively, and have raised particular identity challenges.

It must be noted that among adults engaged with the same Eriksonian psychosocial task, a diversity of meanings will likely be attributed to the same challenging event. Thus, a variety of coping strategies and identity resolutions among these individuals is probable. In the sections to follow, some general research findings on the selected challenges to Erikson's psychosocial tasks of adulthood are presented. Ultimately, however, it must be an appreciation of the specific meaning that an individual attributes to any such challenge that will enable a deeper understanding of his or her unique life history and identity.

Identity and Loss of an Intimate Relationship

> *I know I will never again be married in the way I was married.*
> *. . . I had a belief, I suppose taken from my parents and their*
> *friends, that once you got married, that was it. . . . But suddenly*
> *it dawned on me that while you have unconditional love for*
> *your parents and your children, it is not an appropriate model for*
> *a relationship between partners. I had really got it wrong with*
> *my marriage and kept trying to live by a model of unconditional*

*love. If I left my marriage, I felt as though I wouldn't really
know if I existed, and that felt really dangerous. So I wavered
for three years but then eventually left.*

—38-year-old male retailer

Loss of an intimate relationship can occur for a variety of reasons, each holding different meanings and requiring different adjustments for the remaining partner. A partnership may come to an end through death, divorce, or the breakup of a close relationship. The reason for relational loss, the length of the relationship, the age at which loss is experienced, who initiated the separation, the suddenness of the loss, and other issues such as decisions regarding children and their futures will all affect the adjustments that relational loss brings. Regardless of the reason, however, the loss of an intimate relationship has often been likened to a crushing blow in which one's roles and common ways of orienting to the world and to others are severed, and one is likely to feel disoriented. Recovery, in identity terms, requires becoming reintegrated into life without the lost person, a long, slow, and painful process (Weber & Harvey, 1994).

It is perhaps the loss of an intimate relationship through sudden death that is among the most demanding challenges to the survivor's coping abilities and eventual identity readjustments. Becoming an unexpected widow or widower brings a sudden and sharp finality to a relationship. There is no opportunity for the survivor to finish unfinished business, make plans for the future, or attempt to resolve past conflicts, as there may be in situations of divorce or other forms of terminating a close relationship (Weber & Harvey, 1994). Indeed, bereavement reactions have been shown to be far more severe among those unable to anticipate loss of a partner (Byrne & Raphael, 1994). For those who lose a partner through death in early adulthood, there is often enormous anger and grief over the loss of an anticipated future together.

Becoming a widow or a widower is one of the most stressful and emotionally demanding experiences that one may undergo. The severity of the experience of loss is dependent upon such factors as the length of the relationship, the age of the partner and the children, whether the death was anticipated or unexpected, the nature of the relationship itself, the existence of a support network, and socioeconomic status (Kaslow, 2004). Becoming a widow or widower, in identity terms, means coping not only with the emotional demands of loss and bereavement (even if the marriage was not good or fulfilling) but also the disruption of nearly every aspect of one's life. Many identity-defining routines are lost, and new roles must be performed. Over time, social relations may alter as one is no longer part of a couple, participating in established networks. Furthermore, Lopata (1996) has pointed out that American society, unlike other cultures, lacks a clearly defined social role for the widow or widower beyond the funeral and early stages of widowhood.

Bereaved individuals differ greatly in how much and how long they grieve. Across bereavement studies focusing on the loss of a spouse through death, five basic outcomes have been documented: *common grief, chronic grief, chronic depression, depression followed by improvement,* and *resilience* (Bonanno, Wortman, & Nesse, 2004). Clinical researchers and practitioners have generally assumed that absence of distress following the death of a spouse is an aberration of the normal grieving process. However, a *common grief* reaction (increase in distress following the loss that abates over time) was shown by only about 10 percent of respondents in the Bonanno and colleagues study. One further surprising finding was that nearly half of the sample of bereaved individuals in this investigation showed patterns of resilience in the face of loss, evidencing low levels of depression at prebereavement and at 6 and 18 months following bereavement. Furthermore, this low distress response was associated with good adjustment rather than defensive denial. *Chronic grief* refers to the presence of high levels of both grief and depression after the loss and not diminishing over time. These individuals were often excessively dependent, both on the spouse and others more generally. About 16 percent of the sample evidenced this pattern of reaction. *Chronic depression* (elevated depression prior to the loss that remained elevated over a prolonged bereavement) was evidenced by about 8 percent of the sample. *Depression followed by improvement* reflected a pattern of high preloss depression, which subsided 6 months following the loss. A delayed reaction to grief was nonexistent in the researches' proactive study.

In identity terms, accumulating results from recent studies of bereavement suggest that there are a number of alternative pathways through which one may emerge from the death of a spouse that are indicative of good mental health, and furthermore, that core assumptions that have guided interventions with the bereaved, particularly those that stress the need to grieve and/or experience depression over several years in circumstances of loss, may need to be reevaluated and modified (Bonanno, 2004).

As noted in the last chapter, widowhood is a phenomenon most likely to affect older women. Thus, becoming a widow or widower in young adulthood is an event that few contemporaries are likely to have experienced, and so early widowhood may be an even lonelier experience through lack of opportunity for contact with others in similar situations. Not only are many roles changed, but becoming a widow generally results in more difficult economic circumstances, which, in turn, have identity-related consequences.

Lopata (1996) has found that what happens to a wife after her husband dies depends on her degree of dependence on being married, and being married to that particular partner, the degree of disruption to her various roles, the support systems available, and the cultural status ascribed to widowhood. However, while adjusting to new psychosocial roles and dealing with the emotional turmoil of loss in widowhood, many women have also indicated that they have become stronger through the experience (Umberson, Wortman, & Kessler, 1992).

Bereavement and its impact on the identity of the surviving partner has been the subject of much research. After the funeral and mourning rituals are over and others return to their life routines, the widow or widower must emotionally cope with the personal consequences of losing their partner. Many psychologists have argued that the purpose of grief work is ultimately to release ties with the deceased so that one may be freed for new relationships; however, Faber (1990) and others have noted the importance of maintaining the marital relational bond as a permanent factor in one's sense of identity. Although an actual relationship has ended, some continued emotional attachment to the lost partner is inevitable, even in conflicted relationships, Faber argues. And while continuing relationship to the deceased does lessen with time, it does not disappear. The internalization of positive aspects of an intimate relationship may provide a nourishing link with the past after one's spouse has died.

Indeed, more recent qualitative research has focused on how the psychological mechanisms involved in reconstructing a relationship with a lost loved one via imagination may be vital to the very definition and construction of an identity during late adolescence and early adulthood (Bagnoli, 2003). Bagnoli sought to understand the impact that relational loss through a significant other's death or parental divorce may have on identity construction among youths and young adults in both Italy and England. Bereaved youths and young adults of this investigation who showed the most adaptive functioning managed to reintegrate the lost other into their lives via identification that gave the bereaved a point of self-reference. Through establishing imaginary dialogues, the bereaved could constructively elaborate their loss and use the experience to facilitate self-growth and identity formation.

Whereas death of a spouse or a life partner has been ranked highest among stressful events that one might undergo, divorce has been ranked the second-most stressful life event (Holmes & Rahe, 1967). Certainly, separated and divorced individuals have demonstrated elevated rates of illness and death (Kitson & Morgan, 1990). It is currently estimated that approximately one out of every two first marriages in the United States will end in divorce;

the divorce rate in 2001 per 1,000 among the general population was 4.0, while the marriage rate per 1,000 among the general population was 8.4 (U.S. Bureau of the Census, 2003). The years of early adulthood are those in which most divorces occur. The ending of an intimate relationship through divorce is certainly affecting a large percentage of adults in the United States as well as in other Western nations (U.S. Bureau of the Census, 2003).

The divorce experience has been shown to differ significantly for the person initiating the termination of a marriage compared to the noninitiating spouse (Duran-Aydintug, 1995). Through extensive interviews with some 60 couples aged 19 to 48 years old, this research found that initiators went through a series of well-defined phases in preparation for marital termination, which often occurred over a long period of time. Initially, secret doubts and unexpressed wishes began to cloud the initiators' thoughts regarding future life with the spouse. Eventually, such thoughts solidified and the individual went through a preparation time, getting ready to express his or her wishes to the partner. Going public with the information regarding a separation followed with time, eventuating in new personal and public identity presentations (expressed in forms of the "old" and "new" me). For the noninitiating partner, a time of shock and disbelief were common on news of the partner's wish for separation. A trial time of living apart often produced strong reactions of anger, depression, and hope for the noninitiator. The degree of voluntariness regarding divorce, awareness of partner attitudes, and control over the situation and future options often distinguished those in the two positions noted earlier. Generally, initiators began the role exit process and were more aware of alternative options and support mechanisms than noninitiators.

Additional research has noted some common identity-related trends among those considering divorce and among those undergoing the divorce process. Both marital dissatisfaction and number of divorces have been far higher among those individuals labeled "high self-monitors" (Leone & Hall, 2003). High self-monitors vary their displays of affect, nonverbal behavior, and other means of self-presentation according to the social situation in which they find themselves for purposes of enhancing their self-presentations. Low self-monitors, on the other hand, are especially attuned to their own internal states, attitudes, and feelings. They know themselves well and seek congruence between their inner states and actions. Leone and Hall (2003) conducted several studies to find a direct relationship between self-monitoring and marital dissatisfaction as well as divorce. Indeed the social worlds of high and low self-monitors were structured very differently, with relationships among high self-monitors far more likely to be unsatisfactory and to result in divorce.

Numerous other factors have been associated with marital instability. Incongruence in spouses beliefs about gender-appropriate behavior alongside negative and distancing behaviors in marriage leading to identity disruptions are among the more recent identity-related themes associated with divorce (Pasley, Kerpelman, & Guilbert, 2001). Among those undergoing the divorce process, a reported feeling of loss of identity, the need for moral superiority, and the need to identify positive gain from the divorce experience have characterized attitudes of many (Rossitter, 1991).

What circumstances are associated with one's ability to adjust after divorce? Personal resources important to readjustment include one's financial status, stable psychological functioning, and strong kinship and friendship networks (Bengston, Rosenthal, & Burton, 1990). Divorce, like widowhood, generally means a substantial reduction in income. Where both partners have been employed, the household income is clearly reduced. If one's ex-spouse has been a full-time homemaker, those services must now be hired. And where the only breadwinner has departed, the financial burden upon the remaining ex-partner may be enormous. Adjusting to matters of a greatly reduced income in addition to other family and household responsibilities has made divorce an extremely difficult experience for many women.

Among women undergoing divorce, being employed and having a sense of work identity has been associated with higher self-esteem and lower distress (Bisagni & Eckenrode, 1996) when compared with nonemployed women. For such women, a work identity has provided an alternative avenue for meaningfulness and a sense of purpose in their lives, as well as social interaction and support, productivity, and positive distraction. In terms of psychological functioning, ample social support, high masculinity scale scores, and low levels of bitterness toward the ex-spouse were strong predictors of good adjustment among women following divorce (Bursik, 1991). Unfortunately, little is known about factors leading to positive adjustment among men following divorce.

The breakup of an intimate relationship also brings identity readjustments, although the relationship may not have been as long-standing as one terminated through divorce. Harvey, Weber, and Orbuch (1990) have argued that account making, or generating meanings into a coherent story, plays a vital role in the stress response that an individual undergoes with the dissolution of a close relationship. Account making helps the individual deal with a variety of psychological and physical symptoms. In a study among college students that examined the breakup of a romantic relationship that lasted at least six months, individual account makings were examined in order to learn more about causes and coping behaviors in the termination of a close relationship (Sorenson, Russell, Harkness, & Harvey, 1993).

A relatively complete account making was associated with greater perceived control over the recovery process and feeling good about the breakup; those who initiated the breakup or who felt the breakup was mutual were more likely to give more complete accounts of the loss. These results also indicated that friends and family were not always helpful in the recovery process. Suggestions of possible reconciliation or just talking about the ex-partner were common topics raised by significant others and were actually detrimental to recovery for one trying to disengage from a terminated relationship. Robak and Weitzman (1995) also note a special problem faced by those terminating a close relationship is in the fact that others are likely to minimize the importance of the loss, resulting in disenfranchised grief. Thus, the mourning process for those involved in the relationship breakup is forced to be a private experience. The experience of grief, however, has appeared very similar to that felt by those who have lost a partner through death.

Section Summary and Implications

Loss of an intimate relationship through a partner's sudden death may be among the most demanding of identity challenges. What happens to a wife following her spouse's death is a function of her age, degree of dependence on being married (both emotional and financial), disruption of various life roles, support systems available, and the cultural status given to widowhood. Men's identity readjustments following the death of a spouse are still in need of research.

Among women in the process of a divorce, being employed and having a sense of work identity has been associated with higher self-esteem and lower distress.

The breakup of an intimate relationship also brings identity challenges. Others may minimize the impact of this type of loss, resulting in disenfranchised grief.

Identity and Infertility

We were both a bit older when we married, but a big heartbreak was when we found we were not able to have children. We've really had to work hard at coming to terms with that, so much restructuring of our thinking, and the need to reaffirm ourselves. It's been a very painful process.

—38-year-old male business consultant

Infertility is generally defined as the inability to conceive a pregnancy after one year of engaging in sexual intercourse without contraception; from a recent large national sample in the United States, approximately one out of six (10–15 percent) women of reproductive age desiring to have children experience fertility difficulties (Chandra & Stephen, 1998). Women are about twice as likely to be infertile as men, with causes generally linked to blockage of the oviducts, cervical secretions that are too acidic or thick to enable sperm to pass into the uterus, or hormonal difficulties (Leiblum, 1997). Among men, the leading causes of infertility are low sperm count or the production of too many abnormal sperm cells (Leiblum, 1997). Approximately half of women who seek medical intervention for infertility never give birth to a child (Bergart, 2000). Most couples desiring children assume they will become parents when they are ready, for the attainment of parenthood is central to the identity of many adults. The condition of infertility for couples wishing to conceive may precipitate a life crisis leading to profound feelings of loss, grief, mourning, and identity reconstruction, as the reality becomes apparent that biological parenting may never be a possibility for the couple together. Reality reconsiderations, identity transformations, role readjustments, and the search for finding new ways to best fill creative and nurturant needs without a biological child become the generativity challenges for infertile couples wishing to have children.

Infertility is not a discrete event but rather a long and confusing process for most couples as the reality of their circumstances gradually unfolds into a situation of great loss. In an extensive review of the literature on infertility, Dunkel-Schetter and Lobel (1991) identified several recurrent emotional themes that characterized responses of both men and women. Grief and depression commonly followed the diagnosis of infertility. Feelings of mourning, sadness, disappointment, loss, anger, guilt, disillusionment, and hopelessness were often reported by individuals and observed by others. Anxiety was a further common reaction, particularly as treatment procedures were considered. Also painful to infertile couples may be the fact that others fail to appreciate the extent of the loss that infertility brings, and they may minimize the emotional impact. In fact, infertility is often experienced by couples as not only the death of a child but also the death of all of one's children (Leiblum & Greenfeld, 1997). Stresses in the marriage are inevitable.

Olshansky (1987) has studied the process of how infertile couples that are distressed by their circumstances "take on" an identity as an infertile couple. Such an identity generally becomes central to their lives, as they "work" actively to intervene with the problem. Other previously important identity elements, such as career identity, are likely to be pushed aside while coping with infertility comes to the fore. With time, couples of Olshansky's investigation were able to shed, diminish, or push their infertile identity to the periphery as some form of resolution was found. Paradoxically, however, those distressed by infertility needed to confront their identity as part of an infertile couple in order to make infertility less central to their lives over time.

What are the wider implications of infertility to one's identity? Different writers have pointed to various aspects of one's identity that may be profoundly shaken by infertility. Dunkel-Schetter and Lobel (1991) note how infertile couples seeking treatment may experience two types of loss of control in their lives. Loss of control over one's daily activities, bodily functions, and emotions—in short, loss of control over the present—have been commonly reported, as well as loss of control over the future and the ability to predict, plan, and meet identity-defining life goals. Loss of the ability to direct the present is likely to result from treatment demands that medical intervention brings. Every detail of the couple's sexual activity is subjected to external regulation, often interfering with other work and/or social commitments (Matthews & Matthews, 1986). Infertility may also bring radical changes to perspectives on future goals, as the diagnosis may, for example, mean the biological end of a family name or the death of other dreams. Major reconstructions about the meaning of marriage, parenthood, and indeed existence itself are likely to come under review.

However, many such studies of the potential impact of infertility on identity have not been drawn from large, random samples, but rather small and selective ones (primarily fertility clinic based). In an attempt to overcome this problem, McQuillan, Greil, White, and Jacob (2003) undertook a large survey of 580 Midwestern women to determine whether women with lifetime infertility reported higher levels of distress than women who become mothers. The investigators also examined whether a relationship between infertility and distress depended primarily on role identities (such as motherhood, employment, relational status) or resources (such as education level, income, race/ethnicity). Childless women without fertility problems were not distressed by the absence of children. However, the combination of fertility problems and involuntary childlessness was associated with statistically significant higher levels of psychological distress. The authors argue that the severe, long-term effects of unfulfilled motherhood for this latter group of women in their study supported the argument that frustrated attempts to achieve motherhood threaten a "central life identity" (McQuillan et al., 2003, p. 1015). The authors do caution, however, that from their cross-sectional data they cannot determine the nature of any cause-effect relationship between fertility and psychological distress. Future work also needs to address whether or not blocked parenthood has the same impact for both genders.

Other studies linking identity issues with infertility have noted the threats to one's self-esteem, sexual identity, and gender role identity that may ensue. Feelings of failure, inadequacy, and low self-worth have been commonly reported by those diagnosed as infertile. Furthermore, these attitudes have not been associated with reproductive functioning alone, but rather extended to one's feelings of sexual desirability, physical attractiveness, and performance and productivity in other spheres of life (Dunkel-Schetter & Lobel, 1991). Negative body images have been reported by a number of infertile individuals. Many infertile men and women will also come to question their sexual identity and gender role performance. Infertile women who have defined their identities primarily according to traditional female gender roles in which motherhood figures centrally have shown higher levels of depression, powerlessness, and loss of psychological well-being compared with infertile women who have defined themselves through less traditional gender roles (Morse & Van Hall, 1987).

A couple may, of course, explore a variety of alternatives to biological parenting, including adoption, fostering a child, surrogate mothering, artificial insemination, or deciding to remain childless. Olshansky (1987) identified several different ways young and midlife adults managed their identity as infertile. These strategies included the following:

1. Overcoming the identity of self as infertile by becoming pregnant when the underlying cause of infertility was corrected

2. Circumventing identity of self as infertile by technological intervention through artificial insemination or in vitro fertilization, thereby achieving a pregnancy

3. Reconciling the identity of self as infertile, by choosing to adopt, foster, or remain childless

4. Remaining in limbo, continually failing to conceive without attempting other strategies

This last resolution does not represent an adaptive response to difficulties posed by infertility.

What are the generativity implications of infertility? The four-decade-long study of infertile men, their styles of coping, and the subsequent achievement of generativity, by John Snarey and his colleagues (Snarey, 1988; Snarey, Son, Kuehne, Hauser, & Vaillant, 1987) has pointed to some important patterns. From an ongoing longitudinal study begun in the 1940s, Snarey identified a subsample of 52 men who were diagnosed as infertile during their first marriages in early adulthood. Different styles of coping with infertility were found among the men at this time. All men initially chose substitute activities for parenting, such as lavishing care and attention on a nonhuman object (63 percent), taking part in activities with other people's children (25 percent), or lavishing care and attention upon themselves (12 percent), while they kept trying to conceive. These choices were closely related to how these men later attempted to resolve infertility problems. None of those using self-centered substitutes chose later to adopt. Only a few who used other objects as substitutes eventually decided to adopt. By contrast, over half of those who chose involvement with others' children in early adulthood eventually adopted.

There was a further strong association between early styles of coping with infertility and the attainment of generativity by midlife. Snarey found about one-third of the men in the sample demonstrated a sense of generativity at midlife when he defined generativity according to Erikson's criteria of finding ways to care for the next generation. None of the men who were self-centered in their earlier coping strategies for dealing with infertility were later identified as generative. By contrast, some 75 percent of those who had substituted other people's children in coping with their early infertility were identified as generative at midlife, as were about 25 percent of those who substituted other objects. Although men's early strategies for coping with infertility may be a reflection rather than cause of a view that influenced later development, this important piece of research points to the very strong relationship between coping approaches to early adulthood infertility, parenting decisions, and the development of generativity at midlife.

Section Summary and Implications

Infertility is not a discrete event but rather a long and confusing process as a couple's inability to have children gradually clarifies. Various identity elements may be profoundly shaken by infertility. Loss of control over one's daily life as well as more general life goals, one's sense of self-esteem, and sexual- and gender-role identity all may come into question with the diagnosis of infertility.

Snarey has noted how different styles of coping with infertility in early adulthood have been strongly linked to styles of generativity at midlife. Over half of men who chose involvement with other's children to cope with infertility in early adulthood eventually adopted, whereas none who chose self-centered substitutes later chose to adopt. Identity features of early adulthood appear strongly linked to expressions of generativity at midlife.

Identity and Threats to Physical Integrity

I lost Jan last year. Oh, she's still alive—in a full-time care facility now, but the Jan I knew and loved is no longer with us.

—65-year-old male doctor

Kleinman (1988) has observed that "nothing so concentrates experience and clarifies the central conditions of living as serious illness" (p. xiii). Threats to physical integrity certainly increase with age, particularly among the oldest old. Although serious illness or disability may come at any time, this section will focus particularly on threats to physical integrity among those dealing with issues of Integrity Versus Despair in old age. A number of serious conditions such as hypertension, heart disease, cancer, stroke, arthritis, and diabetes become more prevalent for those over age 65. However, the intention of this section is to focus more generally on threats to bodily integrity that will have a profound impact on one's sense of bodily self, identity, and consequent psychological functioning, particularly during the years of later adulthood.

A number of circumstances affecting the elderly may exacerbate the impact of serious illness or disability and disruption to one's sense of identity and life continuity. Becker (1993) has identified five factors that are readily apparent among many of the oldest old: more limited stamina, limited social support, financial constraints, the impact of other recent losses, and the likelihood that other illnesses or disabilities will also be present. The combination of these varied psychosocial factors makes the onset of an additional serious illness or disability for an elderly person extremely demanding.

Serious illness or sudden disability presents for the older individual a fundamental betrayal of the trust she or he has placed in the body's ability to function. The experience of a severe, disabling illness disrupts the sense of continuity that one has established in one's life, continuity that is so vital to one's ego identity (Erikson, 1968). Those who experience severe illness or disability may realize that one's entire life structure has rested on very fragile physical foundations (that may have previously been merely taken for granted). This recognition often results in both direct and indirect expressions of anger, as well as feelings of hopelessness and helplessness (Viney, 1984–85). For those who have experienced serious threats to physical integrity, questions of how continuity may be reestablished with one's previous sense of identity and role involvements have only recently become the subject of research attention.

The degree of disability one may suffer from any serious threat to physical integrity appears not to be entirely determined by physiological measures alone. Rowe and Minaker (1985) have pointed to the role that behavioral and sociological factors play in the consequences of serious illness. Attitudes and expectations, both of the sufferer and significant others in his or her life, play an enormous role in the level at which the sufferer may function. More recent research has focused on one's cognitive representation of illness and the roles that such factors play in the consequences for one's identity adjustments. One's understandings of the cause of the illness, its perceived duration, expected consequences, and how much control one has over one's own recovery all affect the level of disability one will experience.

Weinman, Petrie, Moss-Morris, and Horne (1996) note how cognitive illness representations determine one's coping ability, and they have developed a questionnaire measure to assess components that have been found to underlie one's cognitive representation of illness. They found that illness representations may, in fact, directly affect mood and adjustment, rather than being mediated by one's ability to cope. Additional research by Moss-Morris, Petrie, and Weinman (1996) has shown how illness perceptions play a greater role in the level of disability experienced and level of psychological well-being than coping strategies used by sufferers to manage their illnesses. Those who believed their illnesses were completely out of their control with very serious consequences experienced greater physical and psychological disability than those with more optimistic views of the same illness. Positive reinterpretation of the illness and seeking social support were related to enhanced psychological well-being.

In identity terms, experiencing serious illness requires a redrawing of relationships between self, body, environment, and daily life (Becker, 1993). When individuals are unable to carry out actions or tasks that were previously associated with the self, then certain aspects of one's identity become lost. The degree of disruption to one's sense of identity depends on the severity and importance of aspects of the self that have been lost, the chances of recovery, one's ability to come to terms with losses, and one's ability to rebuild a sense of oneself around these limitations (Corbin & Strauss, 1988). Oliver Sacks (1987, p. 6) has noted that a disease "is never a mere loss . . . there is always a reaction, on the part of the affected organism or individual, to restore, to replace, to compensate for and to preserve its identity, however strange the means may be."

How do social networks, so vital to the process of identity confirmation change over the course of threats to physical integrity? Recent research by Reinhardt, Boerner, and Benn (2003) has systematically examined the impact of chronic disability on social networks over time. The researchers focused particularly on changes to the friendship and family networks of chronically disabled later-life adults. They found a slight, but statistically significant, average decrease in network supports over time. From this extensive research, closest family members showed the highest levels of stability in support over time, but surprisingly, about 50 percent of friendships also remained supportive over time. What this study was unable to untangle is whether the average decrease in social support for the chronically disabled was due to emotional and physical withdrawal on the part of network members or rather the "proactive stance" of the disabled individual as he or she may seek to reduce contacts with those who offered fewer emotional rewards under the changed and difficult circumstances. An important task of future research is to tease apart these two mechanisms and their potential impact on identity for the chronically disabled.

What identity readjustments to serious illness are commonly experienced? Charmaz (1996) has examined the general process of identity adaptation to physical impairment. Identity adaptation involves changing one's lifestyle and attitudes about the self to accommodate bodily losses as well as finding some resolution to the lost unity between body and self. Charmaz suggests identity adaptation consists of several phases, as an individual struggles with rather than against an illness. Individuals must fully experience and define their impairments to make bodily assessments. Such assessments will consequently enable identity tradeoffs, as losses and gains are evaluated and identity goals revised. And ultimately, individuals must flow with rather than against the experience of impairment. Charmaz points out that for those with chronic illness, adaptation seldom occurs only once; rather, those experiencing serious illness are forced repeatedly into new adaptations as they experience new losses.

Neurological illnesses directly impact upon identity for a number of later life adults; Alzheimer's and Parkinson's diseases are two such illnesses where memory functioning, so vital to identity, becomes increasingly impaired. Platt (2004) has pointed out that little is known about the neurology of identity—about what happens to our sense of who we are when neurological disease causes the brain to slowly disintegrate. Social scientists are, however, beginning to directly address identity in relation to these illnesses, both through qualitative case studies as well as larger scale empirical works. One important study examined whether degree of autobiographical memory impairment is associated with identity changes among Alzheimer's sufferers (Addis & Tippett, 2004). The study assessed 20 individuals with Alzheimer's disease, matched for age with 20 control participants. Several important findings emerged from this work. As anticipated, those suffering from Alzheimer's showed impairments on all autobiographical memory tasks. Impairments for some parts of autobiographical memory (particularly for childhood and early adulthood events) were directly related to strength and quality of identity. Among Alzheimer's sufferers, responses to identity statements were far more vague, abstract, and less definite than nonimpaired controls. The study additionally pointed to the fact that while autobiographical memory impairment may drive identity changes for those with Alzheimer's disease, these two constructs do not directly map onto each other. Awareness of cognitive impairments is also likely to impact identity, and many Alzheimer's participants included such deficits in their self-descriptions.

Additional researches on the neurology of identity have been addressing the impact of an Alzheimer's diagnosis on identity construction of the patients themselves (e.g., Beard, 2004) and the implications for identity support among care facilities for elders with cognitive illnesses (e.g., Wellin & Jaffe, 2004). Those receiving an Alzheimer's diagnosis have highlighted three core themes that were instrumental in making sense of the changes in their lives over the course of their illness: *defining moments,* when memory deficiencies were obvious to the sufferers, *decisions about whether or not to tell of the illness,* and *preservation,* including attempts to manage public impressions and tactics used for ease of communication (Beard, 2004). Both studies by Beard (2004) and Wellin and Jaffe (2004) point to the importance of focusing on who the person with Alzheimer's *is* as well as things that the person with Alzheimer's *can* do as coping strategies, rather than focusing on all that has been lost.

Section Summary and Implications

Serious illness or sudden disability represents for the older individual a betrayal of the trust one has placed in the body's ability to function; such disruption severely affects one's sense of biological continuity and ego identity.

Cognitive representations of illness help to determine one's ability to cope; the degree of disability one may suffer is not determined by physiological measures alone.

Threats to bodily integrity require the redrawing of relationships between self, body, environment, and daily life. Identity reformation may be best facilitated by helping those under threat to create a sense of continuity with their past through redefining a possible life and returning to simple, old roles or pastimes in modified form.

Identity and Coming to Terms With Death

He knew that he was getting sick about this time, and that I would probably have to manage on my own. So Jack began quite actively to say that he would miss my company at home, but he encouraged me to take on interests on my own. My father died in '63, and I remember beforehand we had been saying to

> *my parents, "You know, one day one of you is going to die, and you both really need to practice managing on your own. Why doesn't Dad come over and have dinner with me, so that at least Mom can get some practice eating alone?" My parents thought we were crazy, and we never got very far with that idea then. But I guess somehow Jack wanted me to start practicing being on my own when he became so very ill.*

—73-year-old widow, a retired community worker

The United States has often been identified as a society that denies or avoids thinking about death. Indeed, Ernest Becker's (1973) Pulitzer Prize-winning volume, *The Denial of Death,* addresses the varied ways in which much of our activity is directed toward denying that death is the final destiny of us all. The fear of death has become a prominent part of our psychological makeup, directing much of our activity. Against this background, Erikson (1997) has proposed that a large part of the struggle to balance integrity with despair in old age is coming to terms with the course and conclusion of one's life cycle. He terms this phenomenon an "informed and detached concern with life itself in the face of death itself" (Erikson, 1997, p. 61).

Death brings enormous losses and provides the ultimate experience of aloneness. Becker (cited in Keen, 1977) postulated that because of these enormous losses, each of us constructs a personality, style of life, or character armor to deny death. Thus, we identify with a more powerful person, cause, or material possession in an effort to deny the ultimate loss of life. The pull toward despair would thus seem a powerful force in Erikson's final psychosocial stage. In a moving interview from a hospital bed during the final stage of terminal cancer, Becker described his own sadness in the knowledge that he would be unable to see the impact that his work might have on the lives of future social scientists and philosophers:

> *I am sorry I probably won't get to see [the results]. It's funny, I have been working for 15 years with an obsessiveness to develop these ideas, dropping one book after another into the void and carrying on with some kind of confidence that the stuff was good. . . . Sitting here talking to you like this makes me very wistful that I won't be around to see these things.*

—Becker, in an interview with Keen, 1977, pp. 304–305

Erikson would no doubt view such expressed wistfulness as healthy adaptation to the termination of one's life, finding some dignity and integrity in the acceptance of one's death.

The meaning of one's own death will vary according to a number of dimensions. The age at which death occurs, whether or not death can be anticipated within a particular time frame, the degree of incapacity and/or pain an individual experiences prior to death, one's readiness for death, personality factors, and the degree of control one has over the circumstances of one's death all impact on the process of identity development and coming to terms with Integrity Versus Despair. When death comes prior to old age, it is said to be premature and raises many additional losses related to an unlived life, to unexperienced events, to unfulfilled identity potential, both for the dying individual and his or her survivors (Kalish, 1985). Today, with improved medical treatment, it is common for one to experience a lengthy period of time in which one is able to anticipate death following a terminal illness diagnosis or life-threatening injury. This space of time has important identity implications, both for the person who is dying as well as significant others.

Lindemann (1944) first used the term *anticipatory grief* to describe this time in which both the dying person and close survivors can begin both to grieve as well as to make practical adjustments to the termination of one's life. Researchers have found that anticipatory grieving does not eliminate postdeath grieving, but that the effects of the death may be less overwhelming as some plans and arrangements have already been made (Rando, 1986). However, Rando also points out that there is an optimal *living-dying interval*, or length of time between terminal diagnosis and actual death. If an illness lasts less than six months, the time is generally insufficient to allow any real anticipatory grieving to occur. However, if an illness lasts longer than 18 months, the physical and emotional strain of living in anticipation of death, both for the dying individual and for close, care-providing survivors, is enormous. Normal postdeath grieving in such extended situations may even be delayed for the survivors as they recover from the task of caring for the dying individual (Rando, 1986).

Kübler-Ross (1969, 1981, 1991) has been active in contributing to our understanding of how dying individuals often come to terms with their own impending death. She has proposed a sequence of stages, although many later researchers have found that there is much individual variation in the manner and sequence in which people negotiate these hurdles (e.g., Kastenbaum, 2000). Nevertheless, Kübler-Ross maintains that facing death brings forth the following sequence of feelings and behaviors: denial/isolation, anger, bargaining, depression, and acceptance. *Denial and isolation* generally characterize one's initial response to the news that death will take place; the defense of denial seems to provide an initial cushion before the full implications of one's situation can be understood and confronted. Denial is a common response to terminal illness; the feeling that "this can't be happening to me" is a common reaction. *Anger* often follows, once denial can no longer be maintained. Rage, resentment, envy, and jealousy are common emotions during this time, often directed to members of the hospital staff and the individual's family. *Bargaining* is Kübler-Ross's third stage, in which the dying individual will often develop the hope that death can be somehow delayed in exchange for some type of reformed life. Individuals will often try to bargain with God for more time in exchange for a life more dedicated to service. However, the futility of such efforts becomes apparent as the dying person gradually comes to accept the certainty of death. The fourth stage of *depression* ensues, and the individual is often silent and withdrawn, spending much time grieving and mourning their own impending death. Ultimately, Kübler-Ross suggests that *acceptance* brings a sense of peace, as one ceases struggling against the inevitable. Physical pain may be virtually absent at this time, and one may wish to be left alone.

Contemporary researchers have found that some individuals may continue to deny the impending reality up until death. Others, who may be ready to die, show greater acceptance from the outset (Erikson, Erikson, & Kivnick, 1986). Although Kübler-Ross has pointed to a sequence of feelings and behaviors that may characterize the experience of dying for some, many other individuals will experience only some of these phases as they prepare to meet death. Furthermore, some individuals may alternate back and forth, for example, between anger and depression. Contemporary research finds much individual variation in the manner by which people cope with the knowledge that they are dying (e.g., Kastenbaum, 2000).

For those in the years of later adulthood, struggling with finding some resolution to the task of Integrity Versus Despair, coming to terms with death arouses many issues. Among those themes that researchers have investigated more thoroughly have been personality factors related to facing death, the impact of previous bereavements on death-related attitudes, purpose in life attitudes, and attitudes regarding the meaning of death, and the impact of open awareness of dying.

A number of studies have addressed personality factors in relation to orientation toward death and issues of personal identity. Among active adolescents and young adults under 30, existential contemplation occurs but acceptance of death may be linked more to an uncritical reflection of traditional religious beliefs or to a sense of an extended self. The possibility of death has been associated with high levels of distress, fear, and avoidance, particularly for those in the throes of constructing their own identity (LaVoie & de Vries, 2003–2004). Among later-life adults, specific personality factors have actively been linked with a higher probability of mortality. A number of conflicting results have come from studies addressing the relationship of personality factors to mortality. However, findings have often been confounded by participant differences in socioeconomic status and other health and lifestyle factors. Low socioeconomic status has been an established risk factor for mortality, and people of lower socioeconomic status tend to generally have more negative emotions than people of higher income groups (Gallo & Matthews, 2003). Researchers Wilson, Mendes de Leon, Bienias, Evans, and Bennet (2004) selected a sample of 883 older Catholic clergy members (69 percent women) to study the relationship between selected personality factors and mortality over a period of five years. They choose this group of individuals because of the likelihood of high homogeneity in socioeconomic status and other lifestyle factors that might affect mortality. Over this time, approximately 20 percent of their sample died. Risk of death nearly doubled among those who scored high on a measure of neuroticism compared with those who scored low on this index: risk of death was also approximately halved among those with a high conscientiousness score compared with those scoring low on the measure. Additional studies of personality factors in relation to mortality need to be carried out among other relatively homogeneous populations to see if these clear relationships found by Wilson and colleagues (2004) hold up across studies.

Death anxiety, in particular, has been the focus of a number of investigations of later life adults. From an Eriksonian perspective, Rasmussen and Brems (1996) examined the relationship between age, psychosocial maturity, and death anxiety. Psychosocial maturity was assessed according to degree of resolution to the first six Eriksonian psychosocial stages. Their results indicated psychosocial maturity to be a better predictor of death anxiety than age, although both variables were negatively related to death anxiety. Thus, as degree of psychosocial maturity and age increased, fears of death decreased; degree of psychosocial maturity, however, was a better predictor of death anxiety than was age. In addition, having a sense of purpose in life has been negatively correlated with death anxiety among the elderly (Rappaport, Fossler, Bross, & Gilden, 1993); the greater one's sense of life purpose, the less one's fear of death. The conviction that one has a task to complete seems to add more purpose to one's life in its later stages.

Previous experience with bereavement also impacts the ability to accept one's own death. However, the impact of early and recent losses on one's own attitudes toward death is complex. Florian and Mikulincer (1997) found that both early and recent losses were related to higher levels of fear of personal death among adults. But different kinds of associations were found between each kind of loss and each of the many different fears associated with death. For example, those who had experienced early losses were more likely to attribute their own fear of death to loss of social identity, the impact of their death for family and friends, and the loss of self-fulfillment. However, for those who reported more recent losses, fears of death were more associated with annihilation of the body, the unknown nature of death, and loss of self-fulfillment.

In Britain, Seale, Addington-Hall, and McCarthy (1997) examined the prevalence of different death awareness contexts and their identity implications for a dying individual. Open awareness of dying, where both the dying person and close others know the person is dying, is currently the most common context. This result contrasts with findings from a similar survey done in 1969, when closed awareness (in which the dying person was not informed of his or her condition, although close others know) was most common. Compared with people in closed awareness contexts, those dying in full awareness are best able to make plans for their remaining lives, deaths, and futures of their families. They also expressed satisfaction over the degree of control over their place of death, and they were more likely to die at home in the presence of close others. By contrast, those in closed awareness situations were more likely to die alone. Opportunities for full expression of personal identity were best facilitated in dying contexts of open awareness.

Section Summary and Implications

The meaning of one's own death will vary according to its age of occurrence, whether or not death can be anticipated within a set time frame, one's readiness for death, and the degree of control one has over the circumstances of one's death. All of these issues impact on the process of identity development in old age and coming to terms with Integrity Versus Despair.

Researchers have studied a number of issues related to how the elderly come to terms with death. Findings include the fact that open awareness of dying (where the dying and close others are all aware of the situation) best facilitates both identity and integrity resolutions. Through open awareness, the dying are best able to make plans for their remaining lives, resolve unfinished business, and plan for the futures of their families.

Back to the Beginning

Three questions and the words of an elderly male Alzheimer's disease sufferer introduced this chapter, which has focused on issues that pose threats to Erikson's psychosocial tasks of adult life. The loss of an intimate relationship during the young adulthood stage of Intimacy Versus Isolation, the inability to conceive children during Generativity Versus Stagnation, and experiences threatening physical integrity as well as coming to term's with death during Integrity Versus Despair and their identity implications have been the chapter's themes. The Alzheimer's sufferer poignantly notes how the gradual erosion of his sense of identity was never anticipated before his physical death. Indeed, a heightened sense of one's own individual identity is commonly brought to the fore across all the selected challenges of this chapter.

Answers to Chapter Questions

◈ **How does loss of an intimate relationship affect one's identity in early adulthood?**

The identity impact of relational loss depends on a number of factors, such as the reason for relational loss, length and quality of the relationship, suddenness of the loss, who initiated the separation, and the practical consequences of the loss. Relational loss through sudden death of a partner during early adulthood may pose the most demanding of identity challenges.

◈ **How does infertility affect identity and generativity at midlife?**

Infertility may profoundly shake such identity elements as the ability to plan for and control one's future, one's sense of self-esteem, sexual and gender role identity, and one's construction of the meaning of marriage itself, as well as other existential concerns. Snarey found ways of coping with infertility during early adulthood to be strongly related to the attainment of generativity during midlife.

◈ **Are personality factors linked with a greater likelihood of mortality?**

Preliminary researches controlling for socioeconomic status and other lifestyle factors have found an increased risk of mortality among those scoring high on a measure of neuroticism. Risk of mortality was almost halved among those scoring high on a measure of conscientiousness.

PART IV
Epilogue

I am only a human being. That vocation is quite enough.

—Pär Lagerkvist, in *Godt Sagt*

Epilogue

The study of identity has become a rich focus for theory and research in the social sciences over the course of the last half-century. Indeed, as of late November 2005, a PsycINFO search of the term, identity, yielded nearly 41,000 theoretical writings or empirical researches written since Erikson first introduced the concept into the social sciences literature in the 1950s. This volume has attempted to define Erikson's identity construct and to consider its elements in a number of different ways. To Erikson, identity is a synthetic, adaptive sense of being a person in a complex world. Identity's presence enables one, with all of his or her own biological characteristics, psychological interests, aptitudes, needs, and defenses, to find satisfying vocational, ideological, and relational roles within a particular social setting during a particular historical epoch. Identity provides one with a sense of continuity and meaning in one's life. Simply put, identity is what makes one move with direction and gives one reason to be.

The introductory overview of five different general theoretical approaches to an understanding of identity presented in Chapter 1 of this volume illustrates the varied elements that contemporary theorists and researchers have chosen to emphasize in their inquiries into identity's architecture. All approaches are grounded in Erikson's original identity writings, yet all have selected somewhat different dimensions of this overarching construct in developing models and strategies for elaboration. Ultimately, the value of any particular model of identity must rest in the theorist's or researcher's awareness of the model's predictive and explanatory power in relation to identity in its totality. Erikson proposed identity to be an overarching construct; it will ultimately be the ability of future identity researchers following different theoretical persuasions to dialogue that will further the understanding and applications of this important construct.

Erikson furthermore introduced the notion that while issues of identity generally first begin to demand attention during adolescence, ongoing identity development continues over the course of the adult life span. The remaining chapters have followed the normative courses and contents of identity as expressed throughout the years of adolescent and adult life. In so doing, Erikson's concept of identity as an individual's integration of biological, psychological, and contextual elements has been retained, and researches and theory adding further understanding to the interactions among these elements have been presented. Some important themes regarding the *course, contents,* and *contexts* of identity have emerged through individual chapters of this volume. In addition, some important methodological issues have limited the scope of many research efforts reviewed in the chapters. I would now like to suggest some steps that may help refine identity researches in the decades ahead.

How does identity develop and take shape over time? The past decade has witnessed a number of exciting longitudinal studies aimed at elaborating the *course* of the identity formation process during adolescent and adult life. While in the last edition of this volume, I commented on the need for continuing identity researches beyond adolescence, there now exist several longitudinal studies of identity development extending through early or middle adulthood years. Pulkkinen and her colleagues in Finland (Fadjukoff, Pulkkinen, & Kokko, 2005; Pulkkinen & Kokko, 2000) and Anthis (2002), Cramer (2004), and Josselson (1996) in the United States all have found ongoing identity development beyond the years of adolescence.

However, virtually all longitudinal studies of identity development both during and beyond adolescence have found that substantial numbers of those leaving tertiary education and entering adult roles do so without having constructed a sense of their own identities (attained an achieved identity status). Across some 10 published longitudinal studies that have provided information about intraindividual change, I found that commonly around 50 percent of participants had not engaged in the identity formation process of adolescence that Erikson so vividly described (Kroger, in press). Such findings beg the question, why is identity achievement so elusive?

Interestingly, the fact that so many late adolescents and young adults do not attain higher levels of identity development is completely consistent with results from the related literatures of ego development (Loevinger, 1976), moral reasoning (Kohlberg, 1984), and self-other differentiation (Kegan, 1994). The identity status literature has been linked, empirically, with each of these developmental schemes, and longitudinal studies conducted with each of these models has invariably pointed to the elusiveness of developmental complexity (Kroger, in press). I have offered some hypotheses about possible reasons for the elusiveness of identity achievement, but future longitudinal studies might fruitfully explore factors that seem to be associated with movement toward greater developmental complexity.

What fuels the identity formation process? Over the past 10 years, some researches have begun to explore this issue. Piaget (1972) has pointed to the importance of conflict in stimulating change of cognitive structure; movement from a foreclosed to moratorium to achievement identity position may also arise through experiences of conflict or adversity. Kroger and Green (1996) found that exposure to new contexts and internal change processes to be the two types of events most commonly linked with the transition from less to more mature identity positions. More recently, investigations by Anthis (2002) and Kunnen and Wassick (2003) have both pointed to conflict as a trigger for change. Kunnen and Wassick have also elaborated on possible steps in the process of identity accommodation. Work by Cramer (2004) additionally suggests that personality variables such as the ability to use particular adaptive defense mechanisms and certain types of life experiences are also linked with identity achievement during and beyond adolescence. Some research has also indicated, however, that too much conflict may, in fact, impede optimal identity development (Kroger, 2004). Future studies of identity might fruitfully focus on optimum levels of perceived conflict in association with particular personality variables as well as environmental supports that may be necessary to precipitate identity development for particular groups of individuals.

Archer and Waterman (1988) are among many researchers who have pointed to the important and adaptive value that the open flexibility of an identity-achieved structure brings. The fact that such large percentages of late adolescents appear to be entering young adult life foreclosed or diffuse in identity should give policymakers and human service providers working with late adolescents considerable pause for thought. The ability to accurately predict those likely to remain stable in these less mature identity statuses has received preliminary support; future research along similar lines will have important social implications. Educational, judicial, health care, social welfare, and leisure service providers might well consider interventions aimed to stimulate meaningful identity exploration within a context of respect and support. Interventions that may best engage and facilitate development for those remaining foreclosed or diffuse in identity over late adolescence remains another rich and important area for investigation.

And while identity research has now expanded into the years of early and middle adulthood, the investigation of identity processes and contexts that shape one's identity during the years of late adulthood are greatly needed. Since publication of the first edition of this volume, I have been involved in two exploratory studies of identity processes during late adulthood (Kroger, 2000; Kroger & Adair, unpublished raw data). In the first study, qualitative interviews with small groups of later-life adults illustrated how identity exploration and commitment processes so central to the identity-formation task of adolescence had parallels in identity-revision and maintenance processes of late adulthood. Identity revision processes among late life adults commonly involved reintegration, reevaluation, readjustment, and rebalancing. Identity-maintenance processes also took various forms, including maintaining visible forms of continuity and retaining important identity elements through loss. My second qualitative study with Dr. Vivienne Adair examined the symbolic meanings, in identity terms, of cherished personal possessions that late-life adults carried with them as they left their home environments to move into varied types of residential care. This study illustrates the vital nature of continuity to one's personal identity and how identity's varied elements can help to be maintained. Future in-depth studies with larger numbers of late-life participants may provide rich insights how identity can be maintained and revised in the later years; furthermore, such research has the potential to give human service providers and policymakers important foundations for intervention as they seek to serve increasing numbers of older adults growing even older in the decades to come.

How are varied types of identity resolutions expressed during each of Erikson's adult psychosocial tasks of Intimacy Versus Isolation, Generativity Versus Stagnation, and Integrity Versus Despair? Marcia and his colleagues (Marcia, 2002) have begun to explore such issues by examining the relationships between identity status and qualitatively different styles of resolutions to each of Erikson's psychosocial tasks of adulthood. (For example, as noted in Chapter 6, those young adults who have adopted more complex forms of identity resolutions have also tended to adopt more complex forms of intimacy; those late-life adults who have adopted more complex styles of integrity, have also adopted more complex forms of identity.) To date, however, such studies have been undertaken on a cross-sectional basis only. While promising links between identity resolutions and styles of resolving psychosocial tasks of adulthood have appeared (see Marcia, 2002, for a review), such work now needs to be undertaken on a prospective, long-term, longitudinal basis. Only in this way will it ultimately be possible to test both the epigenetic nature of Erikson's theory as well as the epigenetic nature of elaborations to it.

Further issues involved in the identity-formation process described by Erikson are also in need of future research. While much attention has been directed toward the course of identity exploration and commitment as elaborated in Marcia's work, some promising beginnings have been made in attending to other dimensions of identity and their developments during adolescence and adulthood. Schachter (2004), for example, has examined different ways in which Israeli young adults configure relationships among potentially conflicting identifications in the process of identity formation. His work suggests different types of configurations, including an assimilative and synthesizing configuration, a confederacy of identifications, and a configuration based on the thrill of dissonance. Dunkel (2005) has examined the relationship between measures of identity commitment and continuity. His work indicates that current measures of identity do, in fact, share a significant amount of variance with measures of continuity. Berman, Montgomery, and Kurtines (2004) have focused on the issue of identity distress and developed a means of measuring it, while van Hoof (1999) and Dunkel and Anthis (2003) have focused on identity issues of spatial and temporal continuity. These works represent important efforts to explore some of the many further dimensions of identity that Erikson (1968) describes.

Longitudinal investigations tracing the course of identity from late adolescence into young and middle adulthood have found enormous variety in patterns of identity status movement. Such results are not surprising, given the relatively infrequent time intervals over which data has been collected in all of these investigations (reviewed in Chapters 6 and 7). An initial identity assessment in high school and/or 4 years later in college, 10 to 15 years later in early adulthood, and another 8 to 10 years later in midlife have been characteristic of the time intervals involved in all longitudinal identity investigations of identity status change from adolescence through midlife. Such long gaps between assessments provide us with little information about the more continuous movements of identity over time. Although longitudinal studies are the ideal means of understanding the course of identity over adolescent and adulthood years, assessments are needed at sufficiently frequent time intervals to ensure an understanding of the real continuities and discontinuities of identity pathways. Additionally, longitudinal studies over more than two data collection points are a rarity. Recent, longitudinal research involving five-month (Anthis, 2002) and six-month (Luyckx, Goossens, Soenens, Beyers, & Vansteenkiste, 2005) intervals in assessments provide important additions to an understanding of the identity-formation process. And longitudinal assessments over more than two data collection points are further important additions to the identity-formation literature (e.g., Fadjukoff et al., 2005; Luyckx et al., 2005).

Furthermore, methods of analysis in longitudinal studies must be used that allow the study of individual identity trajectories over time. Analysis of group movements into and out of various identity statuses, which has characterized some of the earlier longitudinal investigations of identity, overlooks much valuable information that the study of individual identity trajectories can provide. With sufficient data collection points, future longitudinal research will be able to describe identity trajectories involving various combinations of progression, regression, and stability. Contexts and events that are associated with these various identity trajectories can be a rich source of information.

Identity *contents,* or the actual domains in which individuals express their own interests, values, and beliefs on a social stage, have shown some remarkable similarities over the years from early adolescence through later adulthood. In both 1968 (when Erikson first wrote extensively about identity) and the present, it is the issue of vocation that appears of primary concern to youth. Evidence reviewed in Chapter 4 suggests that even among unemployed late adolescents, vocation is still regarded as their most important identity element. Similarly, finding meaningful ideologies to guide one's life, satisfying sex roles and forms of sexual expression, and meaningful relationships with others have captured the energy of individuals across both adolescent and adult stages of the life span. However, the study of identity contents in the postretirement years of later adulthood raises a number of interesting questions. When traditional work roles no longer serve identity-defining functions in later life, what identity domains become the psychosocial basis for self-definition? Identity research needs to explore and define what key, identity-defining domains actually are for individuals in their later adulthood years.

Finally, attention must be given to various issues associated with *contexts* in which identities are formed and maintained. One important task is still the need to examine the course and contents of identity in a far greater diversity of contexts than identity research addresses at present. Although research on identity formation among youths of different ethnic backgrounds and cultural groups (reviewed in Chapter 5) has been productive and rapidly expanding, these studies have been undertaken primarily with adolescents in secondary or tertiary educational settings. Studies addressing the identity-formation process for youths not engaged in tertiary study (i.e., those working, homemaking, or unemployed) and for youths reflecting a greater diversity of social classes and non-Western cultures would be welcome additions to the identity literature.

Another important contextual issue is recognition that various historical epochs will shape the contours of identity in different ways for late adolescents entering adult life. Researches by Stewart and Ostrove (1998) and Van Mannen and Whitbourne (1997) have certainly demonstrated that social and historical events experienced by different cohorts of late adolescents and young adults have different effects on identity development by midlife. Such findings point to the need for exercising extreme caution in comparing studies of identity development across different historical time frames. The comparison of identity research conducted in the 1970s with that of the 1980s may provide less information about genuine developmental patterns among late adolescents than about the social forces helping to shape identity development at particular points in time. Ideally, a series of longitudinal studies begun at different points in time (termed cohort-sequential designs) will help us to untangle developmental processes from social forces affecting identity formation. Research conducted by Whitbourne and colleagues (1992) is an excellent example of just how such a cohort-sequential design may be used to study developmental and contextual issues giving shape to the course of identity over time.

In studying various contexts in which the identity-formation process occurs, a final comment must be made about the interpretation of results from such studies. Direct causal factors cannot be ascertained from investigations that find associations between particular patterns of identity development and particular social contexts. For example, some studies have found greater identity exploration among adolescents in families that encourage individuality and connectedness. From such information, however, it is not possible to determine the direction of the relationship between variables. An adolescent's level of identity development may elicit certain parental behaviors that stimulate their continued identity explorations, or certain parental behaviors may evoke particular patterns of identity development for adolescents themselves. One must exercise caution in suggesting causal relationships from such correlational data.

It is my hope that the theory, research, and critiques presented in this volume will serve to stimulate your interest in this exciting and rapidly expanding field of identity research. And for some of you, I hope this volume can also serve as the impetus for your own future investigations of identity over the years of adolescent and adult life. I leave the final comment on identity's contours over time to Maria, a 19-year-old university student, articulating her own identity concerns:

I guess my first identity problem is just knowing who I am, and the second, becoming who I am, wherever and however that will change across my own lifetime.

—Maria, 19-year-old university student

References

Achenbaum, W. A. (1993). (When) did the papacy become a gerontocracy? In K. W. Schaie & W. A. Achenbaum (Eds.), *Societal impact on aging: Historical perspectives* (pp. 204–231). New York: Springer.

Adams, G. R. (1985). Identity and political socialization. In A. S. Waterman (Ed.), *Identity in adolescence: Processes and contents* (New Directions for Child Development, No. 30, pp. 61–77). San Francisco: Jossey-Bass.

Adams, G. R. (1999). *The objective measure of ego identity status: A manual on theory and test construction.* Unpublished manuscript, University of Guelph, Ontario, Canada.

Adams, G. R., & Fitch, S. A. (1983). Psychological environments of university departments: Effects on college students' identity status and ego stage development. *Journal of Personality and Social Psychology, 44,* 1266–1275.

Adams, G. R., & Marshall, S. K. (1996). A developmental social psychology of identity: Understanding the person-in-context. *Journal of Adolescence, 19,* 429–442.

Addis, D. R., & Tippett, L. J. (2004). Memory of myself: Autobiographical memory and identity in Alzheimer's disease. *Memory, 12,* 56–74.

Akers, J. F., Jones, R. M., & Coyl, D. D. (1998). Adolescent friendship pairs: Similarities in identity status development, behaviors, attitudes, and intentions. *Journal of Adolescent Research, 13,* 178–199.

Allison, B. N., & Schultz, J. B. (2004). Parent-adolescent conflict in early adolescence. *Adolescence, 39,* 101–119.

Allison, M. D., & Sabatelli, R. M. (1988). Differentiation and individuation as mediators of identity and intimacy in adolescence. *Journal of Adolescent Research, 3,* 1–16.

Alsaker, F. (1990). *Global negative self-evaluations in early adolescence.* Unpublished doctoral dissertation, University of Bergen, Norway.

Alsaker, F. (1995). Is puberty a critical period for socialization? *Journal of Adolescence, 18,* 427–444.

Anthis, K. S. (2002). On the calamity theory of growth: The relationship between stressful life events and changes in identity over time. *Identity: An International Journal of Theory and Research, 2,* 229–240.

Apter, D., & Hermanson, E. (2002). Update on female pubertal development. *Current Opinions in Obstetrics and Gynecology, 14,* 475–481.

Archer, S. L. (1982). The lower age boundaries of identity development. *Child Development, 53,* 1551–1556.

Archer, S. L. (1985). Identity and the choice of social roles. In A. S. Waterman (Ed.), *Identity in adolescence: Process and contents* (New Directions for Child Development, No. 30, pp. 79–99). San Francisco: Jossey-Bass.

Archer, S. L. (1989). Gender differences in identity development: Issues of process, domain, and timing. *Journal of Adolescence, 12,* 117–138.

Archer, S. L., & Waterman, A. S. (1988). Psychological individualism: Gender differences or gender neutrality? *Human Development, 31,* 65–81.

Archibald, A. B., Graber, J. A., & Brooks-Gunn, J. (2003). Pubertal processes and physiological growth in adolescence. In G. R. Adams & M. D. Berzonsky (Eds.), *Blackwell handbook of adolescence* (pp. 24–47). Oxford, UK: Blackwell.

Arlin, P. K. (1989). Problem solving and problem finding in young artists and young scientists. In M. L. Commons, J. D. Sinnott, F. A. Richards, & C. Armon (Eds.), *Adult development, Vol. 1: Comparisons and applications of developmental models.* New York: Praeger.

Arnett, J. (1992). Reckless behavior in adolescence: A developmental perspective. *Developmental Review, 12,* 339–373.

Årseth, A., Kroger, J., Martinussen, M., & Marcia, J. E. (2005). *Meta-analytic studies of relationships and identity.* Manuscript in preparation.

Augustinus, A. (1991). *Confessions* (H. Chadwick, Trans. and notes). Oxford, UK: Oxford University Press.

Backman, L., Wahlin, A., Small, B. J., Herlitz, A., Winblad, B., & Fratiglioni, L. (2004). Cognitive functioning in aging and dementia: The Kungsholmen Project. *Aging Neuropsychology and Cognition, 11,* 212–244.

Bagnoli, A. (2003). Imagining the lost other: The experience of loss and the process of identity construction in young people. *Journal of Youth Studies, 6,* 203–217.

Bailey, W. T. (1992). Psychological development in men: Generativity and involvement with young children. *Psychological Reports, 71,* 929–930.

Bailey, W. T. (1994). Psychological development in women: Generativity. *Psychological Reports, 74,* 286.

Baltes, P. B., & Kunzmann, U. (2004). The two faces of wisdom: Wisdom as a general theory of knowledge and judgment about excellence in mind and virtue vs. wisdom as everyday realization in people and products. *Human Development, 47,* 290–299.

Baltes, P. B., & Staudinger, U. M. (1993). The search for a psychology of wisdom. *Current Directions in Psychological Science, 2,* 75–80.

Barber, B. K., & Olsen, J. A. (1997). Socialization in context: Connection, regulation, and autonomy in the family, school, and neighborhood, and with peers. *Journal of Adolescent Research, 12,* 287–315.

Bartle-Haring, S., Brucker, P., & Hock, E. (2002). The impact of parental separation anxiety on identity development in adolescence and early adulthood. *Journal of Adolescent Research, 17,* 439–450.

Baruch, G., & Brooks-Gunn, J. (Eds.). (1984). *Women in midlife.* New York: Plenum.

Bateson, M. C. (1989). *Composing a life.* New York: Penguin.

Bateson, M. C. (1994, April). *Women at midlife.* Paper presented at the Radcliffe College conference on Women at Midlife, Cambridge, MA.

Baudouin, A., Vanneste, S., & Isingrini, M. (2004). Age-related cognitive slowing: The role of spontaneous tempo and processing speed. *Experimental Aging Research, 30,* 225–239.

Baumeister, R. F. (1986). *Identity: Cultural change and the struggle for self.* New York: Oxford University Press.

Baumeister, R. F. (1987). How the self became a problem: A psychological review. *Journal of Personality and Social Psychology, 52,* 163–176.

Baumeister, R. F., & Muraven, M. (1996). Identity as adaptation to social, cultural, and historical context. *Journal of Adolescence, 19,* 405–416.

Baumrind, D. (1991). The influence of parenting style on adolescent competence and substance abuse. *Journal of Early Adolescence, 11,* 56–95.

Beard, R. L. (2004). In their voices: Identity preservation and experiences of Alzheimer's disease. *Journal of Aging Studies, 18,* 415–428.

Becker, E. (1973). *The denial of death.* New York: Free Press.

Becker, G. (1993). Continuity after a stroke: Implications of life-course disruption in old age. *The Gerontologist, 33,* 148–158.

Bengston, V., Rosenthal, C., & Burton, L. (1990). Families and aging: Diversity and heterogeneity. In R. H. Binstock & L. K. George (Eds.), *Handbook of aging and the social sciences* (3rd ed., pp. 263–287). San Antonio, TX: Academic Press.

Benson, P. L., Sharma, A. R., & Roehlkepartain, E. C. (1994). *Growing up adopted: A portrait of adolescents and their families.* Minneapolis, MN: Search Institute.

Bergart, A. M. (2000). The experience of women in unsuccessful fertility treatment: What do patients need when medical intervention fails? *Social Work in Health Care, 30,* 45–69.

Berman, S. L., Montgomery, M. J., & Kurtines, W. M. (2004). The development and validation of a measure of identity distress. *Identity: An International Journal of Theory and Research, 4,* 1–7.

Berzonsky, M. D. (1992). *Identity Style Inventory.* Unpublished manuscript, State University of New York at Cortland, New York.

Berzonsky, M. D. (2005). Ego identity: A personal standpoint in a postmodern world. *Identity: An International Journal of Theory and Research, 5,* 125–136.

Berzonsky, M. D., & Adams, G. R. (1999). Reevaluating the identity status paradigm: Still useful after 35 years. *Developmental Review, 19,* 81–98.

Berzonsky, M. D., & Kuk, L. S. (2000). Identity status, identity processing style, and the transition to university. *Journal of Adolescent Research, 15,* 81–98.

Berzonsky, M. D., & Lombardo, J. P. (1983). Pubertal timing and identity crises: A preliminary investigation. *Journal of Early Adolescence, 3,* 239–246.

Beyers, W., Goossens, L., Vansant, I., & Moors, E. (2003). A structural model of autonomy in middle and late adolescence: Connectedness, separation, detachment, and agency. *Journal of Youth and Adolescence, 32,* 351–365.

Bisagni, G. M., & Eckenrode, J. (1996). The role of work identity in women's adjustment to divorce. *American Journal of Orthopsychiatry, 65,* 574–583.

Blane, D., Higgs, P., Hyde, M., & Wiggins, R. D. (2004). Life course influences on quality of life in early old age. *Social Science & Medicine, 58,* 2171–2179.

Bledin, K. (2003). Migration, identity and group analysis. *Group Analysis, 36,* 97–110.

Blos, P. (1967). The second individuation process of adolescence. *Psychoanalytic Study of the Child, 22,* 162–186.

Blos, P. (1979). *The adolescent passage: Developmental issues.* New York: International Universities Press.

Blustein, D. L., Devinis, L. E., & Kidney, B. A. (1989). Relationship between the identity formation process and career development. *Journal of Counseling Psychology, 36,* 196–202.

Blustein, D. L., & Noumair, D. A. (1996). Self and identity in career development: Implications for theory and practice. *Journal of Counseling and Development, 74,* 433–441.

Blustein, D. L., & Phillips, S. D. (1990). Relation between ego identity statuses and decision-making styles. *Journal of Counseling Psychology, 37,* 160–168.

Blyth, D., & Leffert, N. (1995). Communities as contexts for adolescent development: An empirical analysis. *Journal of Adolescent Research, 10,* 64–87.

Bogin, B. (1994). Adolescence in evolutionary perspective. *Acta Paediatrica Supplement, 406,* 29–35.

Bonanno, G. A. (2004). Loss, trauma, and human resilience: Have we underestimated the human capacity to thrive after extremely aversive events? *American Psychologist, 59,* 20–28.

Bonanno, G. A., Wortman, C. B., & Nesse, R. M. (2004). Prospective patterns of resilience and maladjustment during widowhood. *Psychology and Aging, 19,* 260–271.

Booth, F. W., Weeden, S. H., & Tseng, B. S. (1994). Effect of aging on human skeletal muscle and motor function. *Medicine and Science in Sports and Exercise, 5,* 556–560.

Boyes, M. C., & Chandler, M. (1992). Cognitive development, epistemic doubt, and identity formation in adolescence. *Journal of Youth and Adolescence, 21,* 277–304.

Boylin, W., Gordon, S., & Nehrke, M. F. (1976). Reminiscence and ego integrity in institutionalized elderly males. *The Gerontologist, 16,* 118–124.

Bradley, C. L. (1997). Generativity—stagnation: Development of a status model. *Developmental Review, 17,* 262–290.

Bradley, C. L., & Marcia, J. E. (1998a). Generativity—stagnation: A five category model. *Journal of Personality, 66,* 39–64.

Bradley, C. L., & Marcia, J. E. (1998b). *The generativity status measure: Replication and extension in two adult samples.* Unpublished manuscript, Simon Fraser University, British Columbia, Canada.

Branch, C., Tayal, P., & Triplett, C. (2000). The relationship of ethnic identity and ego identity status among adolescents and young adults. *International Journal of Intercultural Relations, 23,* 777–790.

Brandtstädter, J., & Greve, W. (1994). The aging self: Stabilizing and protective processes. *Developmental Review, 14,* 52–80.

Breakwell, G. M., & Millward, L. J. (1997). Sexual self-concept and risk-taking. *Journal of Adolescence, 20,* 29–41.

Brim, O. G. (1992). *Ambition.* New York: Basic Books.

Brodinsky, D. M. (1987). Adjustment to adoption: A psychosocial perspective. *Clinical Psychology Review, 7,* 25–47.

Brooks-Gunn, J. (1991). Maturational timing variations in adolescent girls, antecedents of. In R. M. Lerner, A. C. Petersen, & J. Brooks-Gunn (Eds.), *Encyclopedia of adolescence* (Vol. 2, pp. 609–612). New York: Garland.

Brooks-Gunn, J., & Graber, J. (1999). What's sex got to do with it? In R. D. Ashmore & R. J. Contrada (Eds.). *Self, social identity, and physical health: Interdisciplinary explorations* (pp. 152–182). London: Oxford University Press.

Brooks-Gunn, J., & Paikoff, R. L. (1993). Sex is a gamble, kissing is a game: Adolescent sexuality and health promotion. In S. G. Millstein, A. C. Petersen, & E. O. Nightingale (Eds.), *Promoting the health of adolescents* (pp. 180–208). New York: Oxford University Press.

Brooks-Gunn, J., & Petersen, A. C. (Eds.). (1983). *Girls at puberty: Biological and psychosocial perspectives.* New York: Plenum.

Brooks-Gunn, J., & Ruble, D. N. (1982). The development of menstrual-related beliefs and behaviors during early adolescence. *Child Development, 53,* 1567–1577.

Brooks-Gunn, J., & Warren, M. P. (1988). The psychological significance of secondary sexual characteristics in nine- to eleven-year-old girls. *Child Development, 59,* 1061–1069.

Brooks-Gunn, J., & Warren, M. P. (1989). Biological contributions to affective expression in young adolescent girls. *Child Development, 60,* 372–385.

Brown, A. C., & Orthner, D. K. (1990). Relocation and personal well-being among early adolescents. *Journal of Early Adolescence, 10,* 366–381.

Brown, B. B., Eicher, S. A., & Petrie, S. (1986). The importance of peer group ("crowd") affiliation in adolescence. *Journal of Adolescence, 9,* 73–96.

Brown, B. B., & Klute, C. (2003). Friendships, cliques, and crowds. In G. R. Adams & M. D. Berzonsky (Eds.), *Blackwell handbook of adolescence* (pp. 330–345). Oxford, UK: Blackwell.

Bulcroft, R. (1991). The value of physical change in adolescence: Consequences for the parent-adolescent exchange relationship. *Journal of Youth and Adolescence, 20,* 89–105.

Bursik, K. (1991). Correlates of women's adjustment during the separation and divorce process. *Journal of Divorce and Remarriage, 14,* 137–162.

Butler, R. (1968). The life review: An interpretation of reminiscence in the aged. In B. L. Neugarten (Ed.), *Middle age and aging* (pp. 486–496). Chicago: University of Chicago Press. (Reprinted from *Psychiatry, Journal for the Study of Interpersonal Processes, 26,* 1963)

Buzwell, S., & Rosenthal, D. (1996). Constructing a sexual self: Adolescents' sexual self-perceptions and sexual risk-taking. *Journal of Research on Adolescence, 6,* 489–513.

Byrne, G. J. A., & Raphael, B. (1994). A longitudinal study of bereavement phenomena in recently widowed elderly men. *Psychological Medicine, 24,* 411–421.

Campbell, E., Adams, G. R., & Dobson, W. R. (1984). Familial correlates of identity formation in late adolescence: A study of the predictive utility of connectedness and individuality in family relations. *Journal of Youth and Adolescence, 13,* 509–525.

Canals, J., Vigil-Colet, A., Chico, E., & Marti-Henneberg, C. (2005). Personality changes during adolescence: The role of gender and pubertal development. *Personality and Individual Differences, 39,* 179–188.

Carlson, C., Uppal, S., & Prosser, E. C. (2000). Ethnic differences in processes contributing to the self-esteem of early adolescent girls. *Journal of Early Adolescence, 20,* 44–67.

Carstensen, L. L. (1995). Evidence for a life-span theory of socioemotional selectivity. *Current Directions in Psychological Science, 4,* 151–156.

Carter, M. A. T., & Cook, K. (1995). Adaptation to retirement: Role changes and personal resources. *Career Development Quarterly, 44,* 67–82.

Caspi, A. (1995). Puberty and the gender organization of schools: How biology and social context shape the adolescent experience. In L. J. Crockett & A. C. Crouter (Eds.), *Pathways through adolescence* (pp. 57–74). Mahwah, NJ: Lawrence Erlbaum.

Cavanagh, S. E. (2004). The sexual debut of girls in early adolescence: The intersection of race, pubertal timing, and friendship group characteristics. *Journal of Research on Adolescence, 14,* 285–312.

Cederblad, M., Hook, B., Irhammar, M., & Mercke, A. M. (1999). Mental health in international adoptees as teenagers and young adults: An epidemiological study. *Journal of Child Psychology and Psychiatry, 40,* 1239–1248.

Chandra, A., & Stephen, E. H. (1998). Impaired fecundity in the United States: 1982–1995. *Family Planning Perspectives, 30,* 34–42.

Charles, S. T., Reynolds, C. A., & Gatz, M. (2001). Age-related differences and change in positive and negative affect over 23 years. *Journal of Personality and Social Psychology, 80,* 136–151.

Charmaz, K. (1996). The body, identity, and self: Adapting to impairment. *Sociological Quarterly, 36,* 657–680.

Chavira, V., & Phinney, J. S. (1991). Adolescents' ethnic identity, self-esteem, and strategies for dealing with ethnicity and minority status. *Hispanic Journal of Behavioral Sciences, 13,* 226–227.

Chisholm, L., & Hurrelmann, K. (1995). Adolescence in modern Europe: Pluralized transition patterns and their implications for personal and social risks. *Journal of Adolescence, 18,* 129–158.

Christiansen, S. L., & Palkovitz, R. (1998). Exploring Erikson's psychosocial theory of development: Generativity and its relationship to paternal identity, intimacy, and involvement in childcare. *Journal of Men's Studies, 7,* 133–156.

Chumlea, W., Schubert, C., Roche, A., Kulin, H., Lee, P., Hines, J., et al. (2003). Age at menarche and racial comparisons in U.S. girls. *Pediatrics, 111,* 110–113.

Clair, J. M., Karp, D. A., & Yoels, W. C. (1993). *Experiencing the life cycle: A social psychology of aging.* Springfield, IL: Charles C Thomas.

Clancy, S. M., & Dollinger, S. J. (1993). Identity, self, and personality: I. Identity status and the five-factor model of personality. *Journal of Research on Adolescence, 3,* 227–245.

Cobb, N. (1995). *Adolescence: Continuity, change, and diversity* (2nd ed.). Mountain View, CA: Mayfield.

Coberly, S. (1991). Older workers and the Older Americans Act. *Generations, 15,* 27–30.

Cohen, D., & Eisdorfer, C. (1986). *The loss of self: A family resource for the care of Alzheimer's disease and related disorders.* New York: Norton.

Coleman, P. (1995). Facing the challenges of aging: Development, coping, and meaning in life. In J. F. Nussbaum & J. Coupland (Eds.), *Handbook of communication and aging research* (pp. 39–74). Mahwah, NJ: Lawrence Erlbaum.

Collins, W. A., & Laursen, B. (2004). Parent-adolescent relationships and influences. In R. Lerner & L. Steinberg (Eds.), *Handbook of adolescent psychology* (pp. 331–361). New York: Wiley.

Constantinople, A. (1969). An Eriksonian measure of personality development in college students. *Developmental Psychology, 1,* 357–372.

Cook, E. A. (1991). The effects of reminiscence on psychological measures of ego integrity in elderly nursing home residents. *Archives of Psychiatric Nursing, 5,* 292–298.

Cooper, C. R. (1994). Cultural perspectives on continuity and change in adolescents' relationships. In R. Montemayor, G. R. Adams, & T. P. Gullotta (Eds.), *Personal relationships during adolescence* (Advances in Adolescent Development, Vol. 6, pp. 78–100). Thousand Oaks, CA: Sage.

Cooper, C. R., & Cooper, R. G. (1992). Links between adolescents' relationships with their parents and peers: Models, evidence, and mechanisms. In R. D. Parke & G. W. Ladd (Eds.), *Family-peer relationships: Modes of linkage* (pp. 135–158). Hillsdale, NJ: Lawrence Erlbaum.

Corbin, J. M., & Strauss, A. (1988). *Unending work and care: Managing chronic illness at home.* San Francisco: Jossey-Bass.

Costa, M. E., & Campos, B. (1990). Socioeducational contexts and beginning university students' identity development. In C. Vandenplaus-Holper &

B. P. Campos (Eds.), *Interpersonal and identity development: New directions* (pp. 79–85). Porto, Portugal: Faculty of Psychology and Education.

Costa, P. T., Jr., & McCrae, R. R. (1994). "Set like plaster?" Evidence for the stability of adult personality. In T. Heatherton & J. Weinberger (Eds.), *Can personality change?* (pp. 21–40). Washington, DC: American Psychological Association.

Côté, J. E. (1996). Identity: A multi-dimensional analysis. In G. R. Adams, R. Montemayor, & T. P. Gullotta (Eds.), *Psychosocial development during adolescence: Progress in developmental contextualism* (Advances in Adolescent Development, Vol. 8, pp. 130–180). Thousand Oaks, CA: Sage.

Côté, J. E., & Levine, C. G. (2002). *Identity formation, agency, and culture: A social psychological synthesis.* Mahwah, NJ: Lawrence Erlbaum.

Cotton, L., Bynum, D. R., & Madhere, S. (1997). Socialization forces and the stability of work values from late adolescence to early adulthood. *Psychological Reports, 80,* 115–124.

Covey, H. C. (1988). Historical terminology used to represent older people. *Gerontologist, 28,* 291–297.

Craig-Bray, L., Adams, G. R., & Dobson, W. R. (1988). Identity formation and social relations during late adolescence. *Journal of Youth and Adolescence, 17,* 173–187.

Cramer, P. (1995). Identity, narcissism, and defense mechanisms in late adolescence. *Journal of Research in Personality, 29,* 341–361.

Cramer, P. (1998). Freshman to senior year: A follow-up study of identity, narcissism, and defense mechanisms. *Journal of Research in Personality, 32,* 156–172.

Cramer, P. (2001). Identification and its relation to identity development. *Journal of Personality, 69,* 667–688.

Cramer, P. (2004). Identity change in adulthood: The contribution of defense mechanisms and life experiences. *Journal of Research in Personality, 38,* 280–316.

Cross, W. E. (1987). A two-factor theory of black identity: Implications for the study of identity development in minority children. In J. S. Phinney & M. J. Rotheram (Eds.), *Children's ethnic socialization.* Newbury Park, CA: Sage.

Crouter, A. C., Manke, B. A., & McHale, S. M. (1995). The family context of gender intensification during early adolescence. *Child Development, 66,* 317–329.

Crowder, K., & Teachman, J. (2004). Do residential conditions explain the relationship between living arrangements and adolescent behavior? *Journal of Marriage and the Family, 66,* 721–738.

Cuéllar, I., & Roberts, R. E. (1997). Relations of depression, acculturation, and socioeconomic status in a Latino sample. *Hispanic Journal of Behavioral Studies, 19,* 230–238.

Cumming, E., & Henry, W. (1961). *Growing old: The process of disengagement.* New York: Basic Books.

Cushman, P. (1990). Why the self is empty. *American Psychologist, 45,* 599–611.

Dalen, M., & Sætersdal, B. (1992). *Utenlandsadopterte barn I Norge: Tilpasning, opplæring, identitetsutvikling* [Children adopted from other countries in Norway:

Adaptation, training, and identity development]. Oslo: Spesiallærerhøgskolen, University of Oslo.

Danielsen, L. M., Lorem, A. E., & Kroger, J. (2000). Different vocational roads to an adult identity for Norwegian late adolescents. *Youth and Society, 31,* 332–362.

Danish, S. J., Taylor, T. E., & Fazio, R. J. (2003). Enhancing adolescent development through sports and leisure. In G. R. Adams & M. D. Berzonsky (Eds.), *Blackwell handbook of adolescence* (pp. 92–108). Oxford, UK: Blackwell.

Darling-Fisher, C., & Leidy, N. (1988). Measuring Eriksonian development in the adult: The Modified Erikson Psychosocial Stage Inventory. *Psychological Reports, 62,* 747–754.

de St. Aubin, E., McAdams, P., & Kim, T. C. (2004). *The generative society.* Washington, DC: American Psychological Association.

DeCorte, W. (1993). Estimating sex-related bias in job evaluation. *Journal of Occupational and Organizational Psychology, 66,* 83–96.

Delaney, C. H. (1995). Rites of passage in adolescence. *Adolescence, 30,* 891–897.

Delaney, M. E. (1996). Across the transition to adolescence: Qualities of parent/adolescent relationships and adjustment. *Journal of Early Adolescence, 16,* 274–300.

Dick, D., Rose, R., Pulkkinen, L., & Kapiro, J. (2001). Measuring puberty and understanding its impact: A longitudinal study of adolescent twins. *Journal of Youth and Adolescence, 30,* 385–400.

Domino, G., & Affonso, D. (1990). The IPB: A personality measure of Erikson's life stages. *Journal of Personality Assessment, 54,* 576–588.

Dorn, L. D., Crockett, L. J., & Petersen, A. C. (1988). The relation of pubertal status to intrapersonal changes in young adolescents. *Journal of Early Adolescence, 8,* 405–419.

Dryer, P. H. (1994). Designing curricular identity interventions for secondary schools. In S. L. Archer (Ed.), *Interventions for adolescent identity development* (pp. 121–140). Thousand Oaks, CA: Sage.

Duncan, L. E., & Agronick, G. S. (1995). The intersection of life stage and social events: Personality and life outcomes. *Journal of Personality and Social Psychology, 69,* 558–568.

Dunkel, C. S. (2005). The relation between self-continuity and measures of identity. *Identity: An International Journal of Theory and Research, 5,* 21–34.

Dunkel, C. S., & Anthis, K. S. (2003). The self across time and space in late adolescence: A test of temporal-spatial continuity in identity. In S. P. Shohov (Ed.), *Advances in psychology research* (Vol. 20, pp. 131–143). Hauppauge, NY: Nova Science.

Dunkel-Schetter, C., & Lobel, M. (1991). Psychological reactions to infertility. In A. L. Stanton & C. Dunkel-Schetter (Eds.), *Infertility: Perspectives from stress and coping research* (pp. 29–57). New York: Plenum.

Duran-Aydintug, C. (1995). Former spouses exiting role identities. *Journal of Divorce and Remarriage, 24,* 23–40.

Dyk, P. H., & Adams, G. R. (1987). The association between identity development and intimacy during adolescence: A theoretical treatise. *Journal of Adolescent Research, 2,* 223–235.

Dyk, P. H., & Adams, G. R. (1990). Identity and intimacy: An initial investigation of three theoretical models using cross-lag panel correlations. *Journal of Youth and Adolescence, 19,* 91–110.

Easterlin, R. A., Schaeffer, C. M., & Macunovich, D. J. (1993). Will the baby boomers be less well off than their parents? Income, wealth, and family circumstances over the life cycle in the United States. *Population and Development Review, 19,* 497–522.

Eccles, J. S., Early, D., Fraser, K., Belansky, E., & McCarthy, K. (1997). The relation of connection, regulation, and support for autonomy to adolescents' functioning. *Journal of Adolescent Research, 12,* 263–286.

Eccles, J. S., & Roeser, R. R. (2003). Schools as developmental contexts. In G. R. Adams & M. D. Berzonsky (Eds.), *Blackwell handbook of adolescent development* (pp. 129–148). Oxford, UK: Blackwell.

Eisenhandler, S. A. (1990). The asphalt identikit: Old age and the driver's license. *International Journal of Aging and Human Development, 30,* 1–14.

Eisikovits, R. A. (2000). Gender differences in cross-cultural adaptation styles of immigrant youths from the former U.S.S.R. in Israel. *Youth and Society, 31,* 310–331.

Elias, C. J., & Iniu, T. S. (1993). When a house is not a home: Exploring the meaning of shelter among chronically homeless elderly men. *The Gerontologist, 33,* 396–402.

Elkind, D. (1981). *The hurried child.* Reading, MA: Addison-Wesley.

Erikson, E. H. (1956). The problem of ego identity. *Journal of the American Psychoanalytic Association, 4,* 56–121.

Erikson, E. H. (1958). *Young man Luther: A study in psychoanalysis and history.* New York: Norton.

Erikson, E. H. (1963). *Childhood and society* (2nd ed.). New York: Norton.

Erikson, E. H. (1964). *Insight and responsibility.* New York: Norton.

Erikson, E. H. (1968). *Identity: Youth and crisis.* New York: Norton.

Erikson, E. H. (1969a). *Gandhi's truth.* New York: Norton.

Erikson, E. H. (1969b). The problem of ego identity. *Psychological Issues, 1,* 101–164.

Erikson, E. H. (1975). *Life history and the historical moment.* New York: Norton.

Erikson, E. H. (1982). *The life cycle completed.* New York: Norton.

Erikson, E. H. (1997). *The life cycle completed* (extended version). New York: Norton.

Erikson, E. H., Erikson, J. M., & Kivnick, H. (1986). *Vital involvement in old age.* New York: Norton.

Evans, L., Ekerdt, D., & Bossé, R. (1985). Proximity of retirement and anticipatory involvement: Findings from the Normative Aging Study. *Journal of Gerontology, 40,* 368–374.

Faber, R. S. (1990). Widowhood: Integrating loss and love. *Psychotherapy Patient, 6,* 39–48.

Fadjukoff, P., Pulkkinen, L., & Kokko, K. (2005). Identity processes in adulthood: Diverging domains. *Identity: An International Journal of Theory and Research, 5*, 1–20.

Feather, N. T. (1990). *The psychological impact of unemployment.* New York: Springer-Verlag.

Feather, N. T., & O'Brien, G. E. (1986). A longitudinal study of the effects of employment and unemployment on school-leavers. *Journal of Occupational Psychology, 59*, 121–144.

Federal Interagency Forum on Aging Related Statistics. (2000). *Older Americans 2000: Key indicators of well-being.* Washington, DC: The Data Dissemination Branch of the National Center on Health Statistics. Retrieved July 25, 2003, from http://www.agingstats.gov/chartbook2000/default.htm

Fishman, S. (1992). Relationships among an older adult's life review, ego integrity, and death anxiety. *International Psychogeriatrics, 4*(Suppl. 2), 267–277.

Fitch, S. A., & Adams, G. R. (1983). Ego identity and intimacy status: Replication and extension. *Developmental Psychology, 19*, 839–845.

Flammer, A., & Schaffner, B. (2003). Adolescent leisure across European nations. *New Directions for Child and Adolescent Development, 99*, 65–78.

Flanagan, C. (2004). Institutional support for morality: Community-based and neighborhood organizations. In T. A. Thorkildsen & H. J. Walberg (Eds.), *Nurturing morality* (pp. 173–183). New York: Kluwer Academic/Plenum.

Florian, V., & Mikulincer, M. (1997). Fear of personal death in adulthood: The impact of early and recent losses. *Death Studies, 21*, 1–24.

Flum, H. (1994). Styles of identity formation in early and middle adolescence. *Genetic, social, and General Psychology Monographs, 120*, 435–467.

Flum, H., & Blustein, D. L. (2000). Reinvigorating the study of vocational exploration: A framework for research. *Journal of Vocational Behavior, 56*, 380–404.

Fowler, J. W. (1981). *Faith and human development.* New York: Harper & Row.

Freeman, R. B., & Wise, D. A. (1982). *The youth labor market: Problems in the United States.* Chicago: University of Chicago Press.

Fry, C. L., Dickerson-Putnam, J., Draper. P., Ikels, C., Keith, J., Glascick, J., et al. (1997). Culture and meaning of a good old age. In J. Sokolovsky (Ed.), *The cultural context of aging,* (2nd ed., pp. 99–123). Westport, CT: Bergin & Garvey.

Fryer, D. (1997). International perspectives on youth unemployment and mental health: Some central issues. *Journal of Adolescence, 20*, 333–342.

Fullinwider-Bush, N., & Jacobvitz, D. (1993). The transition to young adulthood: Generational boundary dissolution and female identity development. *Family Process, 32*, 87–103.

Furman, W., & Buhrmeister, D. (1992). Age and sex differences in perceptions of networks of personal relationships. *Child Development, 63*, 103–115.

Furrow, J. L., King, P. E., & White, K. (2004). Religion and positive youth development: Identity, meaning, and prosocial concerns. *Applied Developmental Science, 8*, 17–26.

Gaber, I. (1994). Transracial placements in Britain: A history. In I. Gaber & J. Aldredge (Eds.), *Culture, identity and transracial adoption: In the best interest of the child* (pp. 12–42). London: Free Association Books.

Gaddis, A., & Brooks-Gunn, J. (1985). The male experience of pubertal change. *Journal of Youth and Adolescence, 14,* 61–70.

Galambos, N. L., Almeida, D. M., & Petersen, A. C. (1990). Masculinity, femininity, and sex role attitudes in early adolescence: Exploring gender intensification. *Child Development, 61,* 1905–1914.

Galinsky, E. (1993). *National study of the changing work force.* New York: Families and Work Institute.

Galinsky, E., Bond, J. T., & Friedman, D. E. (1993). *The national study of the changing workforce: Highlights.* New York: Families and Work Institute.

Gallo, L. C., & Matthews, K. A. (2003). Understanding the association between socioeconomic status and physical health: Do negative emotions play a role? *Psychological Bulletin, 129,* 10–51.

Garbarino, J. (1999). *Lost boys: Why our sons turn violent and how we can save them.* New York: Free Press.

Gardner, R. M., Friedman, B. N., & Jackson, N. A. (1999). Hispanic and White children's judgments of perceived and ideal body size in self and others. *Psychological Record, 49,* 555–564.

Gergen, K. J. (1991). *The saturated self: Dilemmas of identity in contemporary life.* New York: Basic Books.

Gillespie, L. K., & MacDermid, S. M. (1993, March). *Is women's identity achievement associated with the expression of generativity: Examining identity and generativity in multiple roles.* Paper presented at the biennial meeting of the Society for Research on Child Development, New Orleans, LA.

Gilligan, C. (1982). *In a different voice: Psychological theory and women's development.* Cambridge, MA: Harvard University Press.

Ginsburg, S. D., & Orlofsky, J. L. (1981). Ego identity status, ego development, and locus of control in college women. *Journal of Youth and Adolescence, 10,* 297–307.

Ginzberg, E. (1972). Toward a theory of occupational choice: A re-statement. *Vocational Guidance Quarterly, 20,* 169–176.

Glenham, M., & Strayer, M. (1994, August). *A focus on elders' relationship status as central to their identity and integrity status in Erikson's psychosocial theory.* Paper presented at the annual meeting of the American Psychological Association, Los Angeles.

Goebel, B. L., & Boeck, B. E. (1986). Ego integrity and fear of death: A comparison of institutionalized and independently living older adults. *Death Studies, 11,* 193–204.

Goodenow, C., & Espin, O. M. (1993). Identity choices in immigrant adolescent females. *Adolescence, 28,* 173–184.

Graber, J. A., Brooks-Gunn, J., & Galen, B. R. (1998). Betwixt and between: Sexuality in the context of adolescent transitions. In R. Jessor (Ed.), *New perspectives on adolescent risk-taking behavior* (pp. 270–316). Cambridge, UK: Cambridge University Press.

Granic, I., Dishion, T. J., & Hollenstein, T. (2003). The family ecology of adolescence: A dynamic systems perspective on normative development. In G. R. Adams & M. D. Berzonsky (Eds.), *Blackwell handbook of adolescence* (pp. 60–91). Oxford, UK: Blackwell.

Greenberger, E., & Steinberg, L. (1986). *When teenagers work: The psychological and social costs of adolescent employment.* New York: Basic Books.

Grotevant, H. D. (1993). The integrative nature of identity: Bringing the soloists to sing in the choir. In J. Kroger (Ed.), *Discussions on ego identity* (pp. 121–146). Hillsdale, NJ: Lawrence Erlbaum.

Grotevant, H. D. (1997a). Coming to terms with adoption. *Adoption Quarterly, 1,* 3–27.

Grotevant, H. D. (1997b). Family processes, identity development, and behavioral outcomes for adopted adolescents. *Journal of Adolescent Research, 12,* 139–161.

Grotevant, H. D. (1998). Adolescent development in family contexts. In W. Damon (Ed.), *Handbook of child psychology* (5th ed., pp. 1097–1149). New York: Wiley.

Grotevant, H. D., & Bosma, H. (1994). History and literature. In H. A. Bosma, T. L. G. Graafsma, H. D. Grotevant, & D. J. deLevita (Eds.), *Identity and development: An interdisciplinary approach* (pp. 119–122). Thousand Oaks, CA: Sage.

Grotevant, H. D., & Cooper, C. R. (1986). Individuation in family relationships: A perspective on individual differences in the development of identity and role-taking skill in adolescence. *Human Development, 29,* 82–100.

Grotevant, H. D., Cooper, C. R., & Kramer, K. (1986). Exploration as a predictor of congruence in adolescents' career choices. *Journal of Vocational Behavior, 29,* 201–215.

Grotevant, H. D., Wrobel, G. M., van Dulmen, M. H., & McRoy, R. (2001). The emergence of psychosocial engagement in adopted adolescents: The family as context over time. *Journal of Adolescent Research, 16,* 469–490.

Grove, K. J. (1991). Identity development in interracial, Asian/White late adolescents: Must it be so problematic? *Journal of Youth and Adolescence, 20,* 617–628.

Grumbach, M. M., & Styne, D. M. (1998). Puberty: Ontogeny, neuroendocrinology, physiology, and disorders. In J. D. Wilson, D. W. Foster, & H. M. Kronenberg (Eds.), *Williams textbook of endocrinology* (pp. 1509–1625). Philadelphia: W. B. Sanders.

Gumbel, P. (2005, October 3). Will Europe ever work? *Time,* 32–37.

Gupta, V., & Korte, C. (1994). The effects of a confident and a peer group on the well-being of single elders. *International Journal of Aging and Human Development, 39,* 293–302.

Hamer, R. J., & Bruch, M. A. (1994). The role of shyness and private self-consciousness in identity development. *Journal of Research in Personality, 28,* 436–452.

Hannah, M. T., Domino, G., Figueredo, A. J., & Hendrickson, R. (1996). The prediction of ego integrity in older persons. *Educational and Psychological Measurement, 56,* 930–950.

Hansen, D., Larson, R., & Dworkin, J. (2003). What adolescents learn in organized youth activities: A survey of self-reported developmental experiences. *Journal of Research on Adolescence, 13, 25–55.*

Harker, L., & Solomon, M. (1996). Change in goals and values of men and women from early to mature adulthood. *Journal of Adult Development, 3, 133–143.*

Harris, D. (1990). *Sociology of aging.* New York: Harper & Row.

Harris, R., Ellicott, A., & Holmes, D. (1986). The timing of psychosocial transitions and changes in woman's lives: An examination of women aged 45 to 60. *Journal of Personality and Social Psychology, 51, 409–416.*

Hart, B. (1989). *Longitudinal study of women's identity status.* Unpublished doctoral dissertation, University of California, Berkeley.

Harter, S. (1990). Causes, correlates and the functional role of global self worth: In J. Kolligian & R. Sternberg (Eds.), *Perceptions of competence and incompetence across the life-span* (pp. 67–98). New Haven, CT: Yale University Press.

Hartung, P. J., Porfeli, E. J., & Vondracek, F. W. (2005). Child vocational development: A review and reconsideration. *Journal of Vocational Behavior, 66, 385–419.*

Harvey, J. H., Weber, A. L., & Orbuch, T. L. (1990). *Interpersonal accounts: A social psychological perspective.* Oxford, UK: Blackwell.

Hauser, S. T., Powers, S. I., Noam, G. G., Jacobson, A. M., Weiss, B., & Follansbee, D. J. (1984). Familial contexts of adolescent ego development. *Child Development, 55, 195–213.*

Hearn, S., Glenham, M., Strayer, J., Koopman, R., & Marcia, J. E. (2006). *Integrity, despair and in between: Toward construct validation of Erikson's eighth stage.* Manuscript submitted for publication.

Heidrich, S. M., & Ryff, C. D. (1993). The role of social comparisons processes in the psychological adaptation of elderly adults. *Journal of Gerontology: Psychological Sciences, 48, 127–136.*

Helson, R. (1992). Women's difficult times and the rewriting of the life story. *Psychology of Women Quarterly, 16, 331–347.*

Helson, R., & Sanjay, S. (2001). Three paths of adult development: Conservers, seekers, and achievers. *Journal of Personality and Social Psychology, 80, 995–1010.*

Hendricks, J. (2004). Public policies and old age identity. *Journal of Aging Studies, 18, 245–260.*

Henninghausen, K. H., Hauser, S. T., Billings, R. L., Schultz, L. H., & Allen, J. P. (2004). Adolescent ego development trajectories and young adult relationship outcomes. *Journal of Early Adolescence, 24, 29–44.*

Hill, J. P. (1973). *Some perspectives on adolescence in American society.* A report prepared for the Office of Child Development, U.S. Department of Health, Education, and Welfare, Washington, DC.

Hill, J. P., & Lynch, M. E. (1983). The intensification of gender-related role expectations during early adolescence. In J. Brooks-Gunn & A. C. Petersen (Eds.), *Girls at puberty: Biological and psychological perspectives* (pp. 201–228). New York: Plenum.

Hoare, C. H. (2002). *Erikson on development in adulthood: New insights from the unpublished papers*. New York: Oxford University Press.

Hodges, E., Boivin, M., Vitaro, F., & Bukowski, W. (1999). The power of friendship: Protection against an escalating cycle of peer victimization. *Developmental Psychology, 35,* 94–101.

Holmbeck, G., & Hill, J. (1991). Conflictive engagement, positive affect, and menarche in families with seventh-grade girls. *Child Development, 62,* 1030–1048.

Holmes, T. H., & Rahe, R. H. (1967). The social readjustment rating scale. *Journal of Psychosomatic Research, 11,* 213–218.

Hoopes, J. L. (1990). Adoption and identity formation. In D. M. Brodinzinsky & M. D. Schechter (Eds.), *The psychology of adoption* (pp. 144–166). New York: Oxford University Press.

Hoyer, W. J., & Roodin, P. A. (2003). *Adult development and aging* (5th ed.). Boston: McGraw-Hill.

Hoyer, W. J., & Rybash, J. M. (1994). Characterizing adult cognitive development. *Journal of Adult Development, 1,* 7–12.

Hunsberger, B., Pratt, M., & Pancer, S. M. (2001). Adolescent identity formation: Religious exploration and commitment. *Identity: An International Journal of Theory and Research, 1,* 365–386.

Hunter, W., & Pratt, M. (1988). What to teach in moral education: Lessons from research on age and sex differences in adult moral reasoning. *The Journal of Educational Thought, 22,* 103–117.

Huston, A. C., & Alvarez, M. (1990). The socialization context of gender role development in early adolescence. In R. M. Montemayor, G. R. Adams, & T. P. Gullotta (Eds.), *From childhood to adolescence: A transitional period?* (Advances in Adolescent Development, Vol. 2, pp. 156–179). Newbury Park, CA: Sage.

Hy, L. X., & Loevinger, J. (1996). *Measuring ego development* (2nd ed.). Hillsdale, NJ: Lawrence Erlbaum.

Irhammar, M. (1997). *Att utforska sitt ursprung* [In search of their origins]. Unpublished manuscript, University of Lund, Sweden.

Jackson, S. (1993). Social behavior in adolescence: The analysis of social interaction sequences. In S. Jackson & H. Rodriguez-Tomé (Eds.), *Adolescence and its social worlds* (pp. 15–45). Hillsdale, NJ: Lawrence Erlbaum.

Johnson, C., & Barer, B. M. (1993). Coping and a sense of control among the oldest old: An exploratory analysis. *Journal of Aging Studies, 7,* 67–80.

Johnson, K. (1996, March 7). In the class of '70, wounded winners. *New York Times,* pp. A1, A20–22.

Johnson, P., Buboltz, W. C., & Seemann, E. (2003). Ego identity status: A step in the differentiation process. *Journal of Counseling and Development, 81,* 191–195.

Johnson, W., & Krueger, R. F. (2004). Higher perceived life control decreases genetic variance in physical health: Evidence from a national twin study. *Journal of Personality and Social Psychology, 88,* 165–173.

Josselson, R. (1980). Ego development in adolescence. In J. Adelson (Ed.), *Handbook of Adolescent Psychology* (pp. 188–210). New York: Wiley.

Josselson, R. (1982). Personality structure and identity status in women viewed through early memories. *Journal of Youth and Adolescence, 11,* 293–299.

Josselson, R. (1987). *Finding herself: Pathways to identity development in women.* San Francisco: Jossey-Bass.

Josselson, R. (1996). *Revising herself: The story of women's identity from college to midlife.* New York: Oxford University Press.

Josselson, R., Lieblich, A., & McAdams, D. P. (Eds.). (2003). *Up close and personal: The teaching and learning of narrative research.* Washington, DC: American Psychological Association.

Jung, C. G. (1969). The structure and dynamics of the psyche. In *The collected works of C. G. Jung* (Vol. 8). Princeton, NJ: Princeton University Press. (Original work published 1931)

Kacerguis, M. A., & Adams, G. R. (1980). Erikson stage resolution: The relationship between identity and intimacy. *Journal of Youth and Adolescence, 9,* 117–126.

Kahn, S., Zimmerman, G., Csikszentmihalyi, M., & Getzels, J. W. (1985). Relations between identity in young adulthood and intimacy at midlife. *Journal of Personality and Social Psychology, 49,* 1316–1322.

Kalish, R. (1985). The social context of death and dying. In R. H. Binstock & E. Shanas (Eds.), *Handbook of aging and the social sciences* (2nd ed., pp. 149–170). New York: Van Nostrand Reinhold.

Kaslow, F. W. (2004). Death of one's partner: The anticipation and the reality. *Professional Psychology: Research and Practice, 35,* 227–233.

Kastenbaum, R. M. (2000). *The psychology of death.* New York: Springer.

Kaufman, G., & Elder, G. H. (2002). Revisiting age identity: A research note. *Journal of Aging Studies, 16,* 169–176.

Keating, D. (1996). Habits of mind for a learning society: Educating for human development. In D. Olson & N. Torrance (Eds.), *The handbook of education and human development: New models of learning, teaching and schooling* (pp. 461–481). Oxford, UK: Blackwell.

Keating, D., & Sasse, E. (1996). Cognitive socialization in adolescence: Critical period for a critical habit of mind. In G. R. Adams, R. Montemayor, & T. P. Gullotta (Eds.), *Psychosocial development during adolescence* (pp. 232–258). Thousand Oaks, CA: Sage.

Keefe, K., & Berndt, T. J. (1996). Relations of friendship quality to self-esteem in early adolescence. *Journal of Early Adolescence, 16,* 110–129.

Keen, S. (1977). The heroics of everyday life: A theorist of death confronts his own end. A conversation with Ernest Becker. In S. H. Zarit (Ed.), *Readings in aging and death: Contemporary perspectives* (pp. 300–305). New York: Harper & Row.

Kegan, R. (1982). *The evolving self: Problem and process in human development.* Cambridge, MA: Harvard University Press.

Kegan, R. (1994). *In over our heads: The mental demands of modern life.* Cambridge, MA: Harvard University Press.

Kegan, R., & Lahey, L. L. (2001). *How the way we talk can change the way we work.* San Francisco: Jossey-Bass.

Kennedy, J. (1999). Romantic attachment style and ego identity, attributional style, and family of origin in first-year college students. *College Student Journal, 33,* 171–180.

Kenny, M. E., Lomax, R., Brabeck, M., & Fife, J. (1998). Longitudinal pathways linking adolescent reports of maternal and paternal attachments to psychological well-being. *Journal of Early Adolescence, 18,* 221–243.

Kim, K., Conger, R., Lorenz, F., & Elder, G. H. (2001). Parent-adolescent reciprocity in negative affect and its relation to early adult social development. *Developmental Psychology, 37,* 775–790.

Kim, Y. K., Kim, E. Y., & Kang, J. (2003). Teens' mall shopping motivations: Functions of loneliness and media usage. *Family and Consumer Sciences Research Journal, 32,* 140–167.

Kinnvall, C. (2004). Globalization, identity, and the search for chosen traumas. In K. Hoover (Ed.), *The future of identity: Centennial reflections on the legacy of Erik Erikson* (pp. 111–136). Boston: Lexington Books.

Kissman, K. (1990). Social support and gender role attitude among teenage mothers. *Adolescence, 25,* 709–716.

Kitson, G. C., & Morgan, L. A. (1990). The multiple consequences of divorce: A decade review. *Journal of Marriage and the Family, 52,* 913–924.

Klaczynski, P. A., Fauth, J. M., & Swanger, A. (1998). Adolescent identity: Rational vs. experiential processing, formal operations, and critical thinking beliefs. *Journal of Youth and Adolescence, 27,* 185–207.

Kleinfield, N. R. (1996, March 4). The company as family, no more. *New York Times,* pp. A1, A12–14.

Kleinman, A. (1988). *The illness narratives.* New York: Basic Books.

Kliegel, M., Moor, C., & Rott, C. (2004). Cognitive status and development in the oldest old: A longitudinal analysis from the Heidelberg Centenarian Study. *Archives of Gerontology and Geriatrics, 39,* 143–156.

Kobak, R. R., & Sceery, A. (1988). Attachment in late adolescence: Working models, affect regulation, and representations of self and others. *Child Development, 59,* 135–146.

Kohlberg, L. (1969). Stage and sequence: The cognitive-developmental approach to socialization. In D. A. Goslin (Ed.), *Handbook of socialization theory and research* (pp. 347–480). Chicago: Rand-McNally.

Kohlberg, L. (1973). Stages and aging in moral development: Some speculations. *The Gerontologist, 13,* 497–502.

Kohlberg, L. (1984). *The psychology of moral development: The nature and validity of moral stages* (Vol. 2). New York: Harper & Row.

Kohlberg, L., & Power, C. (1981). Moral development, religious thinking, and the question of a seventh stage. In L. Kohlberg (Ed.), *The philosophy of moral development* (Vol. 1, pp. 311–372). San Francisco: Harper & Row.

Kohler, J. K., Grotevant, H. D., & McRoy, R. G. (2002). Adopted adolescents' preoccupations with adoption: The impact on adoptive family relationships. *Journal of Marriage and the Family, 64,* 93–104.

Koski, K. J., & Steinberg, L. (1990). Parenting satisfaction of mothers during midlife. *Journal of Youth and Adolescence, 5,* 465–474.

Kotre, J. (1984). *Outliving the self: Generativity and the interpretation of lives.* Baltimore: Johns Hopkins University Press.

Kotre, J., & Hall, E. (1990). *Seasons of life.* Boston: Little, Brown.

Kroger, J. (1983). I knew who I was when I got up this morning. *SET Research Information for Teachers, 1,* 1–6.

Kroger, J. (1986). The relative importance of identity status interview components: replication and extension. *Journal of Adolescence, 9,* 337–354.

Kroger, J. (1988). A longitudinal study of ego identity status interview domains. *Journal of Adolescence, 11,* 49–64.

Kroger, J. (1990). Ego structuralization in late adolescence as seen through early memories and ego identity status. *Journal of Adolescence, 13,* 65–77.

Kroger, J. (1995). The differentiation of "firm" and "developmental" foreclosure identity statuses: A longitudinal study. *Journal of Research on Adolescence, 10,* 317–337.

Kroger, J. (1997). Gender and identity: The intersection of structure, content, and context. *Sex Roles, 36,* 747–770.

Kroger, J. (2002). Identity processes and contents through the years of late adulthood. *Identity: An International Journal of Theory and Research, 2,* 81–108.

Kroger, J. (2004). *Identity in adolescence: The balance between self and other* (3rd ed.). London: Routledge.

Kroger, J. (in press). Why is identity achievement so elusive? *Identity: An International Journal of Theory and Research.*

Kroger, J., & Green, K. (1996). Events associated with identity status change. *Journal of Adolescence, 19,* 477–490.

Kroger, J., & Haslett, S. J. (1987). An analysis of ego identity status changes from adolescence through middle adulthood. *Social and Behavioral Sciences Documents, 17* (Ms. 2792).

Kroger, J., & Haslett, S. J. (1991). A comparison of ego identity status transition pathways and change rates across five identity domains. *International Journal of Aging and Human Development, 32,* 303–330.

Kroger, J., Martinussen, M., & Marcia, J. E. (2006, May). *Developmental dimensions of the ego identity statuses: A meta-analysis.* Paper presented at the 10th biennial meeting of the European Association for Research on Adolescence, Anatalya, Turkey.

Kübler-Ross, E. (1969). *On death and dying.* New York: Macmillan.

Kübler-Ross, E. (1981). *Living with dying.* New York: Macmillan.

Kübler-Ross, E. (1991). The dying child. In D. Papadatou & C. Papadatos (Eds.), *Children and death* (pp. 147–160). New York: Macmillan.

Kulenovic, A., & Super, D. E. (1995). The five major life roles reviewed cross-nationally. In D. E. Super & B. Sverko (Eds.), *Life roles, values, and careers: International findings of the work importance study* (pp. 252–277). San Francisco: Jossey-Bass.

Kunnen, E. S., & Wassink, M. E. K. (2003). An analysis of identity change in adulthood. *Identity: An International Journal of Theory and Research, 3,* 347–366.

Kvernmo, S., & Heyerdahl, S. (1998). Influence of ethnic factors on behavioral problems in indigenous Sami and majority Norwegian adolescents. *Journal of Child and Adolescent Psychiatry, 37,* 743–751.

Kvernmo, S., & Heyerdahl, S. (2002). Acculturation strategies and ethnic identity as predictors of behavior problems in Arctic minority adolescents. *Journal of Child and Adolescent Psychiatry, 42,* 57–65.

Labouvie-Vief, G. (1990). Modes of knowledge and the organization of development. In M. L. Commons, L. Kohlberg, R. Richards, & S. Sinnott (Eds.), *Beyond formal operations: 2. Models and methods in the study of adult and adolescent thought.* New York: Praeger.

Labouvie-Vief, G. (2005). Self-with-other representations and the organization of the self. *Journal of Research in Personality, 39,* 185–205.

Labouvie-Vief, G., & Hakim-Larson, J. (1989). Developmental shifts in adult thought. In S. Hunter & M. Sundel (Eds.), *Midlife myths: Issues, findings, and practice implications* (pp. 69–96). Newbury Park, CA: Sage.

LaFromboise, T. D., & Low, K. G. (1989). American Indian children and adolescents. In J. T. Gibbs & L. N. Huang (Eds.), *Children of color* (pp. 114–147). San Francisco: Jossey-Bass.

Lahey, L., Souvaine, E., Kegan, R., Goodman, R., & Felix, S. (1987). *A guide to the subject-object interview: Its administration and interpretation.* Unpublished manuscript, Harvard Graduate School of Education.

Lang, F. R., & Carstensen, L. L. (2002). Time counts: Future time perspective, goals, and social relationships. *Psychology and Aging, 17,* 125–139.

Längle, A. (2004). Existential questions of the elderly. *Archives of Psychiatry and Psychotherapy, 6,* 15–20.

Lannegrand-Willems, L., & Bosma, H. A. (2006). Identity development-in-context: The school as an important context for identity development. *Identity: An International Journal of Theory and Research, 6,* 85–113.

Lanz, M., Iafrate, R., Rosnati, R., & Scabini, E. (1999). Parent-child communication and adolescent self-esteem in separated, intercountry adoptive and intact non-adoptive families. *Journal of Adolescence, 22,* 785–794.

Lapsley, D. K., Rice, K., & Fitzgerald, D. P. (1990). Adolescent attachment, identity, and adjustment to college: Implications for the continuity of adaptation hypothesis. *Journal of Counseling and Development, 68,* 561–565.

Larson, R., & Richards, M. H. (1994). *Divergent realities.* New York: Basic Books.

LaVoie, J., & de Vries, B. (2003–2004). Identity and death: An empirical investigation. *Omega, 48,* 223–243.

Leiblum, S. R. (1997). Introduction. In S. R. Leiblum (Ed.), *Infertility: Psychological issues and counseling strategies* (pp. 3–19). New York: Wiley.

Leiblum, S. R., & Greenfeld, D. A. (1997). The course of infertility: Immediate and long-term reactions. In S. R. Leiblum (Ed.), *Infertility: Psychological issues and counseling strategies* (pp. 83–102). New York: Wiley.

Lemme, B. H. (1995). *Development in adulthood*. Boston: Allyn & Bacon.

Leone, C., & Hall, I. (2003). Self-monitoring, marital dissatisfaction, and relationship dissolution: Individual differences in orientations to marriage and divorce. *Self and Identity, 2,* 189–202.

Leventhal, E. A. (1996). Biology of aging. In J. Sadavoy, L. W. Lazarus, L. F. Jarvik, & G. T. Grossberg (Eds.), *Comprehensive review of geriatric psychiatry* (2nd ed., pp. 81–112). Washington, DC: American Psychiatric Press.

Levine, J. B., Green, C. J., & Millon, T. (1986). Separation-Individuation Test of Adolescence, *Journal of Personality Assessment, 50,* 123–137.

Levine, S. V. (1982). The psychological and social effects of youth unemployment. *Adolescent Psychiatry, 10,* 24–40.

Levinson, D. J. (1978). *The seasons of a man's life*. New York: Alfred Knopf.

Levinson, D. J. (1996). *The seasons of a woman's life*. New York: Alfred Knopf.

Levitz-Jones, E. M., & Orlofsky, J. L. (1985). Separation-individuation and intimacy capacity in college women, *Journal of Personality and Social Psychology, 49,* 156–169.

Lindblad, F., Hjern, A., & Vinnerljung, B. (2003). Intercountry adopted children as young adults: A Swedish cohort study. *American Journal of Orthopsychiatry, 73,* 190–202.

Lindemann, E. (1944). Symptomatology and management of acute grief. *American Journal of Psychiatry, 101,* 141–148.

Lindenberger, U., & Baltes, P. B. (1997). Intellectual functioning in old and very old age: Cross-sectional results from the Berlin Aging Study. *Psychology and Aging, 12,* 410–432.

Loevinger, J. (1976). *Ego development: Conceptions and theories*. San Francisco: Jossey-Bass.

Loevinger, J., & Wessler, R. (1970). *Measuring ego development* (Vol. 1). San Francisco: Jossey-Bass.

Longino, C. F. (1988). Who are the oldest Americans? *The Gerontologist, 28,* 515–523.

Longino, C. F., & Mittelmark, M. B. (1996). Sociodemographic aspects. In J. Sadavoy, L. W. Lazarus, L. F. Jarvik, & G. T. Grossberg (Eds.), *Comprehensive review of geriatric psychiatry* (2nd ed., pp. 135–152). Washington, DC: American Psychiatric Press.

Lopata, H. Z. (1996). *Current widowhood: Myths & realities*. Thousand Oaks, CA: Sage.

Luyckx, K., Goossens, L., Soenens, B., Beyers, W., & Vansteenkiste, M. (2005). Identity statuses based upon four rather than two identity dimensions: Extending and refining Marcia's paradigm. *Journal of Youth and Adolescence, 34,* 605–618.

Magdol, L. (2003). Is moving gendered? The effects of residential mobility on the psychological well-being of men and women. *Sex Roles, 47,* 553–560.

Mahler, M. S. (1963). Thoughts about development and individuation. *Psycho-analytic Study of the Child, 18,* 307–324.

Malina, R. M. (1991). Growth spurt, adolescent. II. In R. M. Lerner, A. C. Petersen, & J. Brooks-Gunn (Eds.), *Encyclopedia of adolescence* (Vol. 1, pp. 425–429). New York: Garland.

Mallory, M. (1989). Q-sort definition of ego identity status. *Journal of Youth and Adolescence, 18,* 399–412.

Manners, J., & Durkin, K. (2001). A critical review of the validity of ego development theory and its measurement. *Journal of Personality Assessment, 77,* 541–567.

Marcia, J. E. (1966). Development and validation of ego identity status. *Journal of Personality and Social Psychology, 3,* 551–558.

Marcia, J. E. (1967). Ego identity status: relationship to change in self-esteem, "general maladjustment," and authoritarianism. *Journal of Personality, 35,* 118–133.

Marcia, J. E. (1976). Identity six years after: A follow-up study. *Journal of Youth and Adolescence, 5,* 145–150.

Marcia, J. E. (1983). Some directions for the investigation of ego development in early adolescence. *Journal of Early Adolescence, 3,* 215–223.

Marcia, J. E. (1993). The relational roots of identity. In J. Kroger (Ed.), *Discussions on ego identity* (pp. 101–120). Hillsdale, NJ: Lawrence Erlbaum.

Marcia, J. E. (2002). Identity and psychosocial development in adulthood. *Identity: An International Journal of Theory and Research, 2,* 7–28.

Marcia, J. E., & Strayer, J. (1996). Theories and stories. *Psychological Inquiry, 7,* 346–350.

Marcia, J. E., Waterman, A. S., Matteson, D. R., Archer, S. L., & Orlofsky, J. L. (Eds.). (1993). *Ego identity: A handbook for psychosocial research.* New York: Springer-Verlag.

Markovits, H., & Valchon, R. (1990). Conditional reasoning, representation, and level of abstraction. *Developmental Psychology, 26,* 942–951.

Markstom-Adams, C. A., & Smith, M. (1996). Identity formation and religious orientation among high school students from the United States and Canada. *Journal of Adolescence, 19,* 237–261.

Markstrom, C. A. (1999). Religious involvement and adolescent psychosocial development. *Journal of Adolescence, 22,* 205–221.

Markstrom, C. A. (in press). *Empowerment of North American Indian girls: Ritual expressions at puberty.* Lincoln: University of Nebraska Press.

Markstrom, C. A., & Iborra, A. (2003). Adolescent identity formation and rites of passage: The Navajo Kinaalda ceremony for girls. *Journal of Research on Adolescence, 13,* 399–425.

Markus, H., & Nurius, P. (1986). Possible selves. *American Psychologist, 41,* 954–969.

Markus, H. R., Plaut, V. C., & Lachman, M. E. (2004). Well-being in America: Core features and regional patterns. In O. G. Brim, C. D. Ryff, & R. C. Kessler (Eds.), *How healthy are we? A national study of well-being at midlife* (pp. 614–650). Chicago: University of Chicago Press.

Marsiglio, W., & Donnelly, D. (1991). Sexual relations in later life: A national survey of married persons. *Journal of Gerontology: Social Sciences, 46,* S333–S334.

Mattanah, J. F., Hancock, G. R., & Brand, B. L. (2004). Parental attachment, separation-individuation, and college student adjustment: A structural equation analysis of mediational effects. *Journal of Counseling Psychology, 51,* 213–225.

Matthews, R., & Matthews, A. M. (1986). Infertility and involuntary childlessness: The transition to nonparenthood. *Journal of Marriage and the Family, 48,* 641–649.

McAdams, D. P. (1988). *Power, intimacy, and the life story: Personological inquiries into identity.* New York: Guilford Press.

McAdams, D. P. (1996). Personality, modernity, and the storied self: A contemporary framework for studying persons. *Psychological Inquiry, 7,* 295–321.

McAdams, D. P., & de St. Aubin, E. (1992). A theory of generativity and its assessment through self-report, behavioral acts, and narrative themes in autobiography. *Journal of Personality and Social Psychology, 62,* 1003–1015.

McAdams, D. P., & Logan, R. L. (2004). What is generativity? In E. de St. Aubin, D. P. McAdams, & T. C. Kim (Eds.), *The generative society* (pp. 15–31). Washington, DC: American Psychological Association.

McAdams, D. P., Ruetzel, K., & Foley, J. M. (1986). Complexity and generativity at mid-life: Relations among social motives, ego development, and adults' plans for the future. *Journal of Personality and Social Psychology, 50,* 800–807.

McCabe, M. P., & Riccardelli, L. A. (2003). Sociocultural influences on body image and body changes among adolescent boys and girls. *Journal of Social Psychology, 143,* 5–26.

McCarthy, C. (1994). *The crossing.* New York: Alfred A. Knopf.

McIntosh, H., Metz, E., & Youniss, J. (2005). Community service and identity formation in adolescence. In J. L. Mahoney, R. W. Larson, & J. S. Eccles (Eds.), *Organized activities as contexts of development: Extracurricular activities, after-school and community programs* (pp. 331–351). Mahwah, NJ: Lawrence Erlbaum.

McIntosh, W. A., Kaplan, H. B., Kubena, K. S., & Landmann, W. A. (1993). Life events, social support, and immune response in elderly individuals. *International Journal of Aging and Human Development, 37,* 23–36.

McLaren, L., & Kuh, D. (2004). Body dissatisfaction in midlife women. *Journal of Women and Aging, 16,* 35–54.

McQuillan, J., Griel, A., White, L., & Jacob, M. C. (2003). Frustrated fertility: Infertility and psychological distress among women. *Journal of Marriage and Family, 65,* 1007–1018.

Mead, G. H. (1934). *Mind, self, and society.* Chicago: University of Chicago Press.

Meeus, W., Decovic, M., & Iedema, J. (1997). Unemployment and identity in adolescence. *Career Development Quarterly, 45,* 369–380.

Melina, L. R., & Rosnia, S. K. (1993). *The open adoption experience.* New York: HarperCollins.

Michael, R. T., Gagnon, J. H., Laumann, E. O., & Kolata, G. (1994). *Sex in America: A definitive study.* Boston: Little, Brown.

Miller, B., Bayley, B. K., Christensen, M., Leavitt, S. C., & Coyl, B. K. (2003). Adolescent pregnancy and childbearing. In G. R. Adams & M. D. Berzonsky (Eds.), *Blackwell handbook of adolescence* (pp. 415–449). Oxford, UK: Blackwell.

Moen, P., & Wethington, E. (1999). Midlife development in a life course context. In S. L. Willis & J. D. Reid (Eds.), *Life in the middle: Psychological and social development in middle age* (pp. 3–23). San Diego, CA: Academic Press.

Montgomery, M. (2005). Psychosocial intimacy and identity: From early adolescence to emerging adulthood. *Journal of Adolescent Research, 20,* 346–374.

Montgomery, M. J., & Côté, J. E. (2003). College as a transition to adulthood. In G. R. Adams & M. D. Berzonsky (Eds.), *Blackwell handbook of adolescence* (pp. 149–172). Oxford, UK: Blackwell.

Mor-Barak, M. E. (1995). The meaning of work for older adults seeking employment: The generativity factor. *International Journal of Aging and Human Development, 41,* 345–358.

Morash, M. A. (1980). Working class membership and the adolescent identity crisis. *Adolescence, 15,* 313–320.

Morse, C. A., & Van Hall, E. V. (1987). Psychosocial aspects of infertility: A review of current concepts. *Journal of Psychosomatic Obstetrics and Gynaecology, 6,* 157–164.

Mortimer, J. (2003). *Working and growing up in America.* Cambridge, MA: Harvard University Press.

Mortimer, J. T., Zimmer-Gembeck, M. J., Holmes, M., & Shanahan, M. J. (2002). The process of occupational decision-making: Patterns during the transition to adulthood. *Journal of Vocational Behavior, 61,* 439–465.

Moss-Morris, R., Petrie, K. J., & Weinman, J. (1996). Functioning in chronic fatigue syndrome: Do illness perceptions play a regulatory role? *British Journal of Health Psychology, 1,* 15–25.

Muller, J., Nielsen, C. T., & Skakkebaek, N. E. (1989). Testicular maturation and pubertal growth and development in normal boys. In J. M. Tanner & M. A. Preece (Eds.), *The physiology of human growth* (pp. 201–207). Cambridge, UK: Cambridge University Press.

Munro, G., & Adams, G. R. (1977). Ego identity formation in college students and working youth. *Developmental Psychology, 13,* 523–524.

Mutran, E., & Reitzes, D. C. (1981). Retirement, identity and well-being: Realignment of role relationships. *Journal of Gerontology, 36,* 733–740.

Muuss, R. E. (1980). Puberty rites in primitive and modern societies. In R. E. Muuss (Ed.), *Adolescent behavior and society* (3rd ed., pp. 109–128). New York: Random House.

Neubauer, J. (1994). Problems of identity in modernist fiction. In H. A. Bosma, T. L. G. Graafsma, H. D. Grotevant, & D. J. deLevita (Eds.), *Identity and development: An interdisciplinary approach* (pp. 123–134). Thousand Oaks, CA: Sage.

Neugarten, B. L. (1977). Personality and aging. In J. E. Birren & K. W. Schaie (Eds.), *Handbook of the psychology of aging* (pp. 626–649). New York: Van Nostrand Reinhold.

Neugarten, B. L., & Neugarten, D. A. (1986). Changing meanings of age in the aging society. In A. Pifer & L. Bronte (Eds.), *Our aging society: Paradox and promise* (pp. 33–51). New York: Norton.

Neugarten, B. L., & Neugarten, D. A. (1996). *The meanings of age: Selected papers of Bernice L. Neugarten.* Chicago: University of Chicago Press.

Newman, B. M., & Newman, P. R. (2001). Group identity and alienation: Giving the we its due. *Journal of Youth and Adolescence, 30,* 515–538.

Newsom, J. T., & Schulz, R. (1996). Social support as a mediator in the relation between functional status and quality of life in older adults. *Psychology and Aging, 11,* 34–44.

Noack, P., & Buhl, H. M. (2004). Relations with parents and friends during adolescence and early adulthood. *Marriage and Family Review, 36,* 31–51.

Noam, G. G. (1992). Development as the aim of clinical intervention. *Development and Psychopathology, 4,* 679–696.

Nurmi, J. E., Poole, M. E., & Kalakoski, V. (1994). Age differences in adolescent future-oriented goals, concerns, and related temporal extension in different sociocultural contexts. *Journal of Youth and Adolescence, 23,* 471–487.

Ochberg, R. (2003). Teaching interpretation. In R. Josselson, A. Lieblich, & D. P. McAdams (Eds.), *Up close and personal: The teaching and learning of narrative research* (pp. 113–133). Washington, DC: American Psychological Association.

Offer, D. (1991). Adolescent development: A normative perspective. In S. I. Greenspan & G. H. Pollock (Eds.), *The course of life: Adolescence* (Vol. IV, pp. 181–199). Madison, CT: International Universities Press.

Ogletree, M., Jones, R., & Coyl, D. (2002). Fathers and their adolescent sons: Pubertal development and paternal involvement. *Journal of Adolescent Research, 17,* 418–424.

Olshansky, E. F. (1987). Identity of self as infertile: An example of theory generating research. *Advanced Nursing Science, 9,* 54–63.

Ontai-Grzebik, L. L. (2004). Individual and social influences on ethnic identity among Latino young adults. *Journal of Adolescent Research, 19,* 559–575.

Organisation for Economic Co-operation and Development. (1995). *Economic outlook.* Paris: Author.

Organisation for Economic Co-operation and Development. (2004). *Economic outlook.* Paris: Author.

Orlofsky, J. L. (1976). Intimacy status: Relationship to interpersonal perception. *Journal of Youth and Adolescence, 5,* 73–88.

Orlofsky, J. L. (1978). The relationship between intimacy status and antecedent personality components. *Adolescence, 13,* 419–441.

Orlofsky, J. L., & Frank, M. (1986). Personality structure as viewed through early memories and identity status in college men and women. *Journal of Personality and Social Psychology, 50,* 580–586.

Orlofsky, J. L., Marcia, J. E., & Lesser, I. M. (1973). Ego identity status and the intimacy versus isolation crisis of young adulthood. *Journal of Personality and Social Psychology, 27,* 211–219.

Ornstein, S., & Isabella, L. (1990). Age vs. stage models of career attitudes of women: A partial replication and extension. *Journal of Vocational Behavior, 36,* 1–9.

Ozer, E., Macdonald, T., & Irwin, C. (2002). Adolescent health care in the United States: Implications and projections for the new millennium. In J. Mortimer &

R. Larson (Eds.), *The changing adolescent experience: Social trends and the transition to adulthood* (pp. 129–174). New York: Cambridge University Press.

Paikoff, R. L., & Brooks-Gunn, J. (1990). Physiological processes: What role do they play during the transition to adolescence? In R. M. Montemayor, G. R. Adams, & T. P. Gullotta (Eds.), *From childhood to adolescence: A transitional period? Advances in Adolescent Development* (Vol. 2, pp. 63–81). Newbury Park, CA: Sage.

Papini, D. R., Micka, J. C., & Barnett, J. K. (1989). Perceptions of intrapsychic and extrapsychic functioning as bases of adolescent ego identity status. *Journal of Adolescent Research, 4,* 462–482.

Papini, D. R., Sebby, R. A., & Clark, S. (1989). Affective quality of family relations and adolescent identity exploration. *Adolescence, 24,* 457–466.

Parker, S., Nichter, M., Nichter, N., Vuckovic, N., Sims, C., & Ritenbaugh, C. (1995). Body image and weight concern among Afro American and White adolescent females: Differences that make a difference. *Human Organization, 54,* 103–115.

Parks, S. (1986). *The critical years: Young adults and the search for meaning, faith, and commitment.* San Francisco: Harper.

Pasley, K., Kerpelman, J., & Guilbert, D. E. (2001). Gendered conflict, identity disruption, and marital instability: Expanding Gottman's model. *Journal of Social and Personal Relationships, 18,* 5–27.

Paterson, J., Pryor, J., & Field, J. (1995). Adolescent attachment to parents and friends in relation to aspects of self-esteem. *Journal of Youth and Adolescence, 24,* 365–376.

Patterson, G. R., & Fisher, P. A. (2002). Recent developments in our understanding of parenting: Bidirectional effects, causal models, and the search for parsimony. In M. H. Bornstein (Ed.), *Handbook of parenting* (2nd ed., pp. 125–150). Mahwah, NJ: Lawrence Erlbaum.

Patton, W., & Noller, P. (1990). Adolescent self-concept: Effects of being employed, unemployed, or returning to school. *Australian Journal of Psychology, 42,* 247–259.

Paulson, S. E., Marchant, G. J., & Rothlisberg, B. A. (1998). Early adolescents' perceptions of patterns of parenting, teaching, and school atmosphere: Implications for achievement. *Journal of Early Adolescence, 18,* 5–26.

Perosa, L. M., Perosa, S. L., & Tam, H. P. (1996). The contribution of family structure and differentiation to identity development in females. *Journal of Youth and Adolescence, 25,* 817–837.

Perosa, L. M., Perosa, S. L., & Tam, K. P. (2002). Intergenerational systems theory and identity development in young adult women. *Journal of Adolescent Research, 17,* 235–259.

Petersen, A. C., & Leffert, N. (1995). What is special about adolescence? In M. Rutter (Ed.), *Psychosocial disturbances in young people: Challenges for prevention* (pp. 3–36). Cambridge, UK: Cambridge University Press.

Peterson, B. (2002). Longitudinal analysis of midlife generativity, intergenerational roles, and caregiving. *Psychology and Aging, 17,* 161–168.

Peterson, B. E., & Stewart, A. J. (1993). Generativity and social motives in young adults. *Journal of Personality and Social Psychology, 65,* 186–198.

Phillips, S. (2003). Adolescent health. In I. B. Weiner (Ed.), *Handbook of psychology: Health psychology* (Vol. 9, pp. 465–485). New York: Wiley.

Phinney, J. S. (1989). Stages of ethnic identity development in minority group adolescents. *Journal of Early Adolescence, 9,* 34–49.

Phinney, J. S. (1996). When we talk about American ethnic groups, what do we mean? *American Psychologist, 51,* 918–927.

Phinney, J. S. (2000). Ethnic identity. In A. Kazdin (Ed.), *Encyclopedia of psychology* (pp. 254–259). Washington, DC, and New York: American Psychological Association and Oxford University Press.

Phinney, J. S. (2003). Ethnic identity and acculturation. In K. M. Chun, P. B. Organista, & G. Marin (Eds.), *Acculturation: Advances in theory, measurement, and applied research* (pp. 63–81). Washington, DC: American Psychological Association.

Phinney, J. S., & Alipuria, L. L. (1990). Ethnic identity in college students from four ethnic groups. *Journal of Adolescence, 13,* 171–183.

Phinney, J. S., & Chavira, V. (1992). Ethnic identity and self-esteem: A longitudinal study. *Journal of Adolescence, 15,* 271–281.

Phinney, J. S., & Rosenthal, D. A. (1992). Ethnic identity in adolescence: Process, context, and outcome. In G. R. Adams, T. P. Gullotta, & R. Montemayor, (Eds.), *Adolescent identity formation: Advances in adolescent development* (Vol. 4, pp. 145–172). Newbury Park, CA: Sage.

Piaget, J. (1968). *Structuralism.* New York: Harper & Row.

Piaget, J. (1972). Intellectual evolution from adolescence to adulthood. *Human Development, 15,* 1–12.

Pini, R., Tonon, E., Cavallini, M. C., Bencini, F., Di Bari, M., Masotti, G., et al. (2001). Accuracy of equations for predicting stature from knee height, and assessment of statural loss in an older Italian population. *Journals of Gerontology: Biological Sciences, 56,* B3–B7.

Platt, M. M. (2004). Identity and Parkinson's disease: Am I more than the sum of my parts? *Journal of Loss and Trauma, 9,* 315–326.

Podd, M. H. (1972). Ego identity status and morality: The relationship between two developmental constructs. *Developmental Psychology, 6,* 497–507.

Pratt, M. W., Diessner, R., Hunsberger, B., Pancer, S. M., & Savoy, K. (1991). Four pathways in the analysis of adult development and aging: Comparing analyses of reasoning about personal-life dilemmas. *Psychology and Aging, 6,* 666–675.

Pratt, M. W., Diessner, R., Pratt, A., Hunsberger, B., & Pancer, S. M. (1996). Moral and social reasoning and perspective taking in later life: A longitudinal study. *Psychology and Aging, 11,* 66–73.

Prause, J., & Dooley, D. (1997). Effect of underemployment on school leavers' self-esteem. *Journal of Adolescence, 20,* 243–260.

Pulkkinen, L. (1994, June). *An identity status as a component of life orientation in young adulthood.* Paper presented at the biennial meetings of the International Society for the Study of Behavioral Development, Amsterdam.

Pulkkinen, L., & Kokko, K. (2000). Identity development in adulthood: A longitudinal study. *Journal of Research in Personality, 34,* 445–470.

Quick, H. E., & Moen, P. (1998). Gender, employment and retirement quality: A life course approach to the differential experiences of men and women. *Journal of Occupational Health Psychology, 3,* 44–64.

Quintana, S. M., & Lapsley, D. K. (1990). Rapprochement in late adolescent separation-individuation: A structural equations approach. *Journal of Adolescence, 13,* 371–385.

Rabin, D. S., & Chrousos, G. P. (1991). Androgens, gonadal. In R. M. Lerner, A. C. Petersen, & J. Brooks-Gunn (Eds.), *Encyclopedia of adolescence* (Vol. 1, pp. 56–59). New York: Garland.

Ragin, C. C. (1987). *The comparative method: Moving beyond qualitative and quantitative strategies.* Berkeley: University of California Press.

Rando, T. (1986). A comprehensive analysis of anticipatory grief: Perspectives, processes, promises, and problems. In T. Rando (Ed.), *Loss and anticipatory grief* (pp. 269–281). Lexington, MA: Lexington Books.

Rappaport, H., Fossler, R. J., Bross, L. S., & Gilden, D. (1993). Future time, death anxiety, and life purpose among older adults. *Death Studies, 17,* 369–379.

Raskin, P. (1986). The relationship between identity and intimacy in early adulthood. *Journal of Genetic Psychology, 147,* 167–181.

Raskin, P. (1989). Identity status research: Implications for career counseling. *Journal of Adolescence, 12,* 375–388.

Rasmussen, C. A., & Brems, C. (1996). The relationship of death anxiety with age and psychosocial maturity. *The Journal of Psychology, 130,* 141–144.

Rattansi, A., & Phoenix, A. (1997). Rethinking youth identities: Modernist and postmodernist frameworks. In J. Bynner, L. Chisholm, & A. Furlong (Eds.), *Youth, citizenship and social change in a European context* (pp. 121–150). Aldershot, UK: Ashgate.

Reinhardt, J. P., Boerner, K., & Benn, D. (2003). Predicting individual change over time among chronically impaired older adults. *Psychology and Aging, 18,* 770–779.

Reis, H. T., Lin, Y. C., Bennett, M. E., & Nezlek, J. B. (1993). Change and consistency in social participation during early adulthood. *Developmental Psychology, 29,* 633–645.

Reis, H. T., Lin, Y., Bennett, M. E., & Nezlek, J. B. (2004). Change and consistency in social participation during early adulthood. In H. T. Reis & C. E. Rusbult (Eds.), *Close relationships.* New York: Psychology Press.

Reis, O., & Youniss, J. (2004). Patterns in identity change and development in relationships with mothers and friends. *Journal of Adolescent Research, 19,* 31–44.

Reitzes, D. C., & Mutran, E. J. (2002). Self concept as the organization of roles: Importance, centrality, and balance. *Sociological Quarterly, 43,* 647–667.

Reitzes, D. C., & Mutran, E. J. (2004a). Grandparenthood: Factors influencing frequency of grandparent-grandchildren contact and grandparent role satisfaction. *The Journals of Gerontology, 59B,* S9–S16.

Reitzes, D. C., & Mutran, E. J. (2004b). The transition to retirement: Stages and factors that influence retirement adjustment. *International Journal of Aging and Human Development, 59,* 63–84.

Reitzes, D. C., Mutran, E. J., & Fernandez, M. E. (1996a). Does retirement hurt well-being? Factors influencing self esteem and depression among retirees and workers. *Gerontologist, 36,* 649–656.

Reitzes, D. C., Mutran, E. J., & Fernandez, M. E. (1996b). Preretirement influences on postretirement self-esteem. *Journals of Gerontology, Series B, Psychological Sciences and Social Sciences, 51B,* 242–249.

Rennemark, M., & Hagberg, B. (1997). Social network patterns among the elderly in relation to their perceived life history in an Eriksonian framework. *Aging and Mental Health, 1,* 321–331.

Rice, F. P. (1992). *The adolescent: Development, relationships, and culture.* Boston: Allyn & Bacon.

Rice, K. G. (1990). Attachment in adolescence: A narrative and meta-analytic review. *Journal of Youth and Adolescence, 19,* 511–538.

Rice, K. G., & Mulkeen, P. (1995). Relationships with parents and peers: A longitudinal study of adolescent intimacy. *Journal of Adolescent Research, 10,* 338–357.

Richard, J. F., & Schneider, B. (2005). Assessing friendship motivation during preadolescence and early adolescence. *Journal of Early Adolescence, 25,* 367–385.

Robak, R. W., & Weitzman, S. P. (1995). Grieving the loss of romantic relationships in young adults: An empirical study of disenfranchised grief. *Omega, 30,* 269–281.

Roberts, B. W., Caspi, A., & Moffitt, T. E. (2003). Work experiences and personality development in young adulthood. *Journal of Personality and Social Psychology, 84,* 582–593.

Roberts, B. W., & Friend, W. (1998). Career momentum in midlife women: Life context, identity, and personality correlates. *Journal of Occupational Health Psychology, 3,* 195–208.

Roche, A. (1979). Secular trends in stature, weight, and masturbation. In A. Roche (Ed.), *Secular trends in human growth, maturation, and development* (Monographs of the Society for Research in Child Development, pp. 3–27). Chicago: University of Chicago Press.

Roker, D. (1994). School-based community service: A British perspective. *Journal of Adolescence, 17,* 321–326.

Roker, D., & Banks, M. H. (1993). Adolescent identity and school type. *British Journal of Psychology, 84,* 301–317.

Rosenblum, G. D., & Lewis, M. (1999). The relations among body image, physical attractiveness, and body mass in adolescence. *Child Development, 70,* 50–64.

Rosenblum, G. D., & Lewis, M. (2003). Emotional development in adolescence. In G. R. Adams & M. Berzonsky (Eds.), *Blackwell handbook of adolescence* (pp. 269–289). Oxford, UK: Blackwell.

Rosow, I. (1974). *Socialization of the aged.* New York: Free Press.

Rossitter, A. B. (1991). Initiator status and separation adjustment. *Journal of Divorce and Remarriage, 15,* 141–155.

Rotheram-Borus, M. J. (1993). Biculturalism among adolescents. In M. Bernal & G. Knight (Eds.), *Ethnic identity* (pp. 81–102). Albany: SUNY Press.

Roubenoff, R., & Hughes, V. A. (2000). Sarcopenia: Current concepts. *Journals of Gerontology: Medical Sciences, 55,* M716–M724.

Rowe, I., & Marcia, J. E. (1980). Ego identity status, formal operations, and moral development. *Journal of Youth and Adolescence, 9,* 87–99.

Rowe, J. W., & Minaker, K. L. (1985). Geriatric medicine. In C. E. Finch & E. L. Schneider (Eds.), *Handbook of the biology of aging* (2nd ed.). New York: Van Nostrand Reinhold.

Rubert, M. P., Eisdorfer, C., & Loewenstein, D. A. (1996). Normal aging: Changes in sensory/perceptual and cognitive abilities. In J. Sadavoy, L. W. Lazarus, L. F. Jarvik, & G. T. Grossberg (Eds.), *Comprehensive review of geriatric psychiatry* (2nd ed., pp. 113–134). Washington, DC: American Psychiatric Press.

Rybash, J. M., Roodin, P. A., & Hoyer, W. J. (1995). *Adult development and aging* (3rd ed.). Madison, WI: Brown & Benchmark.

Ryff, C. D., & Essex, M. J. (1992). The interpretation of life experience and well-being: The sample case of relocation. *Psychology and Aging, 7,* 507–517.

Ryff, C. D., & Keyes, C. L. M. (1995). The structure of psychological well-being revisited. *Journal of Personality and Social Psychology, 69,* 719–727.

Ryff, C. D., Keyes, C. L. M., & Hughes, D. L. (2004). Psychological well-being in MIDUS: Profiles of ethnic/racial diversity and life-course uniformity. In O. G. Brim, C. D. Ryff, & R. C. Kessler (Eds.), *How healthy are we? A national study of well-being at midlife* (pp. 398–422). Chicago: University of Chicago Press.

Ryff, C. D., Lee, Y. H., Essex, M. J., & Schmutte, P. S. (1994). My children and me: Midlife evaluations of grown children and of self. *Psychology and Aging, 9,* 195–205.

Ryff, C. D., Lee, Y. H., & Na, K. C. (1996). *Through the lens of culture: Psychological well-being at midlife.* Unpublished manuscript.

Sacks, O. (1987). *The man who mistook his wife for a hat.* New York: Harper & Row.

Salinger, J. D. (1951). *Catcher in the rye.* New York: Modern Library.

Sampson, R. J. (1997). Collective regulation of adolescent misbehavior: Validation results from eighty Chicago neighborhoods. *Journal of Adolescent Research, 12,* 227–246.

Savin-Williams, R. C. (2001). A critique of research on sexual-minority youths. *Journal of Adolescence, 24,* 5–13.

Scales, P., Blyth, D., Berkas, T., & Kielsmeier, J. (2000). The effects of service learning on middle school students' social responsibility and academic success. *Journal of Early Adolescence, 20,* 332–358.

Scanlon, E., & Devine, K. (2001). Residential mobility and youth well-being: Research, policy and practice issues. *Journal of Sociology and Social Welfare, 28,* 119–138.

Schachter, E. P. (2004). Identity configurations: A new perspective on identity formation in contemporary society. *Journal of Personality, 72,* 167–199.

Schaie, K. W. (1993). The Seattle longitudinal studies of adult intelligence. *Current Directions in Psychological Science, 2,* 171–175.

Schaie, K. W. (1994). The life course of adult intellectual abilities. *American Psychologist, 49,* 304–313.

Schaie, K. W., Labouvie, G., & Bruech, B. U. (1973). Generational and cohort-specific differences in adult cognitive functioning: A fourteen-year study of independent samples. *Developmental Psychology, 9,* 151–166.

Scharf, M., Mayseless, O., & Kivenson-Baron, I. (2004). Adolescents' attachment representations and developmental tasks in emerging adulthood. *Developmental Psychology, 40,* 430–444.

Schechter, M. D., & Grand, S. (1990). The meaning of search. In D. M. Brodzinsky (Ed.), *The psychology of adoption* (pp. 62–92). New York: Oxford University Press.

Schiedel, D. G., & Marcia, J. E. (1985). Ego identity, intimacy, sex role orientation, and gender. *Developmental Psychology, 21,* 149–160.

Schlegel, A., & Barry, H. (1980). Early childhood precursors of adolescent initiation ceremonies. *Ethos, 8,* 132–145.

Schulenberg, J. E., Bryant, A. L., & O'Malley, P. M. (2004). Taking hold of some kind of life: How developmental tasks relate to trajectories of well-being during the transition to adulthood. *Development and Psychopathology, 16,* 1119–1140.

Schultheiss, D. P., & Blustein, D. L. (1994). Contributions of family relationship factors to the identity formation process. *Journal of Counseling & Development, 73,* 159–166.

Schulz, J. H. (1992). The early retirement time bomb. *Aging Today, 15,* 9.

Seale, C., Addington-Hall, J., & McCarthy, M. (1997). Awareness of dying: Prevalence, causes and consequences. *Social Science Medicine, 45,* 477–484.

Seiffge-Krenke, I., Shulman, S., & Klessinger, N. (2001). Adolescent precursors of romantic relationships in young adulthood. *Journal of Social and Personal Relationships, 18,* 327–346.

Selman, R. (1980). *The growth of interpersonal understanding development and clinical studies.* New York: Academic Press.

Sheldon, K. M., & Kasser, T. (2001). Getting older, getting better? Personal strivings and psychological maturity across the life span. *Developmental Psychology, 37,* 491–501.

Shock, N. W., Greulich, R. C., Andres, R., Arenberg, D., Costa, P. T., Lakatta, E. G., et al. (1984). *Normal human aging: The Baltimore longitudinal study of aging.* NIH Publication No. 84–2450. Bethesda, MD: National Institutes of Health.

Shotter, J., & Gergen, K. J. (Eds.). (1989). *Texts of identity.* Newbury Park, CA: Sage.

Silbereisen, R. K., & Noack, P. (1990). Adolescents' orientations for development. In H. A. Bosma & A. E. Jackson (Eds.), *Coping and self-concept in adolescence* (pp. 112–127). Heidelberg, Germany: Springer-Verlag.

Silbereisen, R. K., & Schmitt-Rodermund, E. (1995). German immigrants in Germany: Adaptation of adolescents' timetables for autonomy. In P. Noack, M. Hofer, & J. Youniss (Eds.), *Psychological responses to social change* (pp. 105–125). Berlin: Walter de Gruyter.

Silverberg, S., & Gondoli, D. M. (1996). Autonomy in adolescence: A contextualized perspective. In G. R. Adams, R. Montemayor, & T. P. Gullotta (Eds.), *Psychosocial development during adolescence: Progress in developmental contextualism.* Advances in Adolescent Development (Vol. 8, pp. 12–61). Thousand Oaks, CA: Sage.

Silverberg, S., & Sternberg, L. (1987). Adolescent autonomy, parent-adolescent conflict and parental well-being. *Journal of Youth and Adolescence, 16,* 293–311.

Simmons, R. G., & Blyth, D. A. (1987). *Moving into adolescence: The impact of pubertal change and school context.* New York: Aldine.

Simmons, R. G., Burgeson, R., Carlton-Ford, S., & Blyth, D. A. (1987). The impact of cumulative change in early adolescence. *Child Development, 58,* 1220–1234.

Skoe, E. E. A. (1998). The ethic of care: Issues in moral development. In E. E. A. Skoe & A. von der Lippe (Eds.), *Personality development in adolescence: A cross national and life span perspective* (pp. 143–171). London: Routledge.

Skoe, E. E. A., Cumberland, A., Eisenberg, N., Hansen, K., & Perry, J. (2002). The influences of sex and gender-role identity on moral cognition and prosocial personality traits. *Sex Roles, 46,* 295–309.

Skoe, E. E. A., & Diessner, R. (1994). Ethic of care, justice, identity, and gender: An extension and replication. *Merrill-Palmer Quarterly, 40,* 272–289.

Skoe, E. E. A., Hansen, K. L., Mørch, W. T., Bakke, I., Hoffman, T., Larsen, B., et al. (1999). Care-based moral reasoning in Norwegian and Canadian early adolescents: A cross-national comparison. *Journal of Early Adolescence, 19,* 280–291.

Skoe, E. E. A., & Marcia, J. E. (1991). A care-based measure of morality and its relation to ego identity. *Merrill-Palmer Quarterly, 37,* 289–304.

Skoe, E. E. A., Pratt, M. W., Matthews, M., & Curror, S. E. (1996). The ethic of care: Stability over time, gender differences, and correlates in mid- to late adulthood. *Psychology and Aging, 11,* 280–292.

Skorikov, V. B., & Vondracek, F. W. (1998). Vocational identity development: Its relationship to other identity domains and to overall identity development. *Journal of Career Assessment, 6,* 13–35.

Slater, C. L. (2003). Generativity Versus Stagnation: An elaboration of Erikson's adult stage of human development. *Journal of Adult Development, 10,* 53–65.

Slugoski, B. R., & Ginsburg, G. P. (1989). Ego identity and explanatory speech. In J. Shotter & K. J. Gergen (Eds.), *Texts of identity* (pp. 36–55). Newbury Park, CA: Sage.

Slugoski, B. R., Marcia, J. E., & Koopman, R. F. (1984). Cognitive and social interactional characteristics of ego identity statuses in college males. *Journal of Personality and Social Psychology, 47,* 646–661.

Smith, E. P., Walker, K., Fields, L., Brookins, C. C., & Seay, R. C. (1999). Ethnic identity and its relationship to self-esteem, perceived efficacy and prosocial attitudes in early adolescence. *Journal of Adolescence, 22,* 867–880.

Smith, J., & Freund, A. M. (2002). The dynamics of possible selves in old age. *Journal of Gerontology, 57B,* 492–500.

Smith, M. B. (1994). Selfhood at risk: Postmodern perils and the perils of postmodernism. *American Psychologist, 49,* 405–411.

Smollar, J., & Youniss, J. (1985). Parent-adolescent relations in adolescents whose parents are divorced. *Journal of Early Adolescence, 51,* 129–144.

Snarey, J. (1988). Men without children. *Psychology Today, 22,* 61–62.

Snarey, J. (1993). *How fathers care for the next generation: A four decade study.* Cambridge, MA: Harvard University Press.

Snarey, J., Son, L., Kuehne, V. S., Hauser, S., & Vaillant, G. (1987). The role of parenting in men's psychosocial development: A longitudinal study of early adulthood infertility and midlife generativity. *Developmental Psychology, 23,* 593–603.

Soederberg Miller, L. M., & Lachman, M. E. (2000). Cognitive performance and the role of control beliefs in midlife. *Aging Neuropsychology and Cognition, 7,* 69–85.

Sorenson, K. A., Russell, S. M., Harkness, D. J., & Harvey, J. H. (1993). Account-making, confiding, and coping with the ending of a close relationship. *Journal of Social Behavior and Personality, 8,* 73–86.

Spear, P. (2000). The adolescent brain and age-related behavioral manifestations. *Neuroscience and Biobehavioral Reviews, 24,* 417–463.

Spencer, M. B., & Dornbusch, S. M. (1990). Challenges in studying minority youth. In S. S. Feldman & G. R. Elliott (Eds.), *At the threshold: The developing adolescent* (pp. 123–146). Cambridge, MA: Harvard University Press.

Spencer, M. B., & Markstrom-Adams, C. (1990). Identity processes among racial and ethnic minority children in America. *Child Development, 61,* 290–310.

Stattin, H., & Magnusson, D. (1990). *Paths through life, Vol. 2. Pubertal maturation in female development.* Hillsdale, NJ: Lawrence Erlbaum.

Stein, J. A., & Newcomb, M. D. (1999). Adult outcomes of adolescent conventional and agentic orientations: A 20-year longitudinal study. *Journal of Early Adolescence, 19,* 39–65.

Steinberg, L. (1987). Impact of puberty on family relations: Effects of pubertal status and pubertal timing. *Developmental Psychology, 23,* 451–460.

Stephen, J., Fraser, E., & Marcia, J. E. (1992). Moratorium-achievement (MAMA) cycles in lifespan identity development: Value orientations and reasoning system correlates. *Journal of Adolescence, 15,* 283–300.

Stewart, A. J., & Healy, J. M. (1989). Linking individual development and social changes. *American Psychologist, 44,* 30–42.

Stewart, A. J., & Ostrove, J. M. (1998). Women's personality in middle age: Gender, history, and midcourse corrections. *American Psychologist, 53,* 1185–1194.

Stewart, A. J., Ostrove, J. M., & Helson, R. (2001). Middle aging in women: Patterns of personality change from the 30s to the 50s. *Journal of Adult Development, 8,* 23–37.

Stewart, A. J., & Vandewater, E. A. (1993). The Radcliffe Class of 1964: Career and family social clock projects in a transitional cohort. In K. D. Hulbert & D. T. Schuster (Eds.), *Women's lives through time: Educated women of the twentieth century* (pp. 235–258). San Francisco: Jossey-Bass.

Stewart, A. J., & Vandewater, E. A. (1998). The course of generativity. In D. P. McAdams & E. de St. Aubin (Eds.), *Generativity and adult development: How and why we care for the next generation* (pp. 75–100). Washington, DC: American Psychological Association.

Super, D. E. (1980). A life-span, life space, approach to career development. *Journal of Vocational Behavior, 16,* 282–298.

Super, D. E. (1990). A life-span, life-space approach to career development. In D. Brown & L. Brooks (Eds.), *Career choice and development* (pp. 197–261). San Francisco: Jossey-Bass.

Super, D. E. (1994). A lifespan, life-space, perspective on convergence. In M. L. Savikas & R. W. Lent (Eds.), *Convergence in career development theories: Implications for science and practice* (pp. 63–74). Palo Alto, CA: USCCP Books.

Susman, E. J., & Rogol, A. (2004). Puberty and psychological development. In R. M. Lerner & L. Steinberg (Eds.), *Handbook of adolescent psychology* (2nd ed., pp. 15–44). New York: Wiley.

Suzman, R. M., Harris, T., Hadley, E. C., Kovar, M. G., & Weindruch, R. (1992). The robust oldest old: Optimistic perspectives for increasing healthy life expectancy. In R. M. Suzman, D. P. Willis, & K. G. Manton (Eds.), *The oldest old* (pp. 341–358). New York: Oxford University Press.

Taft, L. B., & Nehrke, M. F. (1990). Reminiscence, life review, and ego integrity in nursing home residents. *International Journal of Aging and Human Development, 30,* 189–196.

Tanner, J. M. (1991). Growth spurt, adolescent. I. In R. M. Lerner, A. C. Petersen, & J. Brooks-Gunn (Eds.), *Encyclopedia of adolescence* (Vol. 2, pp. 419–424). New York: Garland.

Tesch, S. A., & Cameron, K. A. (1987). Openness to experience and development of adult identity. *Journal of Personality, 5,* 615–630.

Tesch, S. A., & Whitbourne, S. K. (1982). Intimacy and identity status in young adults. *Journal of Personality and Social Psychology, 43,* 1041–1051.

Thomas, J., & French, K. (1985). Gender differences across age in motor performance. *Psychological Bulletin, 98,* 260–282.

Thomas, L. E., DiGiulio, R. C., & Sheehan, N. W. (1988). Identity loss and psychological crisis in widowhood: A re-evaluation. *International Journal of Aging and Human Development, 26,* 225–239.

Tougas, F., Lagacé, M., de la Sablonnière, R., & Kocum, L. (2004). A new approach to the link between identity and relative deprivation in the perspective of ageism and retirement. *International Journal of Aging and Human Development, 59,* 1–23.

Troll, L. E., & Skaff, M. M. (1997). Perceived continuity of self in very old age. *Psychology and Aging, 12,* 162–169.

Tucker, C. J., Marx, J., & Long, L. (1998). "Moving on": Residential mobility and children's school lives. *Sociology of Education, 71*(2), 111–129.

U.S. Bureau of the Census. (2003). *Statistical abstract of the United States.* Washington, DC: Author.

U.S. Department of Labor. (1993). Household data. *Employment and Earnings, 40,* 15–65.

U.S. Senate Special Committee on Aging, American Association of Retired Persons, Federal Council on Aging, and U.S. Administration on Aging. (1991). *Aging America: Trends and projections* (DHHS Publication No. FCoA 91–28001). Washington, DC: U.S. Department of Health and Human Services.

Umaña-Taylor, A. (2004). Ethnic identity and self-esteem: Examining the role of social context. *Journal of Adolescence, 27,* 139–146.

Umberson, D., Wortman, C. B., & Kessler, R. C. (1992). Widowhood and depression: Explaining long-term gender differences in vulnerability. *Journal of Health and Social Behavior, 33,* 10–24.

Vaillant, G. E. (1977). *Adaptation to life.* Boston: Little, Brown.

Vaillant, G. E. (2002). *Aging well.* Boston: Little, Brown.

Vaillant, G. E., & Milofsky, E. (1980). Natural history of male psychological health: IX. Empirical evidence for Erikson's model of the life cycle. *American Journal of Psychiatry, 137,* 1348–1359.

Valde, G. A. (1996). Identity closure: A fifth identity status. *The Journal of Genetic Psychology, 157,* 245–254.

Van Hoof, A. (1999). The identity status approach: In need of fundamental revision and qualitative change. *Developmental Review, 19,* 497–556.

Van Mannen, K. J., & Whitbourne, S. K. (1997). Psychological development and life experiences in adulthood: A 22-year sequential study. *Psychology and Aging, 12,* 239–246.

Vandewater, E. A., Ostrove, J. M., & Stewart, A. J. (1997). Predicting women's well-being in midlife: The importance of personality development and social role involvements. *Journal of Personality and Social Psychology, 72,* 1147–1160.

Vercrysse, N. J., & Chandler, L. A. (1992). Coping strategies used by adolescents in dealing with family relocation overseas. *Journal of Adolescence, 15,* 67–82.

Verhulst, F. C. (2000). Internationally adopted children: The Dutch longitudinal adoption study. *Adoption Quarterly, 4,* 27–44.

Vernberg, E. M. (1990). Experiences with peers following relocation during early adolescence. *American Journal of Orthopsychiatry, 60,* 466–472.

Vernberg, E. M., Ewell, K. K., Beery, S. H., & Abwender, D. A. (1994). Sophistication of adolescents' interpersonal negotiation strategies and friendship formation after relocation: A naturally occurring experiment. *Journal of Research on Adolescence, 4,* 5–19.

Viney, L. L. (1984–85). Loss of life and loss of bodily integrity: Two different sources of threat for people who are ill. *Omega, 15,* 207–222.

Vondracek, F. W. (1992). The construct of identity and its use in career theory and research. *The Career Development Quarterly, 41,* 130–144.

Vondracek, F. W., Hostetler, M., Schulenberg, J. E., & Shimizu, K. (1990). Dimensions of career indecision. *Journal of Counseling Psychology, 37,* 98–106.

Vondracek, F. W., & Porfeli, E. J. (2003). The world of work and careers. In G. R. Adams & M. D. Berzonsky (Eds.), *Blackwell handbook of adolescence* (pp. 109–128). Oxford, UK: Blackwell.

Walaskay, M., Whitbourne, S. K., & Nehrke, M. F. (1983–84). Construction and validation of an ego integrity status interview. *International Journal of Aging and Human Development, 18,* 61–72.

Walker, L. J. (1984). Sex differences in the development of moral reasoning: A critical review. *Child Development, 55,* 677–691.

Walker, L. J. (1986). Sex differences in the development of moral reasoning: A rejoinder to Baumrind. *Child Development, 57,* 522–526.

Walker, L., Gustavson, P., & Hennig, K. (2001). The consolidation/transition model in moral reasoning development. *Developmental Psychology, 37,* 187–197.

Wallace-Broscious, A., Serafica, F. C., & Osipow, S. H. (1994). Adolescent career development: Relationships to self-concept and identity status. *Journal of Research on Adolescence, 4,* 127–149.

Ward, C., & Styles, I. (2003). Lost and found: Reinvention of the self following migration. *Journal of Applied Psychoanalytic Studies, 5*, 349–367.

Warr, P. (1992). Age and occupational well-being. *Psychology and Aging, 7*, 37–45.

Waterman, A. S., Geary, P. S., & Waterman, C. K. (1974). Longitudinal study of changes in ego identity status from the freshman to the senior year at college. *Developmental Psychology, 10*, 387–392.

Waterman, A. S., & Goldman, J. A. (1976). A longitudinal study of ego identity status development at a liberal arts college. *Journal of Youth and Adolescence, 5*, 361–369.

Weber, A. L., & Harvey, J. H. (1994). Accounts in coping with relationship loss. In A. L. Weber & J. H. Harvey (Eds.), *Perspectives on close relationships* (pp. 285–322). Boston: Allyn & Bacon.

Weinman, J., Petrie, K. J., Moss-Morris, R., & Horne, R. (1996). The illness perception questionnaire: A new method for assessing the cognitive representation of illness. *Psychology and Health, 11*, 431–445.

Weinmann, L. L., & Newcombe, N. (1990). Relational aspects of identity: Late adolescents' perceptions of their relationships with parents. *Journal of Experimental Child Psychology, 50*, 357–369.

Wellin, C., & Jaffe, D. J. (2004). In search of "personal care": Challenges to identity support in residential care for elders with cognitive illness. *Journal of Aging Studies, 18*, 275–295.

Werner, E. E., & Smith, R. S. (2001). *Journeys from childhood to midlife: Risk, resilience and recovery.* Ithaca, NY: Cornell University Press.

Westermeyer, J. F. (2004). Predictors and characteristics of Erikson's life cycle model among men: A 32-year longitudinal study. *International Journal of Aging and Human Development, 58*, 29–48.

Wethington, E. (2000). Expecting stress: Americans and the "midlife crisis." *Motivation and Emotion, 24*, 85–103.

Whitbourne, S. K. (1991). Intimacy. In R. M. Lerner, A. C. Peterson, & J. Brooks-Gunn (Eds.), *Encyclopedia of adolescence* (Vol. 1, pp. 557–559). New York: Garland.

Whitbourne, S. K. (1996a). Psychological perspectives on the normal aging process. In L. L. Carstensen, B. A. Edelstein, & L. Dornbrand (Eds.), *The practical handbook of clinical gerontology* (pp. 3–35). Thousand Oaks, CA: Sage.

Whitbourne, S. K. (1996b). *The aging individual: Physical and psychological perspectives.* New York: Springer-Verlag.

Whitbourne, S. K. (2002). *The aging individual: Physical and psychological perspectives* (2nd ed.). New York: Springer.

Whitbourne, S. K. (2005). *Adult development and aging: Biopsychosocial perspectives* (2nd ed.). New York: Wiley.

Whitbourne, S. K., & Tesch, S. A. (1985). A comparison of identity and intimacy statuses in college students and alumni. *Developmental Psychology, 21*, 1039–1044.

Whitbourne, S. K., & Van Mannen, K. W. (1996). Age differences in and correlates of identity status from college through middle adulthood. *Journal of Adult Development, 3*, 59–70.

Whitbourne, S. K., Zuschlag, M. K., Elliot, L. B., & Waterman, A. S. (1992). Psychosocial development in adulthood: A 22-year sequential study. *Journal of Personality and Social Psychology, 63*, 260–271.

Wichstrøm, L. (1999). The emergence of gender difference in depressed mood during adolescence: The role of intensified gender socialization. *Developmental Psychology, 35*, 232–245.

Wiesner, M., Vondracek, F. W., Capaldi, D. M., & Porfeli, E. (2003). Childhood and adolescent predictors of early adult career pathways. *Journal of Vocational Behavior, 63*, 305–328.

Willemsen E. W., & Waterman, K. K. (1991). Ego identity status and family environment: A correlational study. *Psychological Reports, 69*, 1203–1212.

Wilson, R. S., Mendes de Leon, C. F., Bienias, J. L., Evans, D. A., & Bennett, D. A. (2004). Personality and mortality in old age. *The Journals of Gerontology: Series B: Psychological Sciences and Social Sciences, 59B*, 110–117.

Winefield, A. H. (1997). Introduction to the psychological effects of youth unemployment: International perspectives. *Journal of Adolescence, 20*, 237–241.

Winefield, A. H., Tiggerman, M., Winefield, H. R., & Goldney, R. D. (1993). *Growing up with unemployment: A longitudinal study of its psychological impact.* London: Routledge.

Winefield, H. R., & Harvey, E. J. (1996). Psychological maturity in early adulthood: Relationships between social development and identity. *The Journal of Genetic Psychology, 157*, 93–103.

Wrobel, G. M., Ayers-Lopez, S., Grotevant, H. D., McRoy, R. G., & Friedrick, M. (1996). Openness in adoption and the level of child participation. *Child Development, 67*, 2358–2374.

Wrobel, G. M., Grotevant, H. D., & McRoy, R. G. (2004). The family adoption communication (FAC) model: Identifying pathways of adopted related communication. *Adoption Quarterly, 7*, 53–84.

Wu, T., Mendola, P., & Buck, G. (2002). Ethnic differences in the presence of secondary sex characteristics and menarche among U.S. girls: The Third National Health and Nutrition Examination Survey, 1988–1994. *Pediatrics, 110*, 752–757.

Yates, M., & Youniss, J. (1996). Community service and political-moral identity in adolescence. *Journal of Research on Adolescence, 6*, 271–284.

Yoder, A. (2000). Barriers to ego identity status formation: A contextual qualification of Marcia's identity status paradigm. *Journal of Adolescence, 23*, 95–106.

Youniss, J., McLellan, J. A., & Yates, M. (1999). Religion, community service, and identity in American youth. *Journal of Adolescence, 22*, 243–253.

Zeldin, S., & Price, L. A. (1995). Creating supportive communities for adolescent development: Challenges to scholars, an introduction. *Journal of Adolescent Research, 10*, 6–14.

Zimmerman, P., & Becker-Stoll, F. (2002). Stability of attachment representations during adolescence: The influence of ego-identity status. *Journal of Adolescence, 25*, 107–124.

Author Index

Abwender, D. A., 133
Achenbaum, W. A., 199
Adair, V., 244
Adams, G. R., 28, 56, 73, 99, 100, 104, 106, 107, 110
Addington-Hall, J., 237
Addis, D. R., 231
Affonso, D., 207
Agronick, G. S., 161
Akers, J. F., 63, 79
Alipuria, L. L., 126
Allen, J. P., 155
Allison, B. N., 47, 52
Allison, M. D., 79
Almeida, D. M., 50
Alsaker, F., 42, 48
Alvarez, M., 51
Anthis, K. S., 89, 149, 242, 243, 245
Apter, D., 36
Archer, S. L., 21, 38, 64, 65, 111, 141, 144, 243
Archibald, A. B., 35–37, 48, 62
Arnett, J., 62
Årseth, A., 100
Ayers-Lopez, S., 117

Bäckman, L., 197
Bagnoli, A., 221
Bailey, W. T., 157
Bakke, I., 51
Baltes, P. B., 197, 215
Banks, M. H., 81

Barber, B. K., 52, 53, 54, 55
Barer, B. M., 214
Barnett, J. K., 96
Barry, H., 40
Bartle-Haring, S., 96
Baruch, G., 174
Bateson, M. C., 174
Baudouin, A., 197
Baumeister, R. F., 12–14, 66, 67, 93
Baumrind, D., 53
Bayley, B. K., 37
Beard, R. L., 232
Becker, E., 233
Becker, G., 229, 230
Becker-Stoll, F., 77
Beery, S. H., 133
Belansky, E., 52, 55
Bengston, V., 223
Benn, D., 230
Bennett, D. A., 236
Bennett, M. E., 155, 159
Benson, P. L., 118
Bergart, A. M., 225
Berkas, T., 125
Berman, S. L., 245
Berndt, T. J., 54
Berzonsky, M. D., 21, 28, 48, 104
Beyers, W., 77, 104, 245
Bienias, J. L., 236
Billings, R. L., 155
Bisagni, G. M., 223
Blane, D., 210

285

Subject Index

About the Author

Jane Kroger is Professor of Psychology, University of Tromsø, in Tromsø, Norway. She holds a Ph.D. in Child Development. Her current research interests are the study of identity in adolescent and adult development. She has published numerous theoretical and research articles on issues of identity and is author of *Identity in Adolescence: The Balance Between Self and Other* (3rd edition) and editor of *Discussions on Ego Identity*. She has been a visiting scholar at the Erik H. and Joan M. Erikson Center at Harvard University and also at the Henry A. Murray Center for the Study of Lives. She is currently president of the Society for Research on Identity Formation.